DYNAMICS OF BUSINESS AND PROFESSIONAL COMMUNICATION

A CASE-BASED APROACH

HEATHER GRAVES

UNIVERSITY OF ALBERTA

ROGER GRAVES

UNIVERISTY OF ALBERTA

PEARSON

Toronto

Acquisitions Editor: David LeGallais
Marketing Manager: Jennifer Sutton
Project Manager: Andrea Falkenberg
Developmental Editor: Paul Donnelly
Production Services: Kayci Wyatt, MPS North America LLC
Composition: Aptara®, Inc.
Permissions Project Manager: Sue Petrykewycz
Literary Permissions Researcher: James Fortney, Lumina Datamatics
Photo Permissions Researcher: Abdul Khader, Lumina Datamatics
Cover Designer: Anthony Leung
Cover Image: Fancy Photography/Veer

Contents

Preface to *Dynamics of Business and Professional Communication*

Business and professional communication takes place in a dynamic, ever-changing environment. How can we best help students prepare to communicate in such a challenging environment?

This book is our answer. More and more, academic institutions must respond to the needs and demands of their students. Assessment tools for our academic programs often focus on student engagement, active learning, and student interaction with other students. The pedagogies of the twentieth century—lectures, quizzes, and exams—have not kept up to these new demands for student engagement. *Dynamics of Business and Professional Communication* supports more interactive and engaging pedagogies that students find motivating and enlightening. Our online teaching videos demonstrate how to engage students in face-to-face classes through a combination of lectures, discussion, and collaboratively preparing to write the case assignment.

The most prominent feature of *Dynamics of Business and Professional Communication* is the focus on cases. Each module has two or three cases that challenge students to apply the business communication concepts they are learning to a specific set of circumstances. These cases are drawn from real-life communication situations. They are high-interest stories that invite students to think through a communication situation—such as having to write a difficult email message—and then write that message.

To understand the problem that a case presents, students can discuss the case in small groups, as part of a whole class discussion, or online in discussion threads in a learning management system (Moodle, Blackboard, Desire2Learn). The discussion leader for a group may make a short, unscripted presentation to the rest of the class. They might also present in person or post a short, 5-slide formal case analysis to the class.

While your choice of interactive technique may change, the case format supports them all. You may not have taught using cases before; to give you ideas on how to do this, we've prepared two videos that demonstrate how to teach using cases. We also recognize that some students may not be used to learning with cases; we have anticipated this challenge as well, and each module has sections after the case which explain the concepts in the chapter by analyzing the case. We also provide slides that you can use to support your class meetings and ensure that the entire class begins with a shared understanding of the module concepts.

Thinking about moving to the "flipped" classroom model of instruction? We provide narrated slides (screencasts) to support student self-learning online. Students can follow an online lecture that gives them an overview of the module. The *Dynamics of Business and Professional Communication* modules themselves are easily delivered in an online, digital format. Most learning management systems also support online, threaded discussion lists that could be used to host online discussions of the cases.

We hope you'll join us as we create a dynamic, new business communication learning solution for 21st century students.

—**Heather Graves and Roger Graves**

Module 1

Audience, Purpose, and Genre in Business and Professional Communication

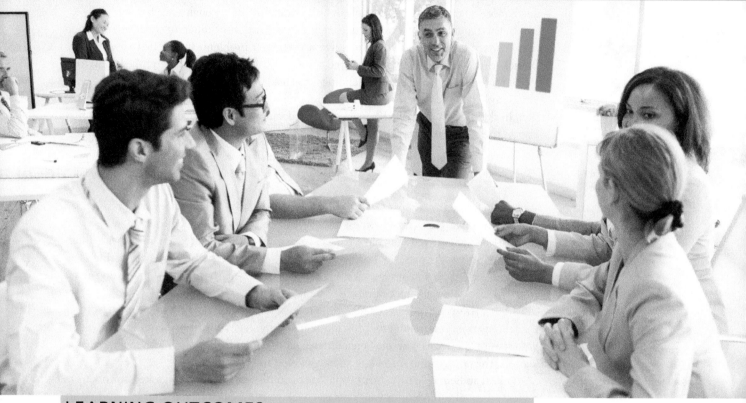

LEARNING OUTCOMES

LO 1 Differentiate between the types of audiences that read documents in an organizational setting

LO 2 Identify the purpose and goals for the message

LO 3 Develop a persuasive strategy that motivates readers to respond to written requests

LO 4 Identify genres and determine how to use them in business and professional communication

GETTING STARTED

Who you write for, why you write to them, and the form you choose to convey your ideas are fundamental factors that affect your success as a writer in the workplace. **Audience** refers to the various individuals who will read a document that you have written. Some people become acutely aware of audience when they post something on a social media page and unexpected readers respond—parents, people from high school whom they had lost contact with, and so on. In business, a text or email to a coworker might be much less formal than a report to a manager who is much higher on the organizational chart.

Audience: The individuals for whom a given document is intended

The **purpose**—why you write—refers to your goals for the document: that is, what you want your audience or readers to learn, understand, or do when they finish reading your document. Before you begin writing, you should have a firm sense of why you are communicating to your audience. If you know *why* you are writing, you will be able to decide *what* to include in your message and, maybe even more importantly, what not to say. By being concise—leaving out unnecessary words—you enhance the power of what you did write.

To accomplish different purposes you should select an appropriate **genre**, or type of document that will reach a particular reader or group of readers to accomplish a specified goal. The key kinds of writing done in workplaces include email messages, text messages, memos, letters, and reports. These are the tools you will use to communicate successfully in the workplace. Learn to pick the appropriate tool and you will find that your career advances much more quickly than those who can only communicate through one channel.

In this module you will meet three people faced with three different situations in which they have to create a document to solve a particular problem. In the first case, Haylee Bostick, a part-time employee at a large commercial bookstore, has been asked to write a memo for her boss to initial before sending it to Head Office. In the second case, Mike Smith has to explain his decision to exceed the limit on his corporate credit card without authorization. In the third case, Mevla Khan creates two documents to inform local residents of a new class at the community centre for which they might be interested in registering.

AUDIENCE IN PROFESSIONAL COMMUNICATION

Audience refers to the groups of readers who are intended to read and who will read (intended or not) a message. Readers of business and professional communication can vary widely. For the same document, you may have readers from diverse cultures, readers who speak different languages (not necessarily English or French), and readers who have contrasting ideas and expectations about your message. For these reasons, you should know something about who will read your message before you write it.

Most correspondence in business and professional communication will be read by more than one person. It is helpful to think in the planning stages of writing about the five different types of audiences who may encounter your document: the initial audience, the gatekeepers, the primary and secondary audiences, and the watchdogs.

Initial audiences are the first people to encounter your draft. If you asked coworkers to review an email intended for your boss to check your tone before you send it out, they are your initial (meaning first) audience. The coworkers are not your *intended* (or primary) readers, but they are still readers of this text.

Gatekeepers are another type of reader. Gatekeepers can prevent your document from being distributed. For example, managers might ask you to draft a message to send out under their name. They will probably review your draft to approve it. If they do not like what you have written, they can veto your message and it will never be distributed. Therefore, your document may need to meet gatekeepers' approval to reach its intended audience.

A third type of audience is your intended or **primary audience**. Primary readers are those people who most need the information and whose names appear on the "To:" line of an email or memo.

Often you have additional readers, known as your **secondary audience**. These readers form the group who may actually implement your message. For example, job applications may be addressed to the director of human resources in an organization (the initial audience), but an administrative assistant sorts the applications from most to least qualified before returning the files to the director. The director may then review only the top five most qualified candidates to select whom to interview. Here the director is the applicants' primary audience, but the administrative assistant is an important secondary reader (he or she reviews and sorts but doesn't make final decisions).

The last type of audience to potentially interact with your message is the **watchdog**. Watchdogs are individuals or groups with political, social, or economic power who can comment on or criticize your message. For example, if you are offended by a particular advertising campaign, you might decide to criticize that organization in conversations with your friends or refuse to buy that company's products to express your disagreement. You can't change that organization's behaviour, but you can speak out against it, so you join a watchdog audience that responds to the organization's actions.

Watchdog audience: Readers who may obtain your document and read it for political, legal, or social reasons

Many organization websites address a variety of audiences. Others target a uniform group, such as the screen capture (Figure 1) from Pearson Learning Solutions website, where all of the links are aimed at educators of some sort. Of course, there are variations among the educators who constitute the primary audience, but few people would visit this site who were not interested in either teaching or training. In contrast, the homepages of city websites such as www.edmonton.ca, www.toronto.ca, or vancouver.ca, address a more diverse group of readers. City residents are the primary audience of such sites, indicated usually by prominent links to "bylaws" or "dog licenses." City websites also include links that target secondary audiences of potential visitors to the city looking for information about attractions or individuals looking to relocate (so links to local jobs appear on many city websites). Other possible links to city expansion plans target watchdog audiences of lawyers or members from municipal governments of surrounding towns or counties.

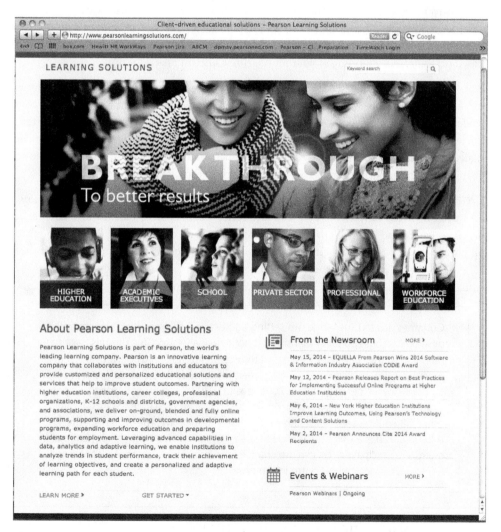

Figure 1 Many but not all organization websites address a variety of audiences.

Source: Home Page screenshot, Pearson Learning Solutions, http://www.pearsonlearningsolutions.com/

UNDERSTAND YOUR AUDIENCE

Once you correctly identify the different groups who make up the audience for your message, consider what might be the best way to present your ideas to these groups. Your goal is to communicate your point so that it helps them accomplish the work they need to do. What aspects of your audience should you consider when preparing to write your message? Evaluate these five areas:

1. Readability and comprehension
2. Power level
3. Obstacles or objections to your message
4. Demographics
5. Communication networks

Readability and Comprehension

Your audience must be able to physically read the words on the page. If they cannot process the words you use, they will not receive your message, so choose words and sentences that match your audience's reading ability. To do this, you must understand your readers well enough to judge the level of language that matches their abilities. In addition to reading your message, your audience must also be able to understand and act on it. To do this, you must provide enough (but not too much) detail so readers can understand your message. Based on their understanding of your message, readers can take action.

Sophisticated Audiences   The passage in Figure 2, taken from the City of Edmonton's City Operations Greenhouse Gas Management Plan, addresses a sophisticated reader—it contains 122 words in five sentences and uses a vocabulary well above the reading level of many citizens. It also uses jargon such as "GHG reduction targets" and conceptually dense language including "the direct engagement of municipalities on climate change," a phrase that is clear to readers who work in high levels of administration.

Broader Audiences   The passage in Figure 3, from the Capital City website, uses 45 words in three sentences. The key difference between this passage and the earlier one, though, is the level of language: "burns gas," "fouls the air," and "save money" are all phrases that most literate citizens can understand quickly. This short section of three

> Countries around the world are setting aggressive GHG reduction targets and developing corresponding plans. Most notably, leaders of G8 countries have recommended that developed countries reduce their emission of GHG by 80% or more by 2050. Moreover, the Government of Canada has set a target to reduce emissions by 17 per cent below 2005 levels by 2020 and 60 per cent to 70 per cent by 2050. Canada's 2020 target is tied to that of the United States, while other G8 countries are targeting even greater reductions. The Government of Alberta also has a Climate Change Strategy which has led to the direct engagement of municipalities on climate change, and the establishment of a Municipal Climate Change Action Centre in the province.

Figure 2 Passage written for a sophisticated audience.

Source: City of Edmonton, Alberta, Canada. http://www.edmonton.ca/environmental/documents/ CityOperationsGHGManagementPlan.pdf

> # Help Stop Idling!
>
> Idling burns gas, fouls the air, and increases health risks. Canadian drivers who leave their engines running needlessly waste millions of dollars yearly and increase global warming. Turn your engine off to save money, create cleaner air in Capital City, and lessen global warming trends.

Figure 3 A passage written for a broader audience.

sentences works because the third sentence motivates readers to take action by showing the benefits for those readers. Direct address—using "you" in a sentence—also makes the writing easier to understand.

Power Level

Assess the status and power level of your readers in relation to yourself. In some organizations, a flat organizational structure (where status and titles are not as important as outcomes) often results in informal communications. For example, in some organizations employees have met the CEO and address him or her by first name. In other organizations, there are many levels of managers between a lower-level employee and the CEO, a structure that often results in a more formal tone and level of language being expected. When writing to your boss or manager, adopt a level of language and tone appropriate to the different power relations. If your boss or manager supervises many people and is above you in status and power, your attitude and language should reflect this "one-up" relationship.

You will also write to coworkers who are your equals in status and power. Your language and tone should therefore reflect this relationship. For example, you might choose a more informal tone when writing to your friend in the next cubicle than to your manager in the corner office. Finally, when you are writing to subordinates, your word choice and tone may also reflect the fact that they are "one-down" to you. For example, you may tell them to do something rather than requesting they do it. That said, your word choice and tone should always treat your readers with courtesy and respect, whatever their status and level of power in the organization.

Obstacles or Objections to Your Message

Think about how your readers' job responsibilities, attitudes, or experiences may affect their responses to your communication. Are there circumstances related to your request that might cause a negative reaction to it? For example, is this the third time you have written to ask for the same piece of information? Do you have a deadline of the end of the day? Does your manager, who is away today, normally handle these requests? If you can anticipate possible objections to your request, you can address these potential problems as you organize and present your message. If you can overcome possible objections as you deliver your message, you are more likely to achieve success. But to anticipate problems, you must understand your readers and their point of view and experience.

Figure 4 appeared taped inside the elevators in a condominium. It is not a good model for communicating for a wide variety of reasons, not the least of which is that many of the people who would view the message rent the units and are not the owners. But even those readers who were owners might object to the additional expense of purchasing a new hot water tank. The only reason given to motivate these owners—that spending a thousand dollars would prevent some inconvenience for others—might not be very persuasive. The

NOTICE TO RESIDENTS

The Corporation is currently dealing with a water damage loss which has affected some common element areas. This will result in some inconvenience while repairs are underway.

We wish to take this opportunity to remind unit owners that older hot water tanks should be replaced in a timely fashion.

NO ORIGINAL TANK SHOULD STILL BE IN USE

If you have any questions or concerns, please relay same via email or drop a note through the office mail slot.

Everyone's cooperation is appreciated.

Board of Directors

Figure 4 Notice to residents. This notice does not motivate readers to comply.

legalistic direction to "relay same via email or drop a note through the office mail slot" increases the emotional distance between the Board of Directors and the unit owners, and that decreases the likelihood that owners will comply with this request.

In the revised memo in Figure 5, the writer states the problem and its result in paragraph one. Paragraphs two and three elaborate on the problem and provide details to help

NOTICE TO RESIDENTS AND OWNERS

Water leaks from older hot water tanks continue to cause damage to common areas and other units. Repairs resulting from this damage are ongoing.

Original hot water tanks (tanks that were installed when the building was new) should be replaced immediately. Original tanks were all Bradford-White models; if you have a different brand in your unit, this notice does not apply to you. If you are unsure, please contact the building office and we'll be happy to take a look to confirm that your hot water tank is not an original one.

If you are not the unit owner, please contact the owner to ensure that the original has been replaced.

With everyone's cooperation, we can avoid unnecessary expenses and the resulting increases in monthly condominium fees.

Board of Directors

Figure 5 Revised notice to residents and owners.

residents determine whether their hot water tank may need replacing. The closing paragraph addresses the renter audience to explain how the situation affects them and aims to motivate readers to replace original hot water heaters by highlighting the consequences of further water damage to the building.

Demographics

Consider the major demographic categories to which your readers belong: race, class, culture, and gender. These aspects of an individual's social identity can affect how they communicate with others. Occasionally, these aspects can present obstacles for your readers in responding to your request. If you consider how these aspects may shape your readers' response to your message, this action can help you prepare your message to better fit their needs or expectations.

Exercise 1: How Does a Diverse Population Affect Communication Processes?

Canada's population is becoming increasingly diverse. Figure 6, drawn from Statistics Canada's website, highlights this diversity. In groups of two or three, review these statistics and consider answers to the following questions:

1. Which statistics are most surprising to you? Why?
2. If these projections are true, how might this diversity change Canadian society?
3. What implications do these changes have for how we should communicate with each other in this country?

Ethnocultural diversity

In 2017, more than one Canadian in five might be foreign-born

- Strong immigration to Canada in recent decades has led to a rise in the number of foreign-born persons and the portion of the population that they represent. Thus, from 1986 to 2006, the immigrant population went from 3.9 million to 6.2 million, accounting for respectively 15.6% and 19.8% of the Canadian population.

- If current immigration trends were to continue in the coming years, the proportion of immigrants in Canada could reach slightly over 22% by 2017. This would be equal to the highest level observed since the beginning of the last century, namely the 22% recorded between 1911 and 1931.

- Few countries have a larger proportion of foreign-born than Canada. In the United States, for example, the proportion of foreign-born was 12.5% in 2006. However, Australia stands out, with immigrants comprising 22.2% of its population.

Figure 6 Ethnocultural diversity in Canada.

Source: Statistics Canada, www.statcan.gc.ca/pub/91-003-x/2007001/4129904-eng.htm.

Communication Networks

Formal communication networks: People you report to for annual reviews; people who show up in a formal organization chart with you

Informal communication networks: People you share information with at work but do not formally report to or work with

All organizations have **formal and informal networks of communication**. Formal networks spread information on the basis of who *should* know. Typically, formal networks consist of reporting structures that make information available through traditional emails and memos within work units. Informal networks move information around without regard to a particular person's status within the organization and tend to consist of chat sessions and email exchanges between workers who may not work in the same unit and have no formal relationship to the information being shared. Understanding where these networks exist and how to use them can help you when you need to spread information across an organization or, instead, keep something quiet. Knowing to which group or groups your readership belongs can help you decide whom to contact when you want a particular message to circulate or stay confidential.

LINK YOUR GOALS WITH READERS' NEEDS

If you think about your readers in terms of the five areas discussed in the previous section, you can begin to understand your readers' needs and goals. Understanding their needs and goals can help you organize and present your ideas in a way that motivates readers to do

Figure 7 Writing from the readers' viewpoint.

what you want them to do. If your readers respond quickly and competently to your request, then your communication with them will succeed.

Typically, the goal of professional communication is to transmit or elicit information. As a writer you will often be requesting readers to do something. However, before readers can comply with a request, they must understand what you need and want. If you link these goals to what your readers want or need, you are most likely to get readers to comply. One strategy is to look at the situation from your readers' viewpoint to ensure that you communicate your ideas in a way that is useful to them. For example, if you use language that reflects their viewpoint, they are more likely to understand why they need to act. Similarly, if you organize your message so that it takes into account their perspective, they will understand how to respond to your request. To understand your readers' viewpoints, pay attention to two areas:

- How you choose words and structure your sentences
- How you organize and present your information

Here are five ways to put your readers' needs first at the sentence level:

1. Emphasize what readers receive, not what you are doing for them.
2. If you are replying, refer specifically to the issue or request raised by the reader.
3. Don't tell readers how *they* are feeling; don't tell readers how *you* are feeling.
4. If your message is positive, use "you" more often than "I."
5. If your message is negative, shun "you" to avoid assigning blame.

Here are four ways to put your readers' needs first at the organization level:

1. Arrange the points in your communication to reflect their needs.
2. Emphasize the points that make your message relevant to your readers.
3. Add headings and lists to visually emphasize main points.
4. Anticipate questions readers might have and include answers.

Case 1★★ BookTime: Unspent Gift Cards

Haylee Bostick had just finished setting up a feature table in the bookstore when her manager, Gwin Patel, approached her. "This display looks terrific, Haylee," said Gwin. Gwin then explained Haylee's next task: an email had arrived earlier from Head Office requesting information about the store's gift card sales. The company chief financial officer wanted figures on the cash value of gift cards sold in 2013 as well as current redeemed dollar totals. Gwin acknowledged that she had asked Haylee to collect and reshelve the unpurchased books, but this new request meant they had to reprioritize to calculate these statistics for Head Office.

Haylee agreed, and Gwin indicated that she would forward the email message to Haylee shortly. "Once you collect the details, you can also draft our response. Send me the draft after lunch so I can send you revisions ASAP. I want our report back to them today."

Haylee said she would do her best. She was familiar with the specialty sales function of the records database, so it shouldn't take long to pull out those figures. First, though, she should look at the email in Figure 8 to see exactly what Head Office was requesting.

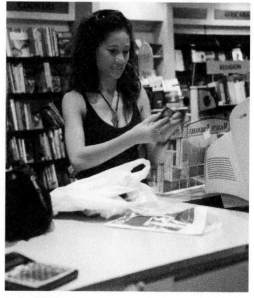
Lucian Coman/Shutterstock

	To:	BookTime Store Managers
Send	**From:**	Diego Battista, Assistant to CFO, Financial
	Re:	Gift Card Redemptions
	Date:	October 3, 2014

The table below shows sales and redemption figures for gift cards, 2011 to 2014. Note that for the gift cards sold in 2013 (line 3), more than $42,000 is still outstanding (as of September 30, 2014).

Year	Gift Cards Purchased	Gift Cards Redeemed
2011	$97,350	$96,975
2012	$102,800	$101,500
2013	$115,750	$72,500
2014	$147,375	$87,025 (to date)

BookTime has never had this large a surplus of unredeemed gift cards before. To reduce this amount, we are launching a marketing campaign in November targeting consumers with unused cards. We need to know which stores are logging the most unredeemed cards to target those areas. To help marketing develop its campaign, we need your sales and redemption figures for 2013 gift cards ASAP. Please also determine whether or not you were the initial seller for redeemed cards.

We appreciate your prompt cooperation, and we anticipate your figures no later than October 8.

Figure 8 Email from Head Office requesting gift card redemption sales for 2013.

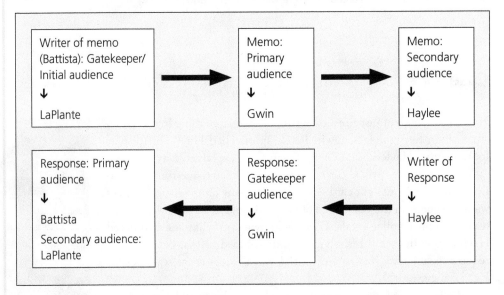

Figure 9 Some audiences for memo from BookTime Head Office and response.

ANALYSIS: AUDIENCE FOR THE BOOKTIME GIFT CARD MEMO

As you can see, the email from Head Office may have been directed to the store manager, Gwin Patel (the primary audience), but she is only *one* of the groups that reads it. Haylee also reads it, as a secondary audience member who assembles the numbers for Store 329.

Before Battista sent it out, he had someone else review it—his boss, Jacques LaPlante, CFO at BookTime, whose priority it is to balance company books for 2013. LaPlante is both the initial audience, who asked Battista to draft the message, and the gatekeeper, who approved the message before its distribution to store managers. In this case, the watchdog audience might include a customer who receives the company promotional materials but responds, "I don't want to use my 2013 gift card to pay for this book for my brother-in-law. I'll use my gift card when *I* want to use it." The customer can postpone using his gift card, but he can't prevent the company's pitch to persuade customers to redeem their cards.

Understanding Haylee's Readers

What Do They Need to Know?   Once she has assembled the figures for Head Office, Haylee opens a new file to draft a message to accompany the numbers. Diego Battista's name might fill the "To:" line as the primary audience, but Gwin will review the message first (the *initial audience*), then approve it, before sending it out under her name (the *gatekeeper*). Haylee decides that Diego Battista will need little explanation with the accompanying figures because he is already familiar with the context for their information; therefore the return memo should be concise and informative.

What Tone and Level of Language Is Appropriate?   Haylee considers that she is writing for Gwin, who is her boss. They have a friendly relationship, so when she does not receive a copy of the memo from head office, her first instinct is to dash off an informal email to remind Gwin. Figure 10 is a draft of this informal message.

Before she clicks "send," Haylee rereads the message and considers that Gwin Patel is clearly above her in status and power, even if they have a good relationship. She decides to revise the draft to make sure she creates a more professional message (see Figure 11).

Haylee also considers the memo that she will draft for Gwin's signature: Gwin is addressing Battista, who is above *her* in power and status. Haylee decides that this situation requires both polite language and a respectful tone while presenting the store figures clearly and concisely.

What Are Possible Objections to the Message?   Haylee next considers possible objections by Head Office (or Battista) to the figures that she will present. Since he initiated this request and issued a tight deadline, he will likely be pleased to receive this message, she reasons. He will also likely skip over the message itself to get to the figures quickly, she concludes, so this means she should probably present the figures so they are easy to find and to process. She has already copied the figures into a spread-sheet as an attachment, but she decides to also copy and paste the table into the email message so there are multiple ways that Battista can find and process the numbers. By

| Send | To: | Gwin |
| | Subject: | Where's the message? |

Hey Gwin,

I haven't gotten the email from Head Office. Did you forget to send it? Any chance you could shoot it my way shortly?

Figure 10 What not to do.

To: Gwin

Subject: Copy of Request from Head Office

Hi Gwin,

I haven't received the email that you were going to forward from Head Office. Would you be able to send it again?

Thanks,

Haylee

Figure 11 What to do.

anticipating his desire to obtain the numbers quickly, Haylee has tried to understand his viewpoint and needs as a reader.

What Do I Know About the Audience for This Message? Haylee's initial and primary audience are Gwin and then Mr. Battista. She considers that both are middle-aged managers who value conciseness and efficiency. She decides that this means her message should be short but clear and the figures easy to locate and understand.

What Unintended Readers Might This Message Reach? Haylee's aunt manages another BookTime store in Winnipeg, MB, and the next time they talk, Haylee will probably mention her work with gift card sales. In this instance, Haylee is a **communication bridge**, because she is moving information from her group or store in London, ON, to her aunt's group or store in Winnipeg.

In the sample message emailed to a client in Figure 12, V. Bhatia organizes his text using the principles of writing for readers described in the preceding section. First, he

> **Communication bridge:** Someone who moves information from one context or work environment to another

To: Client

Subject: Final Step: Receiving approvals

Dear [client]:

I am writing to let you know that there has been a delay in obtaining the final release approvals for your request.

We have the survey results prepared, and I expect that we should receive the necessary approvals to release them early next week.

I apologize for this delay and will be sure to send your survey results by Xpress Post once we do receive those approvals in an effort to get them to you as quickly as possible.

Thank you for your patience,

V. Bhatia
National Marketing Research Coordinator

Figure 12 Email message that considers the writer's audience.

conveys what the client needs to know right away (Principle 1). Then he describes the nature of the delay and offers to send the package using a courier to reduce objections from the client. The message is concise and direct, values that the client possesses (Principle 2). The message also includes an apology and timeline for delivering the product, and these aspects of the letter might help the client if he or she needs to forward the letter to his or her manager to explain the delay (Principle 3). Bhatia knows that timeliness is important to his client, so he arranges to send the package as quickly as possible (Principle 4). The professional tone and formal language of the letter means that if it is seen by other, unanticipated audiences, they will view it as professional and competent (Principle 5).

Exercise 2: What Do Readers Need to Know?

In earlier sections, we discussed making sure that everything readers need to know is present in the initial communication. Examine the memo from Head Office (Figure 8) to determine whether Gwin and Haylee have all the information they need to respond to the request.

1. Review the memo.
2. Make a list of the specific requests made.
3. Do you need any additional information about this request?
4. Brainstorm a list of ways to organize this memo to highlight the information requested.

Exercise 3: Might Readers Have Objections?

In earlier sections, we discussed possible objections or obstacles readers might have to a writer's request. Can you think of any objections that Gwin or Haylee might have to hinder them from responding quickly to Battista's memo?

1. Brainstorm a list of attitudes, events, or responsibilities that might slow them down.
2. Generate a list of ways that Battista could motivate his readers (including Gwin and Haylee) to act promptly.

Exercise 4: Link Your Request to Your Readers' Needs

Reread the memo from Head Office to assess how well the request responds to readers' needs. Use the methods for meeting readers' needs at the sentence and organization level to help you determine how the memo might better meet this objective.

1. What order of ideas would best meet your understanding of Gwin and Haylee's needs?
2. How might you visually emphasize the information requested?
3. What changes would you make at the sentence level to emphasize Gwin and Haylee's viewpoints?

1. Write the Return Memo to BookTime Head Office

Assume the role of Haylee Bostick from Case 1 and draft the follow-up memo for Gwin Patel to send back to Head Office. Figure 13 contains the gift card figures for Store 329. Use the information in earlier sections to help you analyze your reader and then develop an organization and presentation of information that will best meet your readers' needs. Use Haylee's figures as the data in your memo.

Audience: Diego Battista, manager at Head Office, is your primary audience; Gwin Patel, manager of Store 329 and your immediate boss, is your initial/gatekeeper audience

Purpose: To communicate clearly and concisely the information about Store 329 gift card sales

Genre: Informative message sent via email

2. Rewrite Diego Battista's memo

Assume the role of Diego Battista from Case 1 and revise the memo that went out to all BookTime store managers (Figure 8). Use the discussion in the first part of this module to decide what aspects of the memo should be revised to make it better respond to the goals and needs of the readers (use Gwin Patel and Haylee Bostick as representative of some of the audiences for the memo). Focus on presenting the information in a way that will motivate your readers to respond quickly with accurate data.

Audience: Gwin Patel, manager of Store 329, as well as managers of all other BookTime locations

Purpose: To persuade store managers to send the requested information as quickly as possible

Genre: Persuasive message sent through email

Store 329
Cards sold in 2013: 215

	A	B
1	Dollar total of gift cards sold:	$24,575
2	Gift card $$ redeemed:	$18,350
3	Gift card $$ unredeemed:	$6,225
4	Sales from gift cards bought elsewhere:	23%

Figure 13 Haylee's gift card figures for Store 329.

PURPOSE IN BUSINESS AND PROFESSIONAL COMMUNICATION

LO 2 Identify the purpose and goals for the message

Inform: To use language strategies (including definition, statistics, facts) to help your audience understand in detail your topic

Persuade: To use language strategies (including logic, emotion, and credibility) to convince your audience to agree with you

As with all business communication, you need to identify the purpose of your message. Sometimes you will be asked a question or for follow-up information that specifies your purpose by **informing** your audience. In some cases you will be asked to justify or explain a situation, and that requires you to **persuade** your readers.

Most business and professional communication is motivated by some combination of these main goals: to persuade, to inform, to build goodwill, and to minimize follow-up communication. Writers communicate to provide information, to persuade or sell an idea or product, and to create a positive impression for themselves or their company with their readers. A fourth goal may be to ensure that the communication is complete so no follow-up inquiry is necessary. Good writers also aim to build goodwill for themselves as employees and for their organizations. Part of success in business organizations results from motivating readers to read your messages. If you constantly write long-winded email messages that do not get to the point of the message, readers will learn to avoid reading your emails. Motivate readers to read your messages by meeting their information needs.

Motivating Readers to Grant Your Request

What Motivates Your Readers? Readers are motivated by needs. For example, most people work because they need money to buy food and pay rent. These are basic needs—more advanced needs might include feeling competent, being capable of looking after themselves, or even feeling good about accomplishing important work. Needs can be intrinsic or extrinsic. Extrinsic needs are those that come from outside; for example, avoiding a negative performance review. Intrinsic needs are those that come from inside; for example, pride in meeting your sales quota. Not surprisingly, intrinsic needs are more motivating than extrinsic ones. If you can identify and link your request to readers' intrinsic needs, you increase your chances of successful communication. In Figure 14, the client is motivated by wanting to have the project completed as quickly as possible. This knowledge leads the writer to respond by arranging a conference call, an action that should resolve the issues more quickly than email communications.

How Does Your Request Meet Your Readers' Needs? Once you have identified possible needs that may motivate readers, the next step is to decide how your request might connect to your readers' needs. For example, many bosses put a priority on saving time and money. If you see a way that your company can save money by changing one of its current practises, you might pitch your idea to your boss, proposing that you develop the new procedure. Your idea helps make your boss look good by improving company processes and you get approval to work on a new and interesting project. In Figure 14 the message responds to the reader's need to for more information. By arranging for a conference call, the writer moves the information exchange to a priority and ensures that the client knows that the project is important.

| Send | To: | Marcia |
| | Re: | Possible meeting times to discuss your research request |

Dear Marcia,

Would you be available to speak with my manager and me at a time starting between 3:30 and 4:30 (Eastern time; 12:30 to 1:30 Pacific time) this afternoon? I expect that the conversation should only be about 30 minutes.

During this call we can cover the details of your research request, the outstanding documentation that we need from you, and the details of a specification sheet for your research request. *(Reader needs)*

If this time is not convenient for you, we are also available during these times:
- Between 11:30 and 12:30 (Eastern time) today (8:30 and 9:30 Pacific time)
- Between 3:30 and 5:00 (Eastern time) Tuesday (12:30 and 2:00 Pacific time)

We would be happy to call you. Could you please provide a phone number where we can reach you?

Thank you,

Laurie Stewart
Account Representative

Figure 14 A message that responds to readers' needs.

In the email Laurie Stewart motivates her client to respond by making a clear request for a telephone call to clarify the details of a research request. The specific times she offers for the call and the clear indication of the agenda for the call also work to motivate the client to make time for this call. By offering to place the call, Stewart also removes a possible reason for not connecting with her client.

Case 2★★ Arena Boards Canada: Unauthorized Employee Expenses

Dolce Vita/Shutterstock

Arena Boards Canada designs, manufactures, and installs the dasher boards for hockey rinks and indoor soccer fields. Their plexiglass and aluminium boards have revolutionized the industry. Based in a small city in Ontario, they have sold and installed boards in hockey rinks and soccer fields in Canada, the United States, Russia, the United Kingdom, and the Middle East. Now several American investors are interested in buying either part or all of the company. Arena Boards Canada could definitely use the additional capital. It has taken a huge initial investment to install and program the robot to manufacture the arena boards to precise specifications.

The phone rang and Paul Zehr, the majority owner of Arena Boards Canada, heard Mike Smith on the line. Mike was a summer intern who was studying robotics at the local college and the son of one of their first employees. He wanted to work on programming the new robot, but Tom Bender, Paul's partner, had insisted that he spend the first half of the summer on an installation crew. If Mike excelled there, he could help Dave write code for manufacturing the boards.

"What's up, Mike? This has to be fast because I have a meeting starting right away."

Mike explained that he had a bit of a problem on his hands. The trailer axle broke yesterday, and the repair shop wanted $1,500 to fix it. They both knew the company credit card limit is only $500, so Mike had put it on his personal Visa card. Paul interrupted to say that the company credit limit is $500 for this very reason—so employees *can't* charge large unauthorized expenses to it. The question Paul had was why Mike hadn't called yesterday to find out the best way to handle the problem before spending the money.

Mike's explanation did not satisfy Paul. Mike told him that he just didn't think about calling. He thought he needed to get back on the road to make it to the job in Spokane, WA, by Tuesday. Paul had to get to the meeting so he directed Mike to send an email and give him all of the details about what had happened. Paul would read it after the meeting and then figure out what to do.

Paul hung up the phone and thought through the situation quickly. Mike was a hard worker but he lacked judgement. Six months ago the company was on the verge of bankruptcy with employees like Mike purchasing supplies without any oversight. As the owners of Arena Boards Canada, Paul and Tom had issued small-limit credit cards to installation crews so they could take care of the small stuff while they were on the road working on a job. For any expenses over $500, they were supposed to call the office and get an okay from either him or Tom. Fifteen hundred dollars was way out of line for fixing a trailer axle. What was Mike thinking?

ANALYSIS: AIMING TO KEEP THE JOB

When Mike Smith writes his email about the trailer axle repairs to Paul Zehr, co-owner of Arena Boards Canada, what does he want to accomplish with his message? He will need to do several things:

1. Explain what happened
2. Justify his decision not to call the office
3. Get reimbursed for the cost of the trailer repairs
4. Keep his job so he can work on the robot later

His message will need to explain (or inform), justify (or persuade), and placate (or build goodwill). In this situation, he does *not* wish to end further communication with Paul Zehr, but he *does* want to include a full discussion of what happened so that Paul can understand and sympathize with Mike's predicament and decision-making process.

Exercise 5: What Is Mike Smith's Purpose in Writing?

Consider Mike Smith's purpose in the email he must compose to Paul and Tom. Discuss his writing situation using these questions as a guide:

1. To what extent do you think that Mike's task is mainly a persuasive one?
2. To what extent should Mike's message contain informational elements? And which information?
3. How important do you think it is that Mike express his thoughts and feelings about the incident in his message?
4. How heavily would you weigh these aims in what Mike should be trying to accomplish with his memo?

Motivating Readers to Grant Mike's Request

Mike's two primary goals for his email will be to *inform* Paul of what happened to the trailer axle and to *persuade* him that the decisions in handling the repairs were justified. The most challenging part of his message will be the second part, persuading Paul Zehr that he did the right thing. To have any chance of being successful, Mike needs to show in his message how his decision making is actually to Zehr's and Arena Boards Canada's advantage. He needs to explain clearly why it is in the owners' best interests to make an exception to the company policy on this one occasion and to refund the repair costs so that he can pay his personal Visa bill.

LO 3 Develop a persuasive strategy that motivates readers to respond to written requests

To accomplish his goals Mike should follow these two steps:

1. Carefully analyze his audience to determine what motivates his readers: How do they feel? What do they fear? What do they need?
2. Clearly explain to Zehr and Bender how retroactively approving and reimbursing Mike's expense will meet the needs that motivate them.

What Motivates Mike's Readers?   Mike Smith needs to motivate his bosses to refund the repair costs. He needs to identify both intrinsic and extrinsic needs that might help him to persuade them. What kinds of intrinsic and extrinsic needs might Paul Zehr have that Mike can try to meet in his email? As the co-owner of a relatively small manufacturing business with huge capital overhead, one of Zehr's primary needs is to stay in business and make a profit. Mike's expenditure may have jeopardized this need, at least a little, unless he can show how the repairs will help the company profit.

How Does Mike's Request Meet His Readers' Needs?   As noted earlier, many bosses put a priority on saving time and money. If you assume Paul Zehr shares this value, you then explain (writing as Mike Smith) that the trailer axle broke after hitting a piece of debris on I-94 on his way through Chicago. He got a quote for the repairs from the shop that happened to be right across the street, as well as three other local repair shops. You chose the quotation that best combined low price with fast repairs (saving time and money generally) so the breakdown did not affect Arena Boards Canada's arena installation schedule for May (saving time and money specifically). At this point, the need to save time and money has potential as a way to show Paul that Mike was trying to look out for Arena Boards Canada's interests.

How Does Mike Show His Managers That His Request Meets Their Needs?   When you are making a request of readers, you must move clearly from your request to explaining the reasons for your request. In the case of Mike Smith, he needs to move clearly from his request that his bosses reimburse him for the unauthorized trailer repairs to explaining why they should retroactively approve his decision to repair the trailer. This is the point where Smith must make a convincing argument for why he ignored company policy and went ahead with the repairs to show how this decision was in the company's best interests. These points should be concrete and detailed enough that Zehr and Bender can see and (Smith hopes) agree with his problem-solving process.

Let's examine some of the details that Smith can use as evidence to demonstrate he made a good decision. After the amounts are converted into Canadian dollars, here are the four repair quotes that he got:

- Rockford Fix-It had the parts and quoted $1500 with the job completed in 24 hours.
- Busy Bee Auto quoted $800 and a week or more waiting for parts. While Mike waited for the parts, he would also spend six nights in a hotel ($120 per night), plus food ($40 a day).
- Jake's Fix-All was $1250 and three days to express ship parts (plus living expenses).
- Northern Illinois Mechanics was $1100 and a week's wait (plus living expenses).

Smith would then explain that he speculated that Zehr would have chosen the lower total cost and the faster repair job to ensure he arrived at the next installation on schedule. If he were late arriving in Spokane, he would disrupt the tight arena construction schedule for multiple other contractors as well.

Professional Communication Assignments

3. Write Mike Smith's Email

Using the chronology outlined in Figure 15 as well as the details discussed in both the case and the previous section, draft Mike Smith's email to Paul Zehr, explaining how Mike came to spend $1500 of his own money to repair the axle on Arena Boards Canada's trailer. Incorporate the relevant ideas from this module on both audience and purpose to help you make a convincing case for Mike's solution to the problem. Your message should achieve these goals:

1. Inform Zehr of the trailer axle problem and Mike's solution

2. Persuade Zehr that Arena Boards Canada should reimburse him for the $1500 repairs

3. Demonstrate that Mike made a good decision and is a conscientious employee

> **Audience:** Paul Zehr, owner of Arena Boards Canada, who will approve reimbursement of the expenditure
>
> **Purpose:** See three goals above
>
> **Genre:** Persuasive message in email format

4. Write a Memo Explaining New Company Policy on Credit Card Expenditures

In response to the unauthorized expenditure by Mike Smith, Paul Zehr and Tom Bender have decided to explain the company policy more clearly in a memo to distribute to all employees. They usually deliver such information verbally at

05/07	Leave K-W, ON
	Hit debris on I-94 through Chicago, IL
05/08	Rockford (IL) Red Roof Inn: Trailer axle on ground in parking lot
	Got four quotes on repair time/cost
05/09	Flatbed truck took trailer to Rockford Fix-It
05/10	Trailer repairs finished
	Headed north on I-90
05/11	Called Paul Zehr to ask for refund of repair costs

Figure 15 Chronology of Mike Smith's trailer repairs.

meetings, but after the $1500 trailer repair bill, they agree that each employee must receive a clear personal copy of the policy. Writing as Zehr or Bender, draft the memo that explains the company policy on credit card expenses and employee reimbursement on expenses over their employee card limit. Use the information in this module to explain the policy to Arena Boards Canada employees and motivate them to follow the policy at all times.

Audience: All employees at Arena Boards Canada who have a corporate credit card

Purpose: To explain the policy clearly and concisely, motivate readers to follow the policy, and ensure that no one else makes a purchase that exceeds their limit without first gaining manager or owner approval

Genre: Policy memo and persuasive message

BASICS ABOUT GENRE AND GENRE SETS

In addition to audience and purpose, genre shapes how you respond to a situation in business and professional communication. Genre refers to the kind of communication that fits a particular situation. For example, if you want journalists to report on your company's event or new product, you write a press release rather than a memo. Memos are documents that communicate information among employees inside an organization. Memos are less formal documents than letters that go to people outside an organization, usually on company letterhead. The memo, the letter, and the press release may contain the same information, but the information is formatted and presented differently, depending on the genre. Speaking and presenting in person also take place in a variety of genres, such as the impromptu conversation in an elevator, the formal sales presentation, and the webinar. In many ways the genre of a communication is the most important choice a writer makes because the genre then controls the choices that writers and speakers make.

LO 4 Identify genres and determine how to use them in business and professional communication

Readers respond to a document based on its genre. For example, a customer expects a letter; an employee expects a memo. Members of a work group often receive email announcements from human resources, often in the form of flyers. Meet your readers' expectation by using the correct genre to communicate with them.

Business and professional communication genres are often related. They form **genre sets**. Other examples of genre sets in business and professional writing include these documents:

Genre sets: Groups of documents that share a social context and are related to each other by purpose or audience

- Request for proposal (RFP): proposal and report
- The job application package (advertisement, application letter, and résumé)
- Inquiry and response communications (using print or email)

Why Should You Know and Use Genre Conventions?

Know and use genre conventions to show that you are a competent, informed, and credible professional. Readers judge your competence and credibility based on whether you present your ideas in a form that they recognize and expect. You show that you are capable by showing that you know the basics. Use the conventions of business and professional communication so that readers can focus on your great ideas rather than on whether your ideas are as flawed as your presentation of them.

Case 3★ Capilano Community Centre: Advertising a Class for New Immigrants

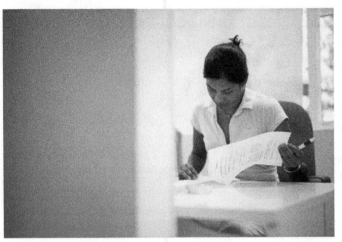

Helen Ashford/GettyImages

Mevla Khan stuck her head in the door of Risa Gomez's office. "Is there anything else that needs to be done?" Mevla had worked her way through the items Risa had given her when she arrived at Capilano Community Centre three hours earlier.

Risa noted that the centre was offering a new English-as-an-Additional-Language class that started August 1. Someone needed to write an email announcement and publicity flyer to be sent out to people who were on the centre's membership list. If Melva felt she could draft that email, Risa could edit it and send it out that day. Risa did a quick search to find two previous email announcements that Melva could use as models for the new one. She then forwarded them to Melva. As for the flyer, Risa directed Melva to the templates in the word processing program and told her to pick one she liked—she just needed to include the Capilano Community Centre logo on it.

Mevla read through the two sample email announcements that Risa gave her as models. The format seemed to be similar in both of them. On a piece of scrap paper, she sketched out the basic format (see Figure 16). Then she made a list of what information was included in the announcement:

Send **To:** _____

Subject: Concise, clear statement of message topic

CC letterhead
Address
Phone numbers

Title of Course

Description: Date, time, who might be interested, focus of course, where/room, costs

Registration information:
Email to events@capilanocc.ca

Figure 16 Basic format for email announcement.

1. News that announcement is about
2. Who cares, why you should care, where, when
3. Summary of event
4. Information about community centre
5. Centre contact information

The task seemed straightforward enough. She gathered up her notes and headed to the staff computer.

ANALYSIS: CONSTRUCTING THE EAL CLASS ANNOUNCEMENT

The announcement and flyer that Risa asks Mevla to create is a genre set. They contain basically the same information, but they are formatted differently.

The Alberta Writes 2 flyer (Figure 17) is an example of a communication about an event. It differs from an email announcement because it has very little text on the page. The email announcement contains much more explanation of what the event is about, who might want to attend, and why they should attend.

Figure 17 Flyer for Alberta Writes 2.

Source: University of Alberta.

ALBERTA
writes 2

Conversations About Writing in Secondary and Post-secondary Contexts

Saturday, April 6, 2013

8:30 a.m. to 4:00 p.m.
Lister Conference Centre,
University of Alberta
$30 includes parking, lunch & snacks

CONTACT:
roger.graves@ualberta.ca

CONFERENCE DETAILS:
www.artsrn.ualberta.ca/conversations/

TO REGISTER:
www.albertawrites2.eventbrite.com/

University of
Lethbridge
Faculty of Education

UNIVERSITY OF ALBERTA
CENTRE FOR TEACHING & LEARNING

Writing
ACROSS THE CURRICULUM

5. Write the Email Announcement to Advertise Capilano Community Centre's English-as-an-Additional-Language Class

Use the information that Mevla gathers from her supervisor in Figure 18 to write the announcement for the Capilano Community Centre's upcoming EAL class. Use the community centre logo in Figure 19 as part of your flyer.

Audience: Immigrants in the community around the Capilano Community Centre who might be interested in improving their spoken English skills

Purpose: To inform readers of the details of the course and to persuade readers who might be interested to attend the class

Genre: Email announcement

6. Create the Flyer to Advertise Capilano Community Centre's English-as-an-Additional-Language Class

Use the information that Mevla gathers from her supervisor to create a flyer to advertise the upcoming EAL class at Capilano Community Centre. Design the flyer to catch the eye of members and nonmembers alike. Make sure that the flyer contains all of the information that interested people will need to sign up for and attend the session.

Audience: Capilano Community Centre members and members of the local community who might want to enrol in an EAL class

Purpose: To attract viewer attention, to inform about the details of the course, and to encourage viewers to enrol

Genre: Poster

English as an additional language class

Aug. 7 to 24 (weekdays)

1:00 P.M. to 4:00 P.M.

Capilano Community Centre, Room 206

Cost: Members $120

         Nonmembers $150

Sponsor: Greater Vancouver YMCA

Leader: Risa Gomez

Contact: 123-4567

Centre Hours: 8:30 A.M.–9:00 P.M.

Figure 18 EAL course information.

Figure 19 Capilano Community Centre logo.

MODULE SUMMARY

■ Audience is a key factor that helps business writers decide what to include and what to exclude from their communications.

■ Audiences vary from the primary reader of a document to various secondary readers; business writers need to keep these secondary readers in mind when they write.

■ Identify your primary purpose for writing before you begin to write: purposes include persuading, informing, and building goodwill.

■ Carefully select the genre or kind of document you will use for your communication; make sure that genre is appropriate and will accomplish your purpose for communicating.

■ Use more than one genre or kind of communication when you need your message to reach different audiences.

Module 2

Argument in Professional Communication

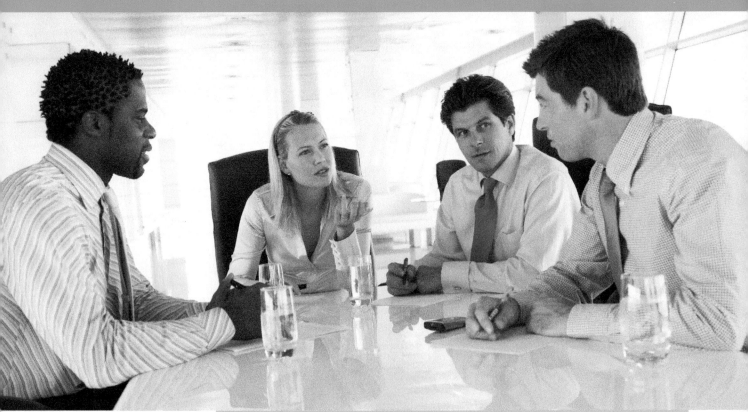

LEARNING OUTCOMES

LO 1 Analyze how to solve a problem or situation to arrive at the best communication solution

LO 2 Demonstrate expertise in writing on a subject so that readers will find you trustworthy

LO 3 Develop argumentative claims to explain and create a convincing case for a recommended solution

LO 4 Synthesize information from supporting documents to create strong arguments

LO 5 Choose the appropriate method of creating an emotional appeal and present the solution in a way that makes readers care about the subject

GETTING STARTED

This module introduces you to the components of argument, an essential skill in business and professional communication. Because this type of communication is primarily persuasive, you need to be able to make a convincing case for your perspective. Most communication in this area requires writers to analyze a problem and present a solution. You need to be able to think through the problem to write clearly about it and make a persuasive case for the action you recommend. To make a persuasive case for your solution, you must be able to use the building blocks of argument: **credibility** (why should readers listen to you?), **logic** (does what you are saying make sense?), and **emotion** (why should readers care?). Of these building blocks, credibility is most important. If readers do not view you as a competent speaker on the subject, they will not be persuaded no matter how good your logic is or how emotionally you speak.

In the first case, you will meet Dan Cooper, who has to manage his credibility in a letter persuading potential clients much older than himself to trust him with their retirement investments. This section shows you how to demonstrate your knowledge of the subject matter and show readers why they should trust you.

The second case introduces you to James Franklin, who has been asked to recommend whether the Prince Edward Island Department of Health Board of Directors should sell the waterfront between a nursing home and the ocean for commercial development. To recommend a course of action to the board, James must study the issues carefully, think through the implications of the sale, and understand the responsibility of the board in making this type of decision. This section explains strategies to help you analyze a problem and develop claims and supporting evidence (reasons) for the argument. It shows you how to motivate readers by linking your arguments to the readers' assumptions, values, and beliefs about the subject matter.

In the third section, Meijing Zhu, a summer intern in the hospitality industry, is asked to draft a letter to summer guests asking them to observe and abide by the resort's rules. This section shows you how to make readers more likely to care about the subject you are discussing. In this case, Meijing must use effective emotional appeals to persuade guests to follow resort rules while they are on vacation.

BASICS ABOUT ARGUMENT

Argument is a central component of good business and professional communication. One of the main purposes of this type of communication is persuasion—for example, if you want coworkers to follow a new policy, issuing a command is unlikely to achieve your result. Instead you need to present the policy and explain why it's important to adopt this policy. Argument or persuasion is about motivating readers to do something. If they want the outcome you are proposing, they may not need much motivation, but if you are proposing an action that they do not value or outright resist, you must work harder to persuade them to act. In essence, you must create an argument for why your coworkers should, for example, clean up any mess they make in the office lunchroom.

Part of motivating readers requires getting them to read the message (emotion) so that you can explain why the change of behaviour is important (logic) and what the advantages are to the change (logic and emotion). They are more likely to read the message if you present the basic information clearly and concisely so they understand the issue and your reasoning makes sense to them (logic and credibility). Once they trust your grasp of the issue, they are more willing to consider your request (credibility), and if you can show them how different behaviour will benefit them and everyone else (emotion), you can motivate them to follow the new policy (persuasion). As you can see, the elements of argument (credibility, logic, and emotion) work together to achieve persuasion. In the first case, Dan hopes to motivate strangers to become his new clients, but his prospecting letter needs a more convincing approach.

Case 1★★★ ES Investment Group: Locating New Clients

Getting a position as an investment services consultant with ES Investment Group (ES) had been a step up from his first professional job at the bank, and Dan Cooper had been happy to leave for something that offered performance-based incentives and a real degree of

Credibility: The sense of trust that you build in your audience through the way you present your document

Logic: The reasons and reasonableness that you convey through what you say in your document

Emotion: The passion, concern, or care you have for your topic

LO 1 Analyze how to solve a problem or situation to arrive at the best communication solution

Professionalism extends from how you dress to how you present yourself in writing.

Andrey_Popov/shutterstock

freedom. ES offered—no, required—that he develop his own group of clients. It was a little like starting up his own business or franchise. ES provided the office, the training, and the support network needed to provide a full range of financial consultation services—a turn-key operation. All Dan had to do was find the clients.

That had turned out to be a challenge. In the six months since he'd started at ES, he'd gone to all the training and marketing seminars. He'd done three seminars on his own with groups of people generated from his immediate social network in the Burlington area—friends of his parents, his friends' parents, and people he knew from growing up in the area. In addition to these contacts, he'd sent out a personalized letter (see Figure 1) to names he had obtained from a marketing firm that ES worked with. The contact list had been limited to individuals and couples living in a section of Burlington with high real-estate values.

ES had a standard letter that he could have used, but Dan felt that it wasn't aggressive enough. He knew he needed to get results, and he wanted to show this potential group of clients that he could do the job—he would be actively working for them to reach their financial goals.

To date, however, the letter's results disappointed him. After sending out the first batch of 20 letters, he had received emails from eight of them and phone messages from five more. None of them had wanted to set up a time for a meeting, and several of them had been aggressively rude in their responses. One had even mentioned that they would never trust their financial future to someone who couldn't use a semi-colon properly, as if that made any sense!

With this as the initial response, Dan knew that he couldn't send the same letter out again next week. He needed to revise it, obviously, but first he needed to figure out why it wasn't working. For help, he turned to his uncle Steve, a management consultant who ran his own one-man company.

Steve read the letter and commented that he understood what Dan was trying to do in it. To help Dan understand how the audience reacted to the letter, he started reading it while saying out loud what he was thinking as he read. "If you want to get anywhere near my money, you'll need, first and foremost, to convince me that you know what you're doing and that you're trustworthy. It seems like every year there is another case of some investment advisor running off with the life savings of all-too trusting friends and relatives. How do I know I can trust you? You work for Edward Schwab. You need to emphasize that in your letter. After the letterhead, you don't mention anything about the company until the third paragraph. They are a great company—over 40 years in the business with a long list of clients. They sponsor baseball and hockey teams in the recreational leagues here. You need to draw more attention to their work in the community. And when you do talk about the company, you need to stress the network of professionals that you have behind you—independent advisors don't have that. It is another major advantage of yours."

Dan started to stand up, but Steve gestured for him to sit back down. Steve made the point that Dan also needed to show readers that *he* was qualified to advise them. Dan needed to give them a specific example of how Dan had helped someone. One example could be the tip Dan gave Steve about borrowing from his own RRSP rather than the bank for a short-term loan. Dan needed to talk more about specific examples of how these people could organize their finances better. By providing help this way Dan wouldn't have to be so aggressive about calling them. They would *want* to call him to see what other tricks he had.

ES Investment Group

Dan Cooper
Investment Services Consultant
dan_cooper@edwardschwab.com

July 4, 2016

John and Joan Pleva
29 Beaver Street
Burlington, ON

Dear Mr. and Mrs. Pleva,

I am Dan Cooper and I am a consultant with ES Investment Group. I am looking to find people who are results-driven, open to new ideas, willing to take advice, and have the ability to look beyond the short term. Smart investors like yourself should be looking to improve your current financial situation by putting in practice innovative new ideas presented to you. These ideas have the potential to increase your overall wealth while reducing risk. To work with these ideas you should have some knowledge of investing. Here are the characteristics of the people who I can help the most; individuals with $400,000 in investable assets, have a mortgage, and have some specific financial goals in mind. Those goals could include paying off a mortgage or taking a vacation every year.

The real estate market over the last couple of years has been up and down but overall up. Increases over time in the GTA has trickled down and allowed even the residents of Burlington and the surrounding area to reap extraordinary growth in the value of their home. This growth however has caused some individuals to become over confident with this market. I'm as excited about the growth in the local real estate market as most home owners but, as we have seen markets go up and down. My job is to help you navigate the turns in the markets through sound financial planning.

My promise is that working with me will bring you the best professional advice and service available. With an unlimited number of specialists, not just at ES Investment Group, but also with a network of professionals, I can assist you. IE – Accountant, Lawyer, etc. Our goal will be to work as a team to create a financial plan and REACH these goals. Are you serious about creating wealth and reducing risk? If so then call me to arrange a ½ hour meeting.

I will be in touch on July 17th, 2016 to set up a time for us to meet together and talk about how I can assist you and if appropriate create an investment plan. To avoid a phone call follow-up please respond via email or leave a telephone message at my office. I look forward to speaking with you in the near future.

Sincerely,

Dan Cooper

Dan Cooper

1159 New Street Burlington, ON L7L 6H9
Ph: 905-333-6666 ● Toll Free 800-333-6666 ● Fax: 905-333-6667

Figure 1 Dan Cooper's letter to prospective clients.

Steve recalled that Dan had been on the investment team at university that came third in the University/College Investment Challenge. He advised Dan to highlight that achievement. It showed that Dan knows what he is doing and may have new ideas that even experienced advisors haven't kept up with. Steve also mentioned the semicolon and advised Dan to proofread the revised letter before he sent it out. Steve also advised Dan to have someone else look at the final draft as well. Steve's point was that people really do judge a book by its cover—or in this case its cover letter. Faulty punctuation suggests that the writer might also be incompetent or sloppy in his financial advice. Right or wrong, this is how people make judgments.

Dan thanked his uncle. As he left, he drew a deep breath. That had been a brutal review of his first attempt at the letter. But Steve's insights really helped him understand why his letter hadn't worked the way he thought it would. His next challenge would be to revise it, and soon, before it cost him any more potential clients.

Basics About Credibility

LO 2 Demonstrate expertise in writing on a subject so that readers will find you trustworthy

Credibility, or the readers' sense that writers know their subject matter, is the first step in creating a persuasive message. If readers are already acquainted with you, their response to your message will be shaped by their prior knowledge, but if your message is their first point of contact, their only basis for judgment is your words and any additional details such as your email address, your job title, or your company letterhead. As they read your message, readers will also assess your level of knowledge of the topic based on how you discuss it. They will judge the reasons you offer for the statements you make, and they will extrapolate from your writing to what you are like as a person. If you seem to know your subject matter and your discussion of the issues is clear and free of errors, they are likely to start believing that you are informed, have a grasp of the issues, and therefore can be trusted. Once readers believe that you are competent, they pay attention to your actual message. On the other hand, if they decide that you are not a credible speaker, it doesn't really matter what you say: they will ignore your message if possible.

Trust: The judgment that you can believe what a person says

This issue of **trust** is important, not only with financial advisors, but also with writing in general. If readers don't trust what you say as a writer, you have no hope of persuading them of your argument. The key to proving yourself trustworthy in writing is demonstrating that you know what you are talking about. Here are four ways to demonstrate your expertise:

- Include details to show your knowledge of the subject
- Describe any opposing viewpoints fairly and accurately
- Show how you and your readers share common ideas about the subject
- Create a feeling of identification (sameness) between yourself and your readers

Show Your Knowledge of the Subject   You can show your knowledge of the subject in several different ways:

1. *Use or define the vocabulary that is central to the discussion.* One way that readers judge your competence is by whether you use the vocabulary associated with your topic. This doesn't mean that your discussion of the topic should be riddled with jargon; it does mean that you should use the terms that convey your understanding. For example, how would you feel about being treated by a doctor that offered you "some stuff for your problem" rather than "some ciprofloxacin for your endocarditis"? Most of us would

Which passage do you think is more credible and trustworthy? Why?	
A recent poll suggests that Canadians expect to work longer than their parents did before they retire. However, once they retire their retirements will last much longer.	A January poll by Simonds Brown found that only 27 percent of 3,017 Canadians 30 to 65 expect to retire fully at 66, down from 51 percent in 2008. "I'm not surprised," says Clive Grant, chief actuary at Fullerton Smythe. "60 years ago, the ratio of working years to retirement years was 5:1, but today it's 1:1 in the public sector and 1.5:1 in the private sector. Today's workers may work five years longer than their parents, but their retirement will last much longer."

Figure 2 Quoting data and experts helps build your credibility as a writer.

prefer to put ourselves in the care of medical professionals who demonstrate their competence by specifically diagnosing and treating our illness. This situation extends to business and professional communication where readers at least partially decide to act based on the perceived competence of the writer.

2. *Quoting data or statistics related to the topic.* Another area that strengthens your credibility, especially in business and professional communication, is including relevant data and statistics. Figure 2 illustrates how the addition of relevant data serves to build trust in addition to developing a logical argument.

3. *Interviewing and quoting experts on the topic.* A third strategy for building trust is to consult experts on the topic and include quotations to illustrate your knowledge of the topic. For example, if you received a mailing from an investment firm inviting you to contact them about managing your investments, would you consider actually contacting them if they illustrated their networks of professional support by quoting some of their experts? How motivated might you be to contact an investment firm if their promotional materials included the first passage in Figure 2?

    The statements in the first version are vague and contain no data or details to strengthen the writer's assertion. The second version includes data and an expert commentator who explains the significance of the statistics. The writer of the second version sounds like someone who understands the situation and who might have useful information to help readers prepare for their retirements.

4. *Presenting new ideas about the topic that show your careful consideration of it.* A fourth way to demonstrate your knowledge of the subject is to include details that show you understand the issues. If you make a point about the topic that readers have not considered, you grab their attention while also showing them that you have given the subject matter some thought. For example, Figure 3 presents the promise of ideas in the first passage compared to a specific idea that illustrates the writer's ability in the second passage. The use of appropriate technical language in describing the idea also serves to build the writer's credibility.

Describe Opposing Viewpoints Fairly   A second way to demonstrate trustworthiness lies in summarizing and addressing viewpoints that are contrary to your own. By acknowledging contrasting perspectives, you show your broad knowledge of the topic. By summarizing them fairly and accurately, you show readers that you are a broadminded thinker who is aware of and makes an effort to understand opposing viewpoints.

Which advisor would you rather invest with?	
Working with me I believe you will receive the best professional advice and service.	In the event of a market downturn, mutual fund management fees of 2 percent or more can significantly reduce your investment returns. For this reason, I only recommend mutual fund companies with management expense ratios (MER) of less than 1 percent.

Figure 3 Demonstrate that you understand the topic by presenting new ideas.

Readers are more inclined to trust writers who are open-minded and sympathetic to new and different ideas.

In the first passage in Figure 4, the writer demonizes supporters of global warming by characterizing them as shrill, fanatical, and hypocritical. The second passage summarizes the viewpoints of global warming supporters more neutrally, without attaching judgments about the members' sanity or morals. In general, we tend to distrust people who characterize others in extreme ways because we perceive them as too emotionally involved to have thought carefully about the issues.

Show How You Share Common Ideas with Your Readers   A third way to gain reader trust is to show that you and your readers share similar beliefs and values. Of course, to do this, you must know what kinds of values and beliefs your readers hold. A careful consideration of your audience can help you figure out what your readers probably value. At the same time, it is unethical to pretend you share readers' values if you do not. Instead, you should keep thinking about the subject until you do find a point about which you and your readers can agree.

Which writer do you find more trustworthy?	
Global warming fanatics, horrified to see their global warming consensus destroyed by scientific facts, have desperately attacked the scientists who contributed to the study. They decry those scientists and engineers as biased because many of them are employed by oil and gas companies in Alberta. These global warmists also emphasize that because these geoscientists are not *atmospheric* scientists they are unqualified to understand the science or speak on global warming. Finally, they assail the skeptical scientists' objectivity while asserting that their own warmist scientists are immune to the influence of employment or sociopolitical factors.	Supporters of androgenetic global warming have questioned whether the scientists and engineers who participated in the study could reach objective conclusions when many of them are employed by oil and gas companies in Alberta. They feel that those scientists may have been pressured by employers to express skepticism about the causes of global warming. Supporters also express reservations about scientists who speak out who are not specialists in atmospheric science, and therefore, may not understand the nuances of the science.

Figure 4 Blatantly biased summaries of opposing viewpoints suggest that writers are narrow-minded and less trustworthy.

Source: Created by H. Graves, © Pearson Education, Inc.

Create a Feeling of Identification Between Yourself and Your Readers

Creating a sense of **identification** between you and your readers contributes a great deal to the process of creating a trustworthy impression and with it, persuasion. If readers feel that they and you are alike, they are much more likely to accept your message. Here is a five-step method to create a sense of sameness between you and your readers:

Identification: The sense that your readers have moved beyond merely agreeing with you to joining your social group

1. List shared beliefs and values

2. Show how your interests are aligned

3. Show how you both "belong" to a privileged group

4. Identify points of conflict between your group and others

5. Invite readers to join you in taking common action

List Shared Beliefs and Values   This strategy is similar to showing how you and your readers share common ground, but it goes beyond that method by detailing a discussion of the values and beliefs that underlie your claims. In Figure 5, the "Core Values" webpage of Christian Dawn explicitly identifies the six values to which the organization adheres. Although readers may not immediately identify with the first value, as they move down the list, they become more and more likely to share Christian Dawn's values. For example, most viewers will agree that people should have priority over money, structure, or systems.

Show How Your Interests Are Aligned   In this step, you show readers how you and they can both benefit from your association. In Figure 5, Christian Dawn starts by emphasizing their values: "Christian values define us." The organization then elaborates these values, using "we": "*We* work with the poor" (emphasis added). Initially, the we

Our core values keep us focused on our mission: to educate, enlighten, and support the poor.

2. Uses "we" to align reader and writer →

Christian Dawn:
Helping the Poor, Spreading the Word

1. Christian values define us.

Our work arises out of our love of God.

2. We work with the poor.

Our faith calls us to work with the poor to alleviate their physical suffering.

3. People matter most.

← 1. Indicates shared value of people over money or systems

Because all people were created by God, we prioritize them over money or other worldly goods.

4. We see ourselves as stewards, not owners.

Our mission requires us to manage assets for the greater good of the poor.

5. Partnership, not high profile, is our goal.

We work with other non-profits to maximize the impact of our work.

6. Action-oriented decision making is our goal.

We actively pursue an action-oriented agenda to get involved where and when we are needed most.

Our Mission

Christian Dawn is a Christian non-profit organization dedicated to helping the world's poor wherever and whenever we can. We aim to alleviate suffering and increase social equality. We serve all people equally, regardless of religion, race, or gender.

How can you help?
1 Find out more about our programs.   2 Learn about our current projects.   3 Donate now.

5. Invites reader to join them in taking common action

Figure 5 This webpage creates identification to demonstrate the trustworthiness of Christian Dawn.

Source: © Pearson Education, Inc.

may not include viewers but as they move down the list, they are likely to see themselves, increasingly, as part of the "we" in "We see ourselves as stewards, not owners," "We work with other non-profits to maximize the impact of our work," and "We actively pursue an action-oriented agenda dedicated to helping the world's poor wherever and whenever we can." Viewers come to see themselves as aligned with Christian Dawn's compassionate interests—that is, to help alleviate the misery of the poor and less fortunate.

Show How You Both "Belong" to a Privileged Group   Psychological research has shown that individuals feel a sense of closeness toward another person if they both share membership in the same group, whether formal or informal. For example, members of the same church (or religion) or service club often form business relationships because they trust one another based on their mutual experiences as members. Figure 6 presents an example of this step in action: the text box in the advertisement for Vulcan Youth Serum presents the series of stages of a typical "VYS user" experience: Skepticism → Reluctance → Conversion → Promotion → Rejection by friends . . . The cycle repeats from 3 onward.

The cyclical stages neatly capture what the reader is probably thinking about the information in the ad. It validates the reader's initial skepticism, but then uses humour to show how this response evolves to enthusiastic support. The writers of the ad try to persuade readers to consider joining this unique group of individuals who found their skepticism about Vulcan Youth Serum misplaced.

Identify Points of Conflict Between Your Group and Others   The next step in creating identification involves building greater cohesion among the members of your group by showing how other groups are in conflict with them. Christian Dawn does not use this strategy in their webpage. Instead they build a partnership with viewers that brings them into the group based on their shared desire to help the less fortunate.

Invite Readers to Join You in Taking Common Action   This is the final step in creating identification and persuasion. When you feel you have established a sense of identity with your readers, you ask them to act in some way that brings your interests together and solves the problem(s) that you've described in your argument. In Figure 5 Christian Dawn concludes its list of values with a summary of "Our Mission," followed by the heading "How can you help?" The three steps invite viewers to join Christian Dawn in taking common action to help the poor.

ANALYSIS: IMPROVING DAN COOPER'S CREDIBILITY

In Case 1, Dan Cooper has 11 replies to his letter seeking new clients, all of them declining to meet with him. One of the callers notes that she would never trust her financial

Figure 6 Create a sense of identification with readers.

future to someone who cannot use a semicolon properly. Dan is stunned that what he regarded as a trivial matter could be the deciding factor in rejecting his offer. But when the written document is the only point of contact between you and your reader (as it is in Dan and his prospective clients' cases), everything that you write becomes data for your readers to analyze in considering whether they find you trustworthy. Readers who don't know Dan use his faulty punctuation as evidence that he will also be careless of the details in handling their money.

As Dan reviews his draft, he realizes that he can improve his credibility by clearly showing his knowledge of investing and financial advising. He assesses his use of technical language in the draft and sees that, although he did use some financial planning vocabulary, he mostly avoids the kinds of specific terms that would demonstrate his extensive education in this area. This is one area that he can improve. For example, in the following passage, he uses the phrases "financial plan," "creating wealth," and "reducing risk"—all laypersons' phrases associated with investment planning: "Our goal will be to work as a team to create a financial plan and REACH these goals. Are you serious about creating wealth and reducing risk? If so then call me to arrange a ½ hour meeting." These phrases are not specialized, so they don't demonstrate his understanding of the technical aspects of investing. Readers are not convinced that he "knows his stuff."

Next, Dan notices that the only figure mentioned in the letter is the amount of assets the readers have to invest (*quote data related to the topic*). Given that his letter is all about data and statistics, he decides he should probably add some attractive ones that will also demonstrate his knowledge. For example, he can quantify the increase in property values in the Burlington area over the last three years to show that he has done his homework on this point.

Another area that he can improve, Dan decides, is his use of experts (*quoting experts*). He considers using a quote from a local investment banker as a way to show his knowledge of and connections with bankers and financial planners in the area. Dan decides he can go one better by also using the local banker's comments to show that he has innovative and ingenious ideas that stodgy, traditional financial planners haven't considered (*present new ideas to show you have considered the topic*).

Next, Dan considers whether there is an opposing viewpoint that he should include, but he decides that this strategy isn't relevant to this letter.

He also considers whether he shares common values with his potential clients and realizes that this is an important area. He sees that he did try to show his readers that they share similar goals with this statement: "Are you serious about creating wealth and reducing risk? If so then call me to arrange a ½ hour meeting." It demonstrates that he does share readers' goals of wanting to increase their wealth and minimize the risks inherent in doing so.

Dan also decides that he can improve his attempts to create a sense of identification between readers and himself. In his original draft, he does not really put into action this strategy for creating credibility. If he does, he can create a hugely persuasive letter. One way to create identification is to better demonstrate shared values. Dan decides to offer his readers a useful tip to help them generate more wealth (for example, Uncle Steve mentioned the point about borrowing from his own retirement rather than the bank for a short-term loan); this tip will demonstrate that Dan is serious about creating more wealth for readers. Giving away useful information backs up his claim to want to help readers increase their wealth. He demonstrates that they share the value of making money for the reader without taking big risks.

In Dan's case, he asks readers to trust him to use their money to make more money for them (and himself, indirectly). He needs to be subtle about showing how his and his readers' interests are aligned. He tried to get at this point in these two sentences: "My promise is that working with me will bring you the best professional advice and service available. With an unlimited number of specialists, not just at ES Investment Group, but also with a network of professionals, I can assist you. IE – Accountant, Lawyer, etc." However, this wording just makes him sound self-important. Instead of *telling* his readers, he needs to *show* them what makes his among "the best professional advice and service." Then they will see how they can work with Dan to improve their investment portfolio. Dan might also show readers how he and they belong to a group by targeting a version of his letter to potential clients that share his religious or political affiliation. For example, he could refer to the volunteer work he has done offering financial consultation to clients of the domestic violence shelter sponsored by the Ben Ezra Synagogue. Another strategy that might be useful for Dan is to rewrite his letter to characterize his clients as a unique group gaining distinct advantages with him as their financial advisor. Readers will want to join this group and receive similar benefits.

Dan may also be able to show how investors working with financial groups other than Dan's form a group that is antithetical to his client group. For example, those investors will find their portfolios being "churned"—that is, assets (stocks or mutual funds) being bought and sold unnecessarily to create commissions for the advisors. The rival group of investors with churning portfolios causes increased fluctuations in the market that affect the volatility of Dan's clients' portfolios. Investors who respond to market fluctuations increase the risk of all investors. Readers will want to join the group with less risk, lower advisor commissions, and more stability, which Dan Cooper now represents (based on his argument in the letter).

Finally, Dan can end his letter by inviting readers to meet with him to review their portfolio (invite reader to join him in taking action), learn some new useful tips, and establish an ongoing financial partnership with him. Notice that he does take this step in his letter in Figure 1, but because he does not adequately establish the process of identification, readers are turned off rather than convinced to act. He has not adequately demonstrated his trustworthiness as a writer or investment advisor through the main body of the letter. He needs to more skillfully and tactfully create an emotional link or sense of identity between his readers and himself. In your revision of his draft, aim to present Dan's credentials in a way that compels readers to give him a chance to sell himself further at the face-to-face meeting.

Professional Communication Assignments

1. Revise Dan Cooper's Letter

Reread Dan Cooper's letter carefully from the perspective of a new client to figure out what specific phrases and details in the letter might have made some of the recipients aggressively rude in their responses to him. Then decide what specific kinds of evidence Dan could add to the letter to strengthen his credibility and trustworthiness. Use some of the details from Dan's résumé (reproduced in Figure 7) to help you develop accurate and detailed evidence that readers will find more persuasive. Then rewrite Dan's letter so that it accomplishes what he would like it to do: bring him new clients. Use all of the information in this module to help you create an effective, logical, and emotional appeal that makes readers want to hear what Dan Cooper has to say about their investments, and an ethical appeal that demonstrates Dan's expertise and trustworthiness in the area of financial planning.

Audience: John and Joan Pleva, and other potential clients who are unclear on why they should trust him with their retirement funds

Purpose: To motivate Mr. and Mrs. Pleva (and other potential clients) to schedule an appointment with Dan to discuss their investments

Genre: Sales letter with persuasive message

2. Create an Information Card

Create an information card to include with the letter listing the services that Dan Cooper provides. For details about what to include on the card, visit the websites of financial services firms. Here are three models to help get you started:

- www.edwardjones.ca
- www.investorsgroup.com
- www.rbcwealthmanagement.com

Audience: Prospective clients who are skeptical of changing investment advisors

Purpose: To offer readers useful free advice that will increase their interest in meeting Dan to discuss their investment portfolio

Genre: Information card

Daniel A. Cooper

Education

2012   BBA, (co-op) concentration in financial planning
                Wilfrid Laurier University, Waterloo, ON

Awards and Honours

2011   3rd place, Canadian University and Colleges Investment Challenge
                200 teams from colleges and universities across Canada entered, three prizes awarded
                Sponsored by Canadian National Trust
2008–2012   Dean's List

Work Experience

2014–present   **Investment Services Consultant**, ES Investment Group, Burlington, ON
                Manage individual portfolio of clients,
                Offer innovative and effective financial solutions to maximize investment potential

2012–2013   **Teller**, Bank of Montreal, Burlington, ON
                Served bank clients
                Prepared end of day statements
                Headed courtesy desk for regular shifts responding to bank customer inquiries

2011   **Administrative Assistant**, Steve Cooper & Associates, Oakville, ON
                Document preparation services
                Reception duties, supply management, book-keeping

2010   **Assistant to Small Business Advisor**, Bank of Montreal, Burlington, ON
                Opened new accounts for new and existing business owners
                Maintained paperwork
                Data entry

2009   **Server**, Kelsey's, Burlington, ON
                Managed tables in section of restaurant
                Took and filled orders, helped with food preparation

Figure 7 Dan Cooper's résumé.

Case 2★★★ Prince Edward Island Health Authority: Writing Is Thinking

Without smiling, Yasmin Blackwell pushed James Franklin's three-page memo report across the desk so that it was in front of him. James's face registered surprise and concern; it was obvious that Ms. Blackwell was not happy. She had read the report last night to prepare for meetings on Monday morning. The problem with the report was that it didn't tell her what she needed to know.

James was puzzled by this response. He had done all the research that Ms. Blackwell asked for, and he tried to lay it out as clearly as he could. He leaned across the desk to pick up the report. He paged through it. He *knew* everything was there that she had asked him to do: comparative figures on similar properties; estimated revenue from the sale; a floor plan of the nursing home as it currently existed; even some figures that she hadn't asked for but that James knew were relevant and important.

Ms. Blackwell acknowledged that James did do the research, but noted that he didn't provide her with a preliminary analysis or recommendations. She needed him to distill it for her. She needed him to make recommendations about what he thought the board should do.

A photo of a wharf similar to the one being proposed for the front of the property.

Zonesix/Shutterstock

As her administrative assistant, he needed to provide her with the tools to do her job. This meant useful analysis *and recommendations.* Even if she did not follow James's recommendations, she pointed out, those recommendations were useful as a starting point for her own analysis of the situation.

Ms. Blackwell noted that she wouldn't need the report until Sunday night or early Monday. That meant James had some time today and over the weekend to rewrite the report. His most important priority should be to add recommendations and elaborate his analysis of the situation. The report wasn't bad: the information and analysis were solid, but it needed to be an *argument* rather than a *description.*

James grimaced and turned to go. He did have plans for the weekend, so he'd have to get the report rewritten today unless he wanted to still be writing when he hit his friend's house in Sackville on Saturday afternoon. He liked working for the Department of Health, but there seemed to be a lot more to the job of administrative assistant than he had thought when he started back in June.

James sat down at his desk, flipping through the pages to see what he'd written. He started to see what Ms. Blackwell meant about the report describing rather than arguing for a position. Wasn't that a lot of responsibility for him—deciding what the board should do? Making a decision meant he'd have to think a lot more carefully about the information that he'd collected.

About six weeks earlier, the Prince Edward Island Department of Health, which oversees the administration and management of Ocean View Retirement Community (as well as 12 other nursing homes across the island), received an offer from Islander Entertainment Group for $100,000 to purchase the 8-metre-wide strip of shoreline between the nursing home and the water's edge. Islander Entertainment was proposing to build a large wharf, restaurant, amusement park, and marina out in front of the nursing home, using the waterfront strip as well as a 10-metre right-of-way along the south side of the building that would give them access to the waterfront. The accompanying photograph came with Islander Entertainment Group's offer. It illustrates the proposed complex in relation to Ocean View, except that the building over the water would be located directly in front of the retirement community, blocking the residents' ocean view.

Basics About Logic

One of the common mistakes that many people make in thinking about writing is that if the grammar is correct, the words are spelled properly, and the commas are where they should be, then it is a good piece of writing. If the text also contains detailed and useful information about the topic, then it's a great piece of writing. Although these aspects of writing may be important in the final proofreading stages, they are secondary to the content and thought in the writing. When you are asked to write a report in an organization, supervisors will rarely have in mind for you to regurgitate the plain facts. Instead they are looking for you to take a stand on the topic, interpret the facts that you collect in your research, and present them with a viewpoint that demonstrates logical analysis, insightful ideas, and clear explanations. These goals are only achieved after careful thinking about the topic.

In business and professional communication, thinking clearly and writing well are especially important because most communication involves analyzing a problem or situation and then presenting a solution. If your manager asks you to study a problem and collect all relevant information needed to solve that problem, he or she also usually expects you to analyze and process the information as well. Your logical analysis of the situation and your proposed perspective on it helps guide your manager's thinking too. Even if he or she disagrees with your perspective, your writing helps clarify the areas of disagreement to help him or her think through the issue. When you think carefully and logically through the subject matter, you improve your own skills, and that will make you a better candidate for promotion.

An argument is different from a description because it takes a stand on an issue. An argument makes claims. To persuade someone of something, you need to present them with a series of related **claims** and supporting **evidence** that they find logical and interesting. To take you seriously, readers must also be convinced that you know your topic well. A good argument is made up of three parts:

1. The ways that you demonstrate your knowledge of the topic (your credibility as a writer)
2. The claims and evidence that present your ideas on the topic (the logic of your argument)
3. The commitment the reader comes to feel toward your topic (the emotional content of the argument)

Claim: Statements that you believe to be true together with reasons that explain why you think the statement is true

Evidence: Facts, narratives, other documents, and/or statistics that back up your claim that a statement is true

The Logic of Your Argument

The logic of an argument refers to its internal consistency. To create an argument that is internally consistent means that you develop a series of claims about the subject that cover its major aspects but do not contradict one another.

LO 3 Develop argumentative claims to explain and create a convincing case for a recommended solution

What Is a Claim?
A claim is a statement in which you give a position and then add a reason that explains that position. The Canadian Cancer Society website (Figure 8) creates an argument about preventing cancer.

> *Example 1:* You can reduce your risk of developing cancer [the claim] *because* half of all cancers can be prevented through healthy living [the stated reason].
>
> *Example 2:* You should learn more about healthy lifestyle choices *because* lifestyle choices can reduce your risk of developing cancer.
>
> *Example 3:* You should find out how to stop cancer early *because* factors in the environment can increase your risk of developing cancer.

In each of these examples, the word *because* joins the claim and the stated reason. Usually, the claim plus a reason relies on a second, unstated reason. For example, the claim "You can reduce your risk of developing cancer *because* half of all cancers can be prevented through healthy living" relies on the assumption (or unstated reason) that you want to live healthily to avoid getting cancer. By making this claim, the Canadian Cancer Society assumes that you agree that avoiding cancer is a good move and something you are willing to work toward by changing your lifestyle. Writers usually assume that their readers share the value(s) implied in the unstated reason.

Making Claims
There are a number of ways that you can create claims that may be useful as you expand your argument on a particular topic. Rather than making up your mind before you think through a situation, you should generate as many ideas as you can about the topic from all perspectives. You want as many arguments for a particular action as you can think of against it. Brainstorm a list of reasons. You can also use general topics that can be adapted to any situation to help you come up with ideas. Although there are a number of general topics that you could use, here are five that are useful in analyzing situations in business and professional communication:

1. *Define or redefine key terms.* For example, what does it mean to "make healthy lifestyle choices"? Does this just mean switching from cream to milk in your coffee and removing the skin from your chicken before you eat it? Does it include taking preventative action to avoid disease? Does it include promoting your choices to friends and family members? These questions try to define what "making healthy lifestyle choices" is.

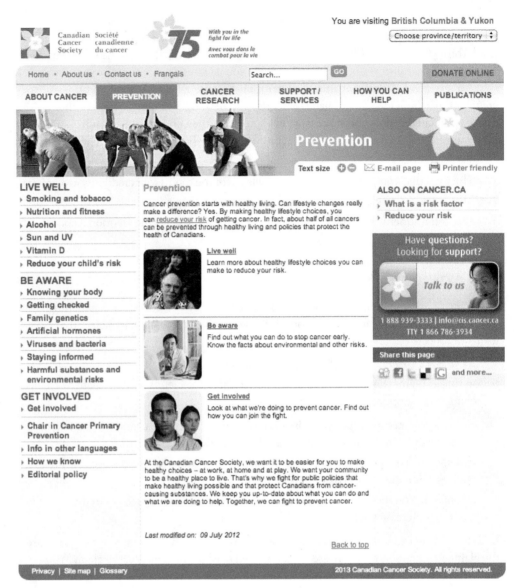

Figure 8 Canadian Cancer Society website creates an argument about how to prevent cancer.

Source: Used with permission of Canadian Cancer Society.

2. *Logically subdivide your topic.* In Figure 8, the Canadian Cancer Society has divided "Prevention" into three separate webpages: "Live well," which examines "making healthy lifestyle choices" in greater detail; "Be aware," which discusses known facts about environmental and other risks; and "Get involved," which invites readers to find out what the Canadian Cancer Society is doing to prevent cancer and to join the Society in its work.

3. *Decide based on precedent.* You can generate ideas using this general topic by researching what others have decided when facing similar circumstances. You can use others' solutions as evidence to support your own position or you can critique them in the light of your perspective on the topic. For example, you might interview a series of people who have survived cancer to discover their views on making healthy lifestyle choices. Their experience might provide inspiration and models for further actions people could take to prevent cancer.

4. *Use the consequences of something as a reason to do or not do it.* For example, if you were researching ways to prevent skin cancer, you might examine evidence supporting the claim that tanning beds produce vitamin D (individuals living in northern climates are often vitamin D deficient). After investigating the types of light rays used in tanning beds, you would conclude that tanning beds produce only harmful UVA rays, not the UVB rays that our bodies use to manufacture vitamin D, so they in fact increase the risk of skin cancer and provide no corresponding benefits.

5. *Take a point of view that contradicts common opinion.* In this strategy you consider the various viewpoints that are possible on your topic. What do you think most people would say about, for example, making healthy lifestyle choices? Perhaps they would complain that making healthy lifestyle choices is boring: eating fruits and vegetables and lean meats, avoiding fast food and refined sugar and flour treats like donuts, pastries, and ice cream. You might consider the ways in which eating healthy food is interesting and tasty so that you could argue for the enjoyable aspects of healthy eating.

Of course, these general topics are useful for helping you generate some claims and reasons, but from there you need to expand these ideas into full-fledged, well-supported claims that build your overall argument.

Expanding Claims

A claim + a stated reason + an unstated (or implied) reason make a good *beginning* for an argument. From this beginning you need to add *evidence* to expand the claim into an argument. Let's expand an earlier example into an argument: You can reduce your risk of developing cancer *because* half of all cancers can be prevented through healthy living. One way to expand this claim is to consider what values or beliefs are assumed in the stated reason. In other words, what does the Canadian Cancer Society value when it states "Because half of all cancers are caused by lifestyle choices, you can reduce your risk of getting cancer by making healthy lifestyle choices"?

LO 4 Synthesize information from supporting documents to create strong arguments

1. It values quality of life—that is, the ability to live cancer-free.
2. It values taking action to achieve the goal of living cancer-free.
3. It values efforts made to reduce the risk of getting cancer.

What Evidence Can We Point to in Support of These Values?   The Canadian Cancer Society demonstrates its valuing of quality of life by devoting a series of webpages to "Prevention"—that is, actions individuals can take to reduce their risk of developing cancer (a severe reduction in quality of life). One page educates readers about the kinds of lifestyle choices they can make to reduce their risk (details about actions that support the Society's position that you can control whether you get cancer). Another page presents facts about "environmental and other risks" (facts that support the Society's contention that environmental factors can contribute to cancer risk). The navigational bar on the left side of the page lists topics related to cancer risk (additional evidence to support the Society's argument in support of cancer prevention). One of the links, "Chair in Cancer Primary Prevention," indicates an expert that is sponsored by the Society that focuses on cancer prevention. Quoting informed people or experts also contributes convincing evidence to support the claim.

Here are three ways of adding evidence to support the values underlying a claim and reason:

1. Add facts (vivid description)
2. Quote comments from experts
3. Cite data and statistics

Sometimes you will need to do some research to locate the evidence that supports your claims and reasons. The Canadian Cancer Society webpage shown in Figure 8 has 13 links to topics related to cancer risk and prevention. These additional webpages all serve as evidence to support the argument that readers can control (to a certain extent) whether they develop cancer by making healthy lifestyle choices. Any research you do to support your claims is worthwhile because data, facts, and quotations from experts strengthen the logic of your argument, making it more persuasive.

Strengthening Your Argument

Once you have developed a claim, a stated reason, and an unstated reason into a well-supported argument, consider it from opposing viewpoints to see where its weaknesses lie. If you can figure out where the opposite perspective might refute your argument, you can decide how best to modify your ideas to take the opposing view into account.

Someone might rebut the Canadian Cancer Society's argument for taking action to reduce cancer risk by focusing on the other 50 percent of cancers that are not lifestyle related. The argument may be made that we could spend our lives making healthy lifestyle choices but still develop a genetically caused cancer. In view of this position, one might qualify the earlier claim to acknowledge that action can prevent only some cancers but point out that it is better to take what action we can rather than wait around to develop a different cancer.

ANALYSIS: JAMES TRANSFORMS DESCRIPTION INTO ARGUMENT

James was shocked when his boss, Yasmin Blackwell, rejected his report because it didn't include what *he* thought about the topic. He started to realize that good writing is good thinking: logical analysis, insightful ideas, and clear explanation. Since he didn't carefully think through his topic, he could not write well about it—not in a way that was useful to his reader. He also realized that he needed to go beyond just thinking carefully about his topic. He should have also translated that thought into a form and presentation that communicated his ideas effectively to Ms. Blackwell to help them both achieve their purposes. She needed an analysis of the information about the Islander Entertainment Group's offer to purchase the shoreline in front of the Ocean View Retirement Community. As chair of the Prince Edward Island Department of Health Board of Directors, she would have to lead the board in making a decision about the offer. She needed to go into the Monday morning meeting with a clear understanding of the offer and a carefully made decision about how best to respond to it. James's careful analysis and recommendations would be a shortcut in her own analysis of the situation.

To rewrite his report, James Franklin has to figure out what he thinks the board members should do. This means re-examining the data that he collected to decide what it means. Here are the major issues that he needs to consider as he decides whether is it better for the board to sell the land or keep it:

- What is the board's mission and responsibility in the larger community?
- How will the sale of this land affect the residents of Ocean View Retirement Community?
- What is the board's responsibility regarding the welfare of the retirement community's residents?
- Is the offer realistically priced?
- Does the board need the money that the sale would generate?
- What are the long-term negative and positive consequences to selling this land?

Figure 9 reproduces the answers that James jotted down to these questions. You can see that the answers themselves start to transform into arguments as he works his way down the

What is board's mission/responsibility in the larger community?

- Responsible for providing quality health care to the citizens of Prince Edward Island
- Also for sound financial management of health care resources (including hospital lands)

How will the sale of this land affect the residents of Ocean View Retirement Community?

- Islander Entertainment's proposed structure will ruin their view of the ocean
- Many won't notice because they are sedated for various problems, including dementia, Alzheimer's, etc.
- Development adds someplace close for residents to go for entertainment (mental stimulation)
- Public right of way (road) on south side of building would greatly increase road noise and traffic beside the dementia wing

What is board's responsibility re: welfare of retirement community residents?

- Provide quality health care: does this include a quiet environment and a good view?
- Many elderly people lack mental stimulation: proposed development (Ferris wheel on wharf and restaurant/pub) would be increased mental stimulation for those residents that need it

Does the board need the money that the sale would generate?

- Some shortfall in funding in last year's budget
- Request for money to refurbish common room at Ocean View not allocated by Department of Health
- $100,000 offer would provide extra funding beyond refurbished common room for updating aging facilities at Ocean View
- Overall, though, the board/department/ministry does **not** need the money that badly

Is the offer realistically priced?

- Conservative offer for oceanfront property
- Could ask for more $$$

What are the long-term consequences to selling this land?

Negatives

- Board (and Ministry) would lose control of further development of land and its usage through selling it
- What if Islander Entertainment goes bankrupt? Board wouldn't control what happens to structure/additional development of the property
- Loss of valuable oceanfront asset: loss of $$ (long-term) and control

Positives

- Increased development of harbour community to draw tourists and locals to downtown centre
- Potential activities for residents of Ocean View and their families/friends who visit
- I can't think of anything else!!!

Figure 9 James Franklin's notes as he analyzes the Islander Entertainment offer.

list. The details that were neutral information in the descriptive version of the report become pieces of evidence in the argument that support his claims.

Logic and James's Argument

James's goal was to create an internally consistent discussion of the proposed waterfront sale. To do this, he needed to develop a series of claims that covered its major aspects without contradicting one another. James developed a series of claims for his report:

> *Example 1:* The Board should sell the waterfront strip [the claim] *because* the money from the sale will pay for improvements to the retirement home common room [the stated reason].
>
> *Example 2:* The Board should not sell the waterfront strip *because* developing this land will ruin the residents' spectacular view of the ocean.
>
> *Example 3:* The Board should sell the waterfront strip *because* the development will bring more tourists and local people to the town harbour to enjoy the waterfront.

In each of these examples, the word *because* joins the claim and the stated reason. As noted earlier, a claim plus a reason relies on a second, unstated reason. For example, "The Board should sell the waterfront strip because the money from the sale will pay for improvements to the retirement home common room" relies on the assumption that improving the common room is important. In making this claim, James assumes that Ms. Blackwell agrees that updating the common room is a priority for the nursing home and, therefore, should be for the board.

To ensure that he thought through the proposal, James decided to make a thorough list of ideas from all perspectives. Figure 10 presents James's analysis using the general topics. Once he had some useful ideas, he decided to expand them into full-fledged, well-supported claims that built his overall argument.

James Expands Claims into Arguments

Adding evidence to a claim produces an argument. James reread his first claim: "The Board should sell the waterfront strip because the money from the sale will pay for improvements to the retirement home common room." To expand this claim, he considered the values or beliefs that are assumed in the stated reason. In other words, what does James value when he writes, "the money from the sale will pay for improvements to the retirement home common room"?

1. The common room update should be a priority for the nursing home
2. If the budget didn't fund the update, we should look for alternative funding
3. Actions that improve the lives of the nursing home residents are good

To support the point that updating the common room is a priority, James evaluates the condition of the room right now, adding vivid details—the peeling, faded paint, the ripped fabric on the chairs, and the duct tape holding several card table legs together. He notes that few residents use the room because it is depressing (fact). He includes a comment from one resident about why she avoids the common room: "Daisy Ellis notes that in the common room these days, 'The sun shines right in there, and it gets too hot. We need blinds that block out the worst of the sun so it's comfortable to sit in there'" (comments from informed people or experts). James also adds a statistic: "Most mornings only two or three of the 125 residents will be sitting in the common room after breakfast." This evidence shows readers the importance of renovating the common room. James intends to persuade the reader to agree with his value that the renovation be a priority at the nursing home.

James used the research that he did for the first version of the report. To be able to quote Daisy Ellis's perspective about the existing common room, however, James would

1. *Define or redefine key terms.* For example, what does it mean for the Health Authority to "provide quality health care"? *Does this just mean providing doctors and facilities to citizens? Does it include taking preventative action to avoid disease? Does it include promoting mental health?* These questions try to define what "health care" is. *What about citizens' spiritual health?* This question begins to redefine "health care."

2. *Logically subdivide your topic.* For example, to explore the possibilities for action that the board could take, James might write: "The board has three options on this issue: 1. Refuse the offer to purchase and retain control of the waterfront; 2. Sell the land and lose control of the waterfront; and 3. Lease the land to Islander Entertainment and maintain control of the property." From here, he could give a cursory analysis of the first two options and then focus on explaining and developing the third, using it as his solution and recommendation in the report.

3. *Decide based on precedent.* To use this general topic, James researches the decisions made by Health Boards across Canada to discover what others have decided when facing a similar proposal. Depending on what he finds, he can use the decisions by other boards to argue in support of his position: "The Board of Directors for the Vancouver Island Health Authority, when faced with a similar offer to purchase the shoreline in front of The Peaks Retirement Village, decided to . . ."

4. *Use the consequences of something as a reason to do or not do it.* For example, James notes that the proposed development will increase traffic noise beside the dementia wing of the nursing home (*consequence*). He argues that the board should reject the offer because more noise will increase the suffering of the dementia patients in that wing (*conclusion*).

5. *Take a point of view that contradicts common opinion.* In this case, James assumes that common opinion would say to sell the land and use the money to improve the facilities for nursing home residents by hiring additional staff or purchasing new equipment that the residents would use. In contrast, he argues for rejecting the sale, highlighting that the quality of the view and the health benefits that generations of residents will get from the peaceful setting are more beneficial than a few dollars that are soon spent. This argument relies on readers valuing the quality of life of nursing home residents from a spiritual perspective rather than purely a medical health standpoint.

Figure 10 James generated some useful ideas using the general topics.

need to either visit the nursing home or call some of the residents. This would be worthwhile because data, facts, and quotations from experts would strengthen his logic, making it more persuasive.

Exercise 1: Analyzing the Values and Beliefs in a Claim Plus Reason

1. Examine the following two claims.
2. Analyze each to identify the unstated reason the claim relies on.
3. Create a list of the assumptions, values, and beliefs that the stated and unstated reasons rely on.

4. Using the previous discussion, identify some specific pieces of evidence that you could use to support these claims.

Claim 1: The Board should not sell the waterfront strip *because* developing this land will ruin the residents' spectacular view of the ocean.

Claim 2: The Board should sell the waterfront strip *because* the development will bring more tourists and local people to the town harbour to enjoy the waterfront.

Generate your own claim plus reason that James could use in his argument. To do this, you may have to decide where you stand on the issue of whether the board should sell the nursing home waterfront. Then analyze your claim to identify the unstated reason or assumption and the values and beliefs that underlie them. Next, develop some evidence that supports your claim. Do some research on the Internet or the library, if necessary, to find appropriate facts or statistics that work as evidence.

Figure 11 expands James's claim into an argument by adding evidence. Note that the italicized text in the figure identifies the various strategies used to create evidence to make the argument more convincing.

Finally, James considered possible rebuttals to his argument, concluding that a good rebuttal would be to ask whether the land sale is the best way to fund the common room renovation. Opposing viewpoints might include the argument that updating the common room will increase the number of users but sacrifice the spectacular view from the windows, a questionable improvement. Users would lose an important reason to sit in there. To respond to this criticism, James could write a follow-up paragraph to this argument that addressed the value of the ocean view to nursing home residents. He could acknowledge the value of the view but argue that updating the common room is more important because of its larger and more real benefits to residents. He might argue that changing the ocean view at the nursing home will affect only a few of the residents because most of them are too ill to notice.

The board should sell the waterfront strip because the money from the sale will pay for improvements to the retirement home common room. Records show that over the last three years, the board has asked for but not received budget funding to improve the Ocean View common room *[Demonstrates that the improvements have been a budget priority not shared by the Department of Health]*. Since then, the quality of the furnishings has continued to degrade to the point that the worn patches of upholstery are actually becoming rips, with the stuffing sticking out. Several card table legs are repaired with duct tape *[Aesthetic reasons to update the room]*. The original curtains can no longer be drawn to keep out the early morning sun, so the room heats up quickly most days. Only a handful of residents (two or three of the 125 total) still use the room, mostly individuals in wheelchairs placed there by nursing home staff *[Statistical evidence]*. Daisy Ellis, a fifteen-year resident of Ocean View, no longer uses the common room *[Expert testimony as evidence]*: "The sun shines right in there, and it gets too hot. We need blinds that block out the worst of the sun so it's comfortable to sit in there" *[Practical reasons to update the room]*. One way to prioritize improvements to the common room is to use some of the proceeds from selling the waterfront strip. We have budgeted $10,000 for these updates in the past. The sale of the land would also provide $90,000 additional money for other projects at Ocean View or elsewhere.

Figure 11 A claim plus a reason expanded to include evidence to create a convincing step in the argument. The italicized text identifies the strategies used to create evidence.

3. Rewrite James Franklin's Report to Make Recommendations

Assume the part of James Franklin. Write a two- or three-page report to Yasmin Blackwell in which you review the offer to purchase the waterfront at Ocean View Retirement Community and argue a particular course of action for the director. Use the discussion in this module on how to create effective appeals to logic, emotion, and credibility to help you analyze the case and present your perspective in a convincing argument. Use the data in Table 1 and Figure 12 as evidence to help you support the arguments that you make.

Audience: Yasmin Blackwell, James Franklin's boss

Purpose: To outline a position about the proposed sale of the Ocean View Retirement Community waterfront that demonstrates careful consideration of the evidence and a well thought out plan that Ms Blackwell can use as a basis for her own analysis and decision.

Genre: Memo report

4. Write a Memo to the Director of Ocean View Retirement Community

As a business communication co-op student working at Ocean View Retirement Community, you have been asked by your boss, Anthony Perkins, director of the facility, to draft a response for his signature to a letter he received from Yasmin Blackwell, a member of the Board of Directors that oversees the facility, about a proposal to sell the waterfront access in front of Ocean View. She has requested advice from Mr. Perkins about how such a commercial development at the retirement community might affect the lives of its residents, and she needs a response by the end of the week. Mr. Perkins has told you that his gut reaction to the proposal is negative, but he is willing to listen to an argument about how it might benefit residents. Evaluate the information from Case 2 to assess how the commercial development might affect the retirement community's residents. Decide whether you think it would benefit or harm residents.

Table 1 Real estate prices for waterfront and nonwaterfront lots around P.E.I.

Location of Properties	Lot size	Water	No Water	Asking Price
Tignish	200 x 150		X	$26,900
Tignish	.7 acres	X		$109,000
O'Connor sub.	.34 acres	X		$60,000
O'Connor sub.	.38 acres		X	$12,000
Cape Traverse	.39 acres	X		$99,500
Cape Wolfe	.5 acres		X	$7,900
Brooklyn	.28 acres		X	$9,900
Seawood	.28 acres		X	$29,700
Fernwood	various		X	$75,000
Fernwood	various	X		$100,000

Source: Based on P.E.I. Real Estate Listings, August, 2007.

Figure 12 Plan of Ocean View Retirement Community and proposed waterfront development.

You have two options:

1. Draft the letter to Yasmin Blackwell explaining how the development will affect facility residents.

   OR

2. Draft a memo to Mr. Perkins trying to convince him that the commercial development will benefit facility residents.

Audience: For option 1, your initial audience is Mr. Perkins, your immediate supervisor; your primary audience is Ms. Blackwell, Chair of the Board of Directors of Ocean View Retirement Community. For option 2, your primary audience is your manager, Mr. Perkins, who is opposed to the idea but willing to entertain opposing viewpoints.

Purpose: For option 1, to educate Ms. Blackwell on the range of impacts that developing the waterfront will have on the residents and employees at the retirement community; a secondary purpose will be to demonstrate your competence and intelligence to your supervisor, Mr. Perkins, and finally, to make Mr. Perkins look good, because he will ultimately sign and send your draft. For option 2, your main purposes are to speak for the residents of the retirement community, to demonstrate your competence and intelligence to your immediate supervisor, and to serve as an opposing viewpoint to help Mr. Perkins explore the proposal more fully.

Genre:

Option 1: Persuasive letter

Option 2: Persuasive memo report

Case 3★★ Persuading Guests to Observe the Rules at Brandywine Falls Inn and Cottages

Zurijeta/Shutterstock

Meijing Zhu slammed the car door shut and then took a deep breath of the cold, fresh air as she looked around. There was still more than a hint of winter in the knife-edged wind but the sun was shining brilliantly, lighting up the branches of the towering pine trees that surrounded her. There were worse ways of spending the summer than working at a resort in Muskoka, but in early May summer was definitely several weeks off yet. She shivered and retrieved her backpack from the backseat just as the black flies found her. Slinging it onto her back, she made a dash for the main office at Brandywine Falls Inn, 30 metres away from the parking lot.

Meijing bolted in the office door, slamming it quickly and firmly behind her. "Boy, those black flies are vicious first thing in the morning!"

"Their appetites don't weaken as the day goes on," replied Helen Hurley, the wife side of the husband-and-wife team that owned and operated Brandywine Falls Inn and Cottages, located just off Highway 69 south of Parry Sound. Mrs. Hurley got up from the desk behind the counter with a file folder that she held out to Meijing.

Mrs. Hurley began to give an overview of the materials in the folder. They had decided that every room should have a letter that told guests about resort improvements over the winter, as well as reminding them to follow the house rules. There had been a lot of trouble at the end of last summer with rowdy, thoughtless guests. The letter was one attempt to be firmer about the rules, with the risk being the loss of reputation as a family resort if they didn't get the guests under control. Both owners agreed that making sure guests have a clear list of the rules at the start of their visit was a priority. Guests could be given the letter at the registration desk when they checked in or they could find a copy with the information binders in each unit.

Meijing liked the idea and suggested that the letter could be given out at the registration desk as well as appear in the binder. She had done an assignment like this in her business communication course at George Brown College last year. She offered to draft the letter.

That sounded great to Mrs. Hurley. She gave Meijing a list of some of the improvements made over the winter and directed her to the website to find a copy of the rules of the resort. Mrs. Hurley noted that they didn't want this letter ordering people to follow the rules. That didn't work last year. She wanted Meijing's draft to try to make them feel like they wanted to follow the rules. The hope was that by explaining the reasons for the rules in more detail, the resort might get more guests to comply with them.

Meijing stood in front of the computer, which had the main page for the Inn onscreen, and clicked on the "rates and policies" link. After scanning the page, she noticed that rules were combined with other information on the page. She opened a word processing file and began copying and pasting the policies into the blank document. Figure 13 reproduces her finished list of rules; Figure 14 shows the list of renovations and updates to the Inn.

It will take a bit of writing to transform these terse statements into a persuasive argument, she thought as she worked.

Figure 13 Meijing's list of policies at Brandywine Falls Inn and Cottages.

HIGH SEASON is from June 15 to September 21, all long weekends and holidays, and some additional weekends

TOWELS: Bring your own beach, pool, and whirlpool towels

HOT TUB: Skinny dipping permitted after 8 P.M.

VISITORS: Limit of four visitors per unit allowed at a time

PARKING: Please park in visitor's parking lot at entrance gate

OFF SEASON: Clothing optional permitted

HIGH SEASON: Clothing optional not permitted

REGISTRATION: For your security, all your visitors must register at office before going to any unit

PETS: Because some of our guests have pet allergies, we have had to strictly enforce our ban on pets. For this reason, we have a **no pets** rule at Brandywine Falls Inn and Cottages. Local kennels are available.

QUIET TIME: From 11:00 P.M. to 8:30 A.M. Please respect everyone's right to a quiet, peaceful holiday.

To ensure everyone's enjoyment, we reserve the right to accept, reject, or terminate a reservation at any time.

Figure 14 Meijing's completed list of renovations to Brandywine Falls Inn.

Improvements and Updates at Brandywine Falls Inn and Cottages
✓ All units painted and new blinds
✓ New awnings or porches on all cottage units
✓ Rec hall renovated, Sony PS 4 console and games added
✓ Two computer terminals with email and computer game links
✓ Wireless internet connection in all units, as well as rec hall lounge and library
✓ Addition of two trampolines and three barracudas for more water fun
✓ New 5 km marked and maintained hiking trail
✓ 15 m^2 of new white beach sand

Basics About Emotional Appeals

Though the logic of your argument is important, there are two other parts to persuasion that are essential if you hope to have people act on your message: your emotional appeal and your credibility as a speaker on your topic. The **emotional appeal** refers to writing your argument in a way that makes readers care about your message. Your credibility, as stated previously, refers to whether readers think that you know what you are talking about—do they trust you? As well as establishing your credibility and developing a consistent and well-supported series of claims with evidence, you want to connect with readers on an emotional level so that they want to act in the way that you propose. To connect with readers, you can choose from among or use all of several strategies to develop an emotional appeal:

- Conscious word choice
- Concrete examples and vivid details
- Appropriate analogies or metaphors

Word Choice   You are probably already aware that you can use a variety of words to talk about any particular subject. Some words add a positive slant to your topic (positive connotation); different words can convey a negative or critical attitude toward it (negative connotation). Let's look at an example of how word choice affects the development of the logic of an argument. Figure 15 is part of a pitch by the Canadian

Figure 15 Note the primarily logical appeals in the CAA page on distracted driving.

Source: Text is reproduced and adapted from Canadian Automobile Association (CAA) website.

Neutral Word Choice	Negative Connotations
If you are driving on a residential road, this means that you may have **missed** 85 parked cars, 36 houses, or five intersections. Maybe you **didn't see** the vehicle that was backing down a driveway or maybe **it was** the young cyclist who may have suddenly turned into your path.	If you are driving on a residential road, this means that you may have **side-swiped** 85 parked cars, passed 36 houses or run 5 intersections. Maybe you **T-boned** the vehicle that was backing down a driveway or maybe you **smashed** into the young cyclist who may have suddenly turned into your path.

Figure 16 Compare the connotations of the word choices in each passage.

Source: Text is reproduced and adapted from Canadian Automobile Association (CAA) website.

Automobile Association to discourage viewers from texting while driving. The CAA takes a logical approach, using facts and figures to convince readers: "Based on a recent CAA time trial, replying to a text message takes an average of 33.6 seconds. If you are driving on a residential road, this means that you may have missed 85 parked cars, 36 houses or 5 intersections. Maybe you didn't see the vehicle that was backing down a driveway or maybe it was the young cyclist who may have suddenly turned into your path. Just imagine what else you may have missed, and the consequences that could follow." In this passage, the word choice is neutral: "you may have missed . . . you didn't see . . . or maybe it was. . . Just imagine what else you may have missed and the consequences that could follow." In this statement, the emotional appeal comes in the final sentence where readers must use their imaginations to confront possible catastrophic outcomes. Figure 16 presents an alternative version that replaces neutral verbs with descriptive ones, creating a vivid image of the catastrophic outcomes that leaves little to the imagination.

Use Concrete Examples and Vivid Details A second way to develop an effective emotional appeal in an argument is to use concrete examples and vivid details. Of course, these are also useful for fully informing your readers about the information you want them to know. But they also help readers to become more interested and invested in what you are saying.

In Figure 17, note the concrete details used in the advertisement, "Why love one . . . but eat the other?" by www.iVegan.ca, persuading readers to shun pork. Context for the question comes from photographs of a Jack Russell terrier and a piglet, both smiling and making eye contact with viewers. The specific fact, "mother pigs sing to their piglets while nursing," for example, surprises viewers and demonstrates the writer's knowledge. Statistics, "26 million pigs" and "2-feet wide crates," also build credibility. Additional concrete details build emotional *and* logical appeals: "pigs are the smartest domestic animals, with intelligence beyond that of a 3-year-old human child," "pigs dream, recognize their names, and form affectionate loyal bonds." These facts show that pigs are actually smarter and better companion animals than dogs, yet viewers are inexplicably repulsed at the idea of eating dogs but not pigs.

Figure 17 Logical appeal appears in the text, whereas emotional appeal appears in both text and image.

Source: iVegan.ca

Exercise 2: How Concrete Examples and Vivid Details Create Emotions

1. Examine the advertisement for the humanity of pigs (Figure 17) and identify concrete examples and vivid details that add to its impact and its argument.

2. List the phrases that you consider examples and details.

3. Analyze the phrases to determine the kind of emotion that each phrase or the phrases taken together are intended to create in the reader.

4. What other techniques does this advertisement use to pique the reader's interest in its message?

5. Write a one-half to one-page summary of your analysis of how the concrete examples and vivid details create an emotional appeal that builds interest in the argument.

Develop Appropriate Analogies and Metaphors   The third way to develop effective emotional appeals in an argument is to use comparisons such as analogies or metaphors that make your issue or product come alive for your readers.

Analogies: Comparisons that emphasize the similarities between two things or situations

Analogies are comparisons that emphasize the similarities between two things or situations. For example the "Why love one . . . but eat the other?" advertisement in Figure 17 uses an analogy to compare a dog to a pig. The ad does this by posing this question and then detailing facts about pigs that viewers must measure against what they know about dogs.

The facts about pigs summarized in the ad highlight their intelligence and inner lives, knowledge that also highlights ways in which pigs exceed dogs in intelligence, nurturing behaviour, and emotional attachments. This comparison, where pigs exceed dogs in admirable qualities, creates cognitive dissonance in readers who believe they are entitled to allow mistreatment and consumption of these smart, sensitive animals. This strategy strengthens viewer engagement in the subject and creates an emotional appeal intended to motivate readers to feel guilt about eating pork.

Metaphors are comparisons that describe an unfamiliar idea in terms of a familiar idea. For example, the advertisement, "Why love one . . . but eat the other?," illustrates through the extensive list of facts and information the ways in which pigs have human qualities: mothers pigs sing to their piglets as they nurse; they form affectionate bonds with one another and other species including humans; they are smarter than 3-year-old humans, and they understand some human language (for example, their names). These human-like qualities are then juxtaposed against the treatment that pigs receive in industrial pig farming, which is horrifying, especially if viewers, in light of what they have just learned about pigs, substitute dogs or humans into the photographs that illustrate some of the experiences of pigs in contemporary industrial pig farming. The emotional content arises from the readers' response to the basis for comparison. Base your word choice on what you want to accomplish with the comparison: to educate, inform, persuade, entertain, and so on.

Metaphors: Comparisons that describe an unfamiliar idea in terms of a familiar idea

ANALYSIS: MEIJING MOTIVATES READERS TO FOLLOW THE RULES

Meijing knows that the logic of her argument will be important, but it will be even more important to have readers act on her message. To have any hope of motivating them to follow the rules, she knows that she needs to develop her credibility and emotional appeals effectively—that is, readers will have to accept her argument and care about her request. Let's look at her audience and purpose first. In Meijing's case, she wants guests to read and understand the resort's rules, but she also wants them to remember and comply with them later (audience analysis). To persuade guests to follow the rules, she needs to convince them that it is important—that they *want* to act in those ways. First, she needs to develop good reasons to show readers why they should follow the rules (her logical argument). Not only does she want to present good reasons to follow the rules, she also wants guests to decide to act according to the rules. She wants to encourage those readers who were always inclined to behave appropriately as well as inform those readers who were unaware that there are rules, and she wants to reinforce for readers who may have other ideas that a certain standard of behaviour is expected (her purposes).

To change or reinforce the way readers respond to the rules, Meijing knows that she should pay attention to her word choice in the message, use concrete examples and vivid details and, where appropriate, include analogies and metaphors, all strategies that will engage her readers. Meijing thought about word choice: she would have to choose carefully when to use positive and negative slant to her topic. She selected one of the rules from her file and drafted two more versions of it:

- HOT TUB, bathing suits optional after 8 P.M.
- HOT TUB, nude bathing permitted after 8 P.M.
- HOT TUB, skinny dipping allowed after 8 P.M.

She considered how each phrasing conveyed a different idea about the activity. The wording for "bathing naked" seemed neutral in the first statement, hypercorrect in the second, and colloquial (informal or even slang) in the third one. She analyzed the emotions attached to each phrasing: "Bathing suits optional" seemed least emotional, being mainly

> A number of guests at Brandywine Falls Inn have serious pet allergies, so we are maintaining our pet-free status at the Inn again this year. This policy is strictly enforced. At the same time, we do realize that it is often a problem for guests to find family members or friends willing to look after pets while they are on vacation, so we have an arrangement with two local kennels who will provide excellent, loving care to your pets during your stay here at the Inn. Present one of our guest coupons to the Muskoka Country Club for Pets or the Four Paws Inn for a 15% discount on your kenneling fees. The coupons are available at the registration desk.

Figure 18 Meijing's first draft of an argument explaining the no-pets policy at the Inn.

descriptive. "Nude bathing permitted" sounded stuffy and hoity-toity, whereas "skinny dipping allowed" sounded like harmless, adolescent fun. Meijing concluded that whichever choice she made would reinforce or undercut in her readers' minds the point that Brandywine Falls Inn and Cottages is a family resort.

Next, Meijing considered how word choice might affect the development of the logic of her argument. Her rules list contained the bare bones of an argument explaining why pets were not allowed at the Inn: "Since some of our guests have pet allergies, we have had to strictly enforce our ban on pets. For this reason, we have a 'no pets' rule at Brandywine Falls Inn and Cottages. Local kennels are available." This rule informs and demands that readers follow the rule, attempting persuasion in an unforgiving way. Meijing decided that it needed rewriting if she was to persuade readers in her letter to board their pets. Rewritten, it should help readers understand and make them want to cooperate with the rule, she concluded.

She analyzed the argument to develop a more persuasive one. First she identified the claim and stated reason: "We have had to strictly enforce our ban on pets because some of our guests have pet allergies." The unstated reason underlying this claim is something like "We want to offer our allergic guests facilities that are not contaminated with pet allergens." If the owners wanted to make both pet-owning guests and pet-allergic guests welcome, they could designate some of their units as pet friendly and others as pet free. That seemed not to be the case. The target audience for this rule, Meijing decided, was guests who own pets, not guests with pet allergies. She contemplated various ways that she might expand the claim into an argument to which pet owners might respond positively. Figure 18 reproduces Meijing's first draft attempt.

Exercise 3: Analyze the Word Choice in Meijing's First Draft

1. Examine the words that Meijing has used in her first draft in Figure 18.
2. Pick out the words that you think contribute most directly to creating the tone in the paragraph.
3. Classify each word according to whether it has positive, negative, or neutral connotations.
4. Substitute more negative or more positive words to change the overall tone of the argument.
5. Rewrite the paragraph emphasizing the negative tone.
6. Write it again emphasizing the positive tone, based on your choice of words to express ideas.

Meijing further developed her emotional appeal by considering how she might incorporate concrete examples and vivid details. She considered whether prospective guests of Brandywine Falls Inn and Cottages who were exploring the activities available at the resort might be more interested in statement 1 or 2 as they researched its facilities:

1. All guests may use the water equipment.
2. All guests may use the paddleboats, kayaks, barracudas, canoes, rowboats, and mountain bikes.

She decided that 1 is too vague: "water equipment" could be anything from plastic donut floats to paddleboards to powerboats. The list of equipment went much further toward persuading viewers to book a room because of its description and specificity. In fact, she thought, potential guests might decide to spend a week's vacation at Brandywine Falls Inn and Cottages because they could kayak up the river and see the scenery on the mountain bikes. Or parents would want to tour the river below the falls in a paddleboat with their children.

Finally, Meijing considered whether to use analogies or metaphors to develop effective emotional appeals in her argument. She jotted down ideas: "You wouldn't hide your grandmother in the closet at the hotel to avoid paying for her, so why would you hide your dog to avoid the 'no pets' rule at Brandywine Falls Inn and Cottages? Instead, get Grandma her own adjoining room and board Fido at the Muskoka Country Club for Pets, so both they (and you) can enjoy a comfortable, stress-free vacation." Meijing gauged the effectiveness of this comparison in motivating guests to follow the rule on pets: Would they respond positively to the invitation to avoid being someone who abused their grandma or their pet? She also considered whether any terms needed defining. She thought of someone being unfamiliar with the term *barracuda*: "What is a barracuda? A barracuda is a pedal-powered jet ski." She decided that most readers booking a holiday at a Muskoka resort would be familiar with a jet ski. This metaphor isolates the main similarity (body design) as well as the main difference (human vs. engine powered) between the two watercraft to introduce readers to the new concept.

Professional Communication Assignments

5. Write the Letter to Brandywine Falls Inn and Cottages Guests

Assume the role of Meijing Zhu. Write the letter to resort guests telling them about the improvements that were made to the facilities over the last winter and persuading them to read and follow the resort's rules. Use the discussion in this module to help you develop a logical, well-supported, and persuasive argument. Refer to Figures 13 and 14 for summaries of the basic information you wish to convey in your letter. When you have written a first draft of the letter that you are happy with, revise the draft, paying special attention to the emotional and credibility appeals that you are creating through your word choice and argument strategies.

> **Audience:** Your primary audience for this letter is the guests who will visit the resort this summer; secondary audience includes Mr. and Mrs. Hurley, whose voices will be represented in the letter

Purpose: Primarily to persuade readers (the resort guests) to follow the resort policies and to feel goodwill toward the resort; secondarily to demonstrate your competence and ability to your employers

Genre: Persuasive letter

6. Redesign Brandywine Falls Inn and Cottages' Policies Webpage

As Meijing Zhu noted after a cursory examination, the guest rules at Brandywine Falls Inn are presented among additional information and room rates so that there is no quick, easy reference for Inn guests to find and review the rules. Redesign and rewrite a "Rates and Policies" page so that the rates and the rules are presented separately on it. Find a resort on your own or use this link to search for resorts anywhere in Canada:

www.resortsandlodges.com/lodging/canada/index.html. Remove any extra information that you think might confuse or distract guests from finding and reading the important rules. Rewrite any rules that you think could be improved or clarified. Your purpose in revising this page is not only to inform but also to persuade readers to follow the rules. Your revision should display the resort rules and policies clearly, prominently, completely, and persuasively. Hand in both the page you found and your revision of it.

Audience: Primarily potential and returning guests to the resort who will visit the webpage to review the rules and to decide whether to book a vacation there; secondary audiences could include rival resort owners checking out Brandywine Falls' policies

Purpose: To provide a clear and quick reference to viewers to communicate the resort's rates and policies; to motivate viewers to choose this resort for their vacation destination

Genre: Webpage displaying resort amenities and policies

Using the strategies laid out in this module, you can create arguments that may move readers to respond in the way that you want. You greatly increase the chance that readers will do what you want when you give them a clear and well-supported argument with details that demonstrate your knowledge and expertise on the subject and that emphasizes the importance of the topic and their contribution to it through acting. Make your point through persuasive arguments tailored to your readers.

MODULE SUMMARY

- Successful arguments use three basic strategies to persuade readers: credibility, logic, and emotion.
- Writers build credibility both through knowledge, fairness, and shared values or identification with readers.
- Writers create logical arguments by making claims and then supporting those claims with evidence such as experts, definitions, precedents, consequences, examples, and statistics.
- Writers employ emotion in argument through their choice of words, selection of vivid details or examples, inclusion of eye-catching visuals, and use of metaphors and analogies.

Module 3

Style in Business and Professional Writing

Dennis Chan revising his report.
jianying yin/Getty Images

LEARNING OUTCOMES

LO 1 Analyze communication situations and create appropriate written responses to them

LO 2 Use concepts and techniques from plain language to determine reader needs, present key ideas clearly, and eliminate jargon

LO 3 Understand and apply methods for presenting negative information as positively as possible, while still presenting it clearly and ethically

LO 4 Apply techniques for improving cohesion, concision, and emphasis

LO 5 Read source texts carefully and use knowledge gained from them to create appropriate professional documents

GETTING STARTED

Style—the word immediately brings to mind images of colourful fashion, crazy hairstyles, and innovative music. In business and professional writing, style means writing in ways that help readers understand your message. In this module, we introduce you to five topics that will improve your written style in business and professional communication: plain language, positive emphasis when delivering bad news, coherence, emphasis, and conciseness.

Concepts from **plain language** help organize documents and present information so that it is clear and comprehensible. You will also learn how to use positive language to present your ideas and report bad news while also reporting it ethically. You will also learn how to improve the flow or cohesion of your sentences and how to add emphasis to the important information in individual sentences as well as paragraphs. Together, these techniques will improve the quality of your writing.

In the first case, you will meet Dennis Chan, who finds that many of his clients are unable to read and understand their insurance policies because of the legal jargon they contain. He finds a solution in plain language, a global movement to make legal, health, financial, and other important information more accessible to readers. In the second case, Toula Stephanos has to report a higher-than-average return rate for unsold eyeglass frames. Because her manager helped design some of the unsold frames, she has a challenging rhetorical situation, writing a report that puts as positive a spin as possible on bad news that directly affects her boss. The third case finds Jayson Morito revising a report to improve its style. Although the content is solid, it needs revision to improve its organization, its conciseness, and the cohesion of sentences within paragraphs. By working your way through these cases, you will learn ways to communicate clearly and concisely with your readers.

Case 1★★ Plain Language, Insurance Contracts, and the Client's Right to Know

Monday morning was never the best time of the week, but Dennis Chan had never had this many calls. The callers shared a common theme—everyone was asking questions that they should have been able to answer just by reading their policies.

Sure, some of the questions were being asked by people who just couldn't be bothered to read the documents that the insurance companies sent, but some of the others—most of them, in fact—were real questions asked by very frustrated clients. Dennis knew that if he wanted to keep these customers and grow his business, he had to find a way to help his clients locate information quickly.

All these calls were also cutting in to the time, he needed to spend looking for new clients, and referrals from his existing customers were an important part of finding those new clients. He needed to deal with the information problem, and soon.

For example, Mrs. Leung's question about the part of the insurance agreement shown in Figure 1 would puzzle just about anybody on their first reading.

First of all, the sentence in Part 4 is one long sentence—77 words. Dennis wasn't a language expert, but he knew that shorter sentences were often easier to understand. He wondered how Mrs. Leung was supposed to sort her way through such a long sentence. The real problem, he decided, was that Mrs. Leung wasn't supposed to be reading this document at all—lawyers were the real audience. He wondered why these companies could not write a policy that their customers could understand.

Dennis decided that the policy writers probably forgot about customers when they started worrying about the legal details. What his customers needed, he realized, was a guide or summary sheet of the policy that made the agreement clear. When he offered to draft this document, Mrs. Leung responded that she thought it would be wonderful—and the sooner the better, because she had to pay her bill by the end of the month. Dennis explained that it would probably take him a week or so, because he would have to get approval from company lawyers.

Figure 1 A passage from Mrs. Leung's car insurance policy.

Source: H. Graves, © Pearson Education, Inc.

Dennis thought more about the policy language. It surely didn't qualify as an explanation of how insurance works that was easy for his clients to understand. He knew there were codes of consumers rights that described the rights and responsibilities for all parties involved in the business–consumer relationship (See Figure 2).

On the other hand, the text in the policy wasn't all impenetrable. The "What We Will Pay For" section (shown in Figure 3) was not bad, starting with the title.

Codes of Consumer Rights

Many industries have developed codes of consumer rights in an attempt to identify for both businesses and consumers what the rights and responsibilities are for all parties. These codes generally suggest that businesses have the responsibility to treat consumers fairly and to not drag the process of responding out for a long time. The federal courts have backed this up with their recent decisions that outline the responsibility of businesses to act ethically.

These rights are balances with consumer responsibilities to also act fairly in their dealings with businesses. This means that consumers must also act ethically by providing accurate and complete information when they sign contracts.

The details of fair dealing vary from one circumstance to the next, but the essence remains the same: both businesses and consumers have rights and responsibilities. For an example, see Insurance Bureau of Canada, www.ibc.ca, click on Resources at the top of the page, and then Consumer Rights and Responsibilities on the right.

Figure 2 Many industries have developed codes of consumer rights.

Source: © Pearson Education, Inc.

WHAT WE WILL PAY FOR

2.1 Once we receive payment for your insurance, we will refund any reasonable charges you incur when renting a similar vehicle. We will also refund any sensible expenditures for taxis or public transit.

Figure 3 A passage from Mrs. Leung's car insurance policy that is written clearly.

So it could be done, concluded Dennis. The legal language could be revised into plain language. But he also knew that the car insurance policy was a legal contract between the company and the client, so the obscure parts had to be revised carefully in the summary sheet so as not to jeopardize the legalities. But the first step was to write a clear draft and then have the lawyers at Pacific Mountain Mutual verify that all legal points were covered and the summary sheet correctly reflected the contract.

LO 2 Use concepts and techniques from plain language to determine reader needs, present key ideas clearly, and eliminate jargon

STYLE IN BUSINESS AND PROFESSIONAL COMMUNICATION
Plain Language in Professional Documents

Plain language is language that is clear. It contains specific information that is relevant to readers, and it is logically arranged and easy to follow. Governments, including the Government of Canada (see Figure 4), the legal and medical professions, and businesses have grown increasingly interested in using plain language after recognizing that many of their documents were too difficult for the average person to understand. The plain language movement evolved to promote the rewriting of important public documents so that intended audiences could access the information they contained. Legal documents, insurance contracts, tax documents, medical information, product information, and guarantees are some of the targets of this movement to ensure that ordinary readers can understand and follow them.

An institution's duty to inform the public includes the obligation to communicate effectively. Information about policies, programs, services, and initiatives must be clear, relevant, objective, easy to understand, and useful.

To ensure clarity and consistency of information, plain language and proper grammar must be used in all communication with the public. This principle also applies to internal communications, as well as to information prepared for Parliament or any other official body, whether delivered in writing or in speech.

Figure 4 Using plain language is the official policy of Government of Canada.

Source: Communications Policy of the Government of Canada http://www.tbs-sct.ac.ca/pol/doc-eng.aspx?id=12316&section=text, Treasury Board of Canada Secretariat, 2012. Reproduced with the permission of the President of the Treasury Board of Canada, 2014

Plain language is also good and effective business communication style. When you are writing business documents, use these principles to help you communicate effectively with your readers:

- Use short sentences and simple words
- Write so that readers can understand your message in one reading
- Be simple and direct but not simplistic or patronizing

To apply these principles to your document, follow these four steps:

1. Determine the needs of your audience: Are there different groups of readers who will need their own version of the document?
2. Organize the information to meet these readers' needs: Is chronological order suitable, or should you use another organizational pattern?
3. Check the accessibility of the vocabulary: See stylistic advice in this module.
4. Test your draft: Who might give you useful feedback to determine whether the message is clear?

Determine Your Readers' Needs   To determine the needs of your readers, approach the document from their point of view. What do they want to know? For example, if you were writing a message to employees in your organization to remind them to renew their confidentiality agreement for the upcoming year (see Figure 5), what would the different groups in your organization need or want to know? Regular employees will have signed this agreement in previous years, so they will be familiar with the form and the request. New employees may not have encountered this practice before, so they may need more detail than established employees. The contract workers (e.g., external consultants) may want to know whether they need to sign this form since they are not permanent employees.

Good morning,

[1] As announced by President Dustin Pearce earlier this month, all employees, including external consultants who work with Marbury Associates' data, are required to renew their annual *Confidentiality Agreement* at this time. [2] This is part of our obligation to data providers, and it serves as a way to demonstrate to them our commitment to maintaining their privacy and security.

[3] Close to 70% of staff have already completed this agreement. [4] If you've not already done so, please renew your *Confidentiality Agreement* here. [5] It only takes a few minutes and the deadline for renewal is **January 31**.

[6] Please also take a few minutes to visit our new webpage, January is Privacy Awareness Month at Marbury, on the MarburyFreeway and download and read the latest edition of MarburyNews. [7] We invite you to join us in celebrating Privacy Awareness Month!

[8] Thank you for continuing your commitment to maintaining and strengthening Marbury's ongoing reputation as a culture of privacy.

Alex LeCourt
Director of Privacy
Privacy and Legal Services/Vie privée et Services juridiques
Marbury Associates
123, rue Champlain Road, Ste. 123
Ottawa, Ontario K3L 4R9

Figure 5 Plain language and determining your readers' needs.

As you examine the needs of your readers, consider whether they form a homogenous group. Will a single version of the document serve all readers' needs or should you think about readers as different groups? For example, are the needs of contract employees identical to permanent employees when they contemplate signing the agreement? How might the differences affect the way you write the request?

Organize the Information to Respond to Readers' Needs   After determining your readers' needs for a particular document, you have a blueprint for deciding how best to organize information to meet those needs. You can choose from several organizing principles:

- Chronological order
- Most important to least important
- General to specific or specific to general

Use a principle that best organizes the information your readers need. For example, in requesting coworkers to renew their confidentiality agreement, you might use a specific to general pattern of organization. In this case, you begin with the reminder that the agreement must be renewed by month's end, describe the process for renewing it, inform them of more general information associated with privacy in the organization, and conclude by thanking them for their cooperation.

Effective Style in Business Communication   Writing effectively means attending to what you say at the level of word choice. For example, keep sentences short and focus each paragraph on a single idea. Here are some tips for good business writing at the level of words.

Use Active Voice   Active voice means putting people and things into the subjects (usually at the beginning) of your sentences. For example, the following sentence uses active voice:

Mrs. Leung requested *that Dennis Chan explain paragraph 4 of her insurance policy.*

This sentence uses passive voice:

An *explanation of paragraph 4 in her insurance policy* was requested by Mrs. Leung *of Dennis Chan.*

Note that the passive sentence structure is longer (it uses 17 words instead of 13). It also makes readers wait until the end for all the details they need to understand the sentence. Use active voice to improve conciseness and clarity.

Use Present Tense   Present tense is the simplest form for a verb in English. Using the simplest form reduces wordiness and makes ideas clearer and more immediate. For example, using the conditional tense (verbs using *would* and *should*) makes readers work harder to understand: "If you would need to make a claim, you should contact one of our insurance adjustors at 604-123-4567." Instead, say "If you *need* to make a claim, *contact* one of our insurance adjustors at . . . ." Using present tense makes the point fast and easy to grasp—the whole point of good business communication.

Use "You" to Address Readers   Using "you" to address readers creates a closer relationship between writer and reader, and it produces clear, concise prose. For example, which sentence would you rather read?

1. Policy holders should verify the details of their auto insurance policy before submitting their payment.

2. Please verify the details of your auto insurance policy before you pay your bill.

In the first version, the writer addresses someone else ("the policy holder"), not me. I have to place myself into the third person (they) to see whether this directive applies to me or not. In the second version, I immediately know I should read through my policy before I pay the insurance company.

Use Short, Simple Words   English has many words for the same ideas and concepts. When you choose a word, use the shortest and simplest one for a particular concept. For example, both these sentences mean the same thing:

1. Peruse all documents in advance of any submission of remuneration.

2. Read this form before you pay your bill.

Many readers have to read the first sentence twice to understand it. Some may use a dictionary to look up one or two words. Most readers will read the second sentence once and understand it. When you have a choice, choose the short, simple word.

Use the Same Word to Refer to the Same Object   In some writing situations, you may want to show your rich and varied vocabulary (in an academic essay for your history class, perhaps). In most business and professional communication, avoid using synonyms: use the same word for the same object, concept, or idea throughout a document. Synonyms can confuse readers because they wonder if the different words mean the same thing or something else. To inform readers of specific information clearly and concisely, reuse the same terms.

Avoid Jargon   Jargon is specialized language used to impress, not to inform. Distinguish between technical and legal *language* and technical and legal *jargon*. For example, the first sentence below uses technical jargon; the second uses technical language:

1. The purpose of the consultation was to dialogue with the communities and key stakeholders of Perth-Grand Valley and the Northern Townships on the need for a Regional Hospital Service Delivery model with in-depth discussion on how this could best be achieved.

2. We consulted with communities and stakeholders of Perth-Grand Valley and the Northern Townships to discuss whether they needed a Regional Hospital Service and how best to achieve it.

Technical terms are often essential to a topic. If so, include definitions so readers know what the terms mean. If you can, translate a technical term into simpler language. Never use technical jargon to impress in good business communication.

Sentences   Here are some tips for writing effectively at the level of sentences.

Keep Sentences Short (between 14 and 22 words)   Long sentences tax reader memory. If readers get lost, they may not reread to follow your point. They may also lose interest when they forget the beginning of the sentence. Most short-term memories can only process about 25 words in a chunk, so use 25 words as your limit for sentences. Aim for lengths of between 14 and 22 words. One exception is a topic that only makes sense in a longer sentence. But revise to make the sentence as clear and readable as possible. Use parallel structure and lists and avoid interruptive phrases.

How do you shorten sentences? Limit yourself to one or two topics per sentence. If you need to qualify or modify an idea, do so in separate sentences. Break complex ideas into smaller units. Avoid coordinating conjunctions such as *and, but, yet, or, so, for,* and *nor*. The conjunctions encourage long sentences because they enable you to connect ideas in one long sentence.

The paragraph in the left column of Figure 6 is four sentences that contain 128 words—31 words a sentence on average, which is too long if we are aiming to write in plain language.

Coordinating conjunctions can create long, complex sentences.	Revising coordinating conjunctions can simplify and clarify sentences.
[1] Many people do not think of writing as a technology, **yet** it is a tool that humans have used for several thousand years to develop, record, and communicate their thoughts, ideas, and knowledge about themselves and the world around them. *(40 words)* [2] Scholars believe that humans use writing as a way to think, that writing facilitates complex thought **and** that it has enabled our species to make the advances that we have in science, medicine, technology, and the arts. *(37 words)* [3] **And yet**, writing is rarely mentioned in wide-ranging discussions of technology, the more likely focus being on the internet, artificial intelligence, or nanoscale inquiry. *(25 words)* [4] At the same time, writing makes possible many of the innovations that humans develop, **and** it also makes possible the dissemination of knowledge around these innovations. *(26 words)*	[1] Many people do not think of writing as a technology although it is a tool that humans have used for several thousand years. *(23 words)* [2] They have used writing to develop, record, and communicate their ideas about themselves and the world around them. *(18 words)* [3] Scholars believe that humans use writing as a way to think. *(11 words)* [4] They argue that writing helps humans think complex thoughts. *(9 words)* [5] It has also enabled humans to advance our knowledge of science, medicine, technology, and the arts. *(16 words)* [6] Yet writing is rarely mentioned in discussions of technology. *(9 words)* [7] Instead, discussion focuses on technology related to the internet, artificial intelligence, or nanoscience. *(13 words)* [8] All the while, writing makes possible many of the innovations that humans develop while also making it possible to inform people about this new technology. (25 words)

Figure 6 How do you shorten long sentences?

Each sentence contains 25 words or more. The paragraph uses four coordinating conjunctions to join ideas that make the sentences long. If these conjunctions are used as points at which to separate the ideas or if they are removed altogether, the four sentences become eight, and each idea is contained in a separate sentence.

In the paragraph on the right, the coordinating conjunctions have been divided to shorten the sentences and simplify the language. The same passage is now 8 sentences between 9 and 25 words long, 15 words on average. Most of the ideas from the coordinating conjunctions (*but, yet, and*) have been placed in separate sentences.

However, write longer sentences if a longer sentence is more direct. Don't omit transitions as a way to shorten sentences. Transitional words help readers connect ideas and follow your points.

Exercise 1: Shorten Long Sentences

Use the advice on shortening sentences to revise the long sentences in Figure 5.

1. Count the number of words in each sentence and decide which ones are too long.
2. Use the techniques described previously to shorten those sentences that you decide are too long.
3. Make any other changes to the letter that you think make the content clearer and easier to understand.
4. Be prepared to explain what you revised and why.

Vary the Length of Your Sentences   When every sentence is 14 words, your writing becomes boring. Include short, medium, and long sentences (up to 25 words) to keep your ideas fresh and interesting. For example, the sentences in the revised version of Figure 6 contain sentences between 9 and 25 words long.

State Ideas Positively and Avoid Double Negatives   Introducing negatives into your writing increases the complexity of the ideas and the mental gymnastics needed by readers to understand your thoughts. Stating points positively and negatives clearly can keep your writing clear and comprehensible. For example, in Figure 5 the clause "If you've *not* already done so" can be stated positively and more clearly: "If you have already done so, thank you. Otherwise, please renew your Confidentiality Agreement here." A further example from Figure 6, "Many people *do not think* of writing as a technology," may be revised "Many people *overlook* the fact that writing is also a technology."

Paragraphs

Cover One Topic in a Paragraph   Discuss one idea or topic in a paragraph. Subdividing your ideas helps keep your paragraphs short. Short paragraphs help you create a page that is clearly laid out with lots of white space. They also invite readers into your writing. For example, the writer of Figure 5 uses short paragraphs for each topic: the first paragraph reminds readers to renew their confidentiality agreement. The second paragraph asks readers to act and emphasizes the deadline. The third paragraph informs readers where they can learn more about the privacy policy, and the last paragraph thanks readers for acting.

Use Short Paragraphs (150 words, 3 to 8 sentences)   Keep paragraphs short—between 3 and 8 sentences and no more than 150 words. When you are revising a document, scan for long paragraphs. Often a longer paragraph will signal a change of topic that means you need a new paragraph. As with sentence length, vary the length of paragraphs. Varying paragraph lengths adds visual interest to the page. It gives you a chance to add more white space, and it allows you to include more headings that help readers and create an inviting layout. Sometimes the occasional one-sentence paragraph will add emphasis and visual impact to your writing.

Use Topic Sentences   A topic sentence states clearly and simply what the main subject is for that paragraph. When the topic sentence appears first in a paragraph, you aid readers by enabling them to skim your document, reading only the first sentence and still getting an overview of your subject. In Figure 7, sentence a in each paragraph is a topic sentence. The rest of the paragraph then elaborates on the ideas introduced in the topic sentence. For example, in paragraph 1 the topic is "I have handled all KWIK messages quickly and accurately." Sentence b then defines what the writer means by "quickly and accurately." Sentence c further explains her actions on messages where a one-week complete response was not feasible. This sentence ends with a specific example of one such occasion. Sentence d supplies information about the writer's interactions with coworkers to whom she has delegated some messages to ensure that they too respond efficiently and consistently.

Use Transitions   Help readers follow your shifts of thought by including transitions between paragraphs. **Transitions** are words that forecast to readers where you are taking the discussion next. Time-based transitions—*first, second, third, in conclusion*—help readers track the progress of your argument or discussion. Each transition signals that you have finished one part of the subject and are moving on to the next. Other transitions such as *also, in contrast, in addition*, and *however* help readers understand the relationships between your ideas. Transitional words and phrases have been highlighted in Figure 7 using bold text. Like transitions between sentences, transitions between

Transitions: Words and phrases used to connect one paragraph to another

[1] (a) Over the past year I have handled all KWIK messages quickly and accurately. (b) I have acknowledged all KWIK messages within 48 hours and followed up with a full email response within 1 week where possible. (c) In cases where a longer response period was necessary, I provided as much information as possible to the client as soon as it was available and communicated the expected timelines for a full response (**for example**, Healthy Pathways, Lianna Garcia's request for updated information on a read-mission JxL produced by Marbury). (d) I **also** consult with team members to whom KWIK messages have been delegated to ensure they are handled efficiently and consistently, especially around interpreting the mandate section of the data request form and producing timelines.

[2] (a) A **second** important area in which I have excelled has been to consistently review all data requests assigned to me for potential problems with the data requested. (b) **For example**, in Raymond LaFrance's (MRAD) request for Spinal Stenosis Mobility, I identified a problem with the RES-16-MN/ABC codes provided by Data Control before we sent out the data. (c) This change resulted in additional work for both teams, but ultimately provided the requestor with much higher quality data that was usable for his study. (d) I have **also** worked with Augustus to mitigate any risk associated with supplying client data that is sensitive (NWT Support Life) or that requires aggregate data in a very tight timeline (CSPHL).

[3] (a) **In addition**, I have developed procedures to reduce potential errors in process. (b) **For example**, I have created two checklists for the data request process: one for aggregate and one for record level requests. (c) I have updated these checklists with common errors that have been made in the process previously to ensure that the same mistakes do not continue to be made. (d) I have shared these checklists with the new analysts on the team.

Figure 7 An excerpt from a sample year-end self-evaluation.

paragraphs help readers predict and anticipate what follows in the discussion. Paragraph 2 begins with a transitional sentence: "A second important area in which I have excelled has been to consistently review . . ." This longer transition reminds readers of the document's goal of presenting a self-evaluation and signals a shift from one area of accomplishment to another one. Don't sacrifice transitions to keep your sentences or paragraphs short.

Page Layout and Effective Communication   Use document design to present information effectively. Put some thought into how and where you place information on the page to help readers follow and understand your ideas. Lots of **white space** around headings, paragraphs, and visuals can emphasize the important elements of your document. Formatting elements such as headings and lists can also add emphasis and visual interest. Part of the challenge of getting people to read government forms, medical information, legal contracts, and insurance documents is extending the invitation into the document. An attractive page layout can invite readers in and good business style can encourage them to continue reading.

White space: The space not occupied by text or images on a page

ANALYSIS: DENNIS WRITES A SUMMARY OF THE INSURANCE POLICY

LO 1 Analyze communication situations and create appropriate written responses to them

Dennis remembered learning about writing and plain language in his business communication class a few years ago. A quick Internet search turned up some relevant websites, a definition, and some useful pointers. After a quick tour through several plain language sites, Dennis planned four steps for writing a summary sheet to help explain the auto insurance policy:

1. Determine the needs of my audience (Mrs. Leung and others like her): Will different groups of readers need their own version of the policy?

2. Organize the information to meet these readers' needs: Is chronological order suitable or should I use some other organizational pattern for the policy information?

3. Use stylistic advice to revise the policy language.

4. Test my summary of the policy: Which two or three current clients should I ask to read my summary to see whether the message is clear?

Dennis thought about what his readers would want to know about the auto insurance that they were purchasing. Then he generated a list of questions his readers would want answered as they read through their insurance policy: Would a single summary sheet serve all his readers' needs or would it be more effective to think about readers as forming different groups? Would the needs of non-native speakers of English be the same as native speakers of English? How might any differences affect the way he wrote the summary?

Exercise 2: Determine the Needs of Auto Insurance Policy Readers

Before beginning this exercise, review Case 1 and reread Figures 1 and 3 closely, if you need to. In groups of two or three, discuss the case to determine what owners of the insurance policy would want to know as they read through the passages reproduced in this case. As a group, generate a list of questions that you think policy holders would have about their insurance coverage (related to these excerpts). Identify the topics that the excerpt covers. Do these topics answer the questions that policy holders would have about the information in the excerpt? Is there any additional information that readers would want about these topics? Using points raised in your discussion, summarize the needs of Dennis Chan's auto insurance policy readers.

LO 5 Read source texts carefully and use knowledge gained from them to create appropriate professional documents

- www.plainlanguage.gov: This is the website of the American government Plain Language Organization. It contains a wealth of valuable and useful information about plain language, including definitions and some history.

- www.plainlanguagenetwork.org: This website is sponsored by the Plain Language Association International. It provides information about projects, conferences, and many other topics associated with plain language in several different languages.

- http://en.wikipedia.org/wiki/Plain_language: Wikipedia's definition of plain language provides a quick overview of the movement and its goals.

- www.centreforliteracy.qc.ca/node/188: This page contains an excellent overview of the controversy surrounding readability and tests for readability, one aspect of plain language.

Figure 8 Sources for additional information about plain language.

Professional Communication Assignments

1. Revise the Excerpt from the Insurance Policy

Revise the text in Figure 1 so that it is written in plain language and clients like Mrs. Leung can understand it. Use the discussion about style and plain language covered in this module to help you revise the excerpt. Also be sure that your revision fulfills the promise to the consumer described in the Code of Consumer Rights in Figure 2. Because you are probably not a lawyer, you can't reasonably assess whether your revision maintains the legal integrity of the original policy, but do your best to clarify the excerpt without radically altering the intent of the original.

Audience: Clients such as Mrs. Leung who wish to know what they are paying for in their insurance coverage

Purpose: To clearly and concisely communicate the important details about insurance coverage

Genre: Excerpt from an insurance agreement

2. Revise an Insurance Document for Yourself or a Family Member

Find a copy of an insurance document of your own or of a family member and revise a 500-word chunk of it. Use the information in this module to help you with your revision. Hand in a copy of the original excerpt from the insurance policy along with your revision. Make sure you clearly mark the section that you revised.

Audience: You or your family members who want to understand the insurance coverage that they are purchasing

Purpose: To clearly and concisely communicate important details about insurance coverage

Genre: Excerpt from an insurance agreement

Case 2★★★   Style! Eye Fashions: Selling Bad News

LO 1 Analyze communication situations and create appropriate written responses to them

Irina Nemcova explained to the visiting sales representative that the whole product line was unpopular—nobody liked these eyeglass frames. Patients would try on a set of frames from the Casanova line, but they ended up choosing something else. The eyeglass frames looked good on the display, but when the customer put them on the fit or proportion just wasn't right.

Toula Stephanos grimaced and noted that her manager had had high hopes for that collection when it came out. She started putting the small pile of rejected eyeglass frames into her leather display cases. Irina pointed out that perhaps the name, the Casanova line, was part of the problem.

Irina Nemcova models frames in the display.
Picture-Factory/Fotolia

Toula was quick to emphasize that marketing named the lines, not her. But she was glad that Irina wanted some of her other frames. Those were some of her favourites from the new fall collection, the Cool Dudz line. She pointed to a second group that Irina had selected from the samples of new frames during the sales presentation. Irina explained that she liked the unusual but subtle details that made the Cool Dudz line attractive.

Irina asked Toula how her sales trip was going so far. Toula admitted that it was disappointing. The optometrists across Saskatchewan were also returning the Casanova line. She noted that Dr. Bhathal in Prince Albert had sold several frames, but she had only ordered 12 pairs. Toula snapped the clasps shut on her display cases and placed them on the floor. The order for the Cool Dudz line was a bright light. Toula noted to herself that she would have to start her trip report that evening. She had to submit the report before she caught a plane to Milan for European Fashion Week on Sunday.

Toula was more disappointed with this sales trip than she had let on to Irina. She knew her manager, Gaston Papineau, would be particularly upset because so many units from the Casanova line were coming back to them. He had really pushed her to sell that line because he had been involved in some of the designs. At least the Cool Dudz and the MyFrames lines had interested nearly all of the doctors in both Manitoba and Saskatchewan that she'd visited on this trip. Maybe their orders would soften the return of—how many unsold frames? There were four or five dozen, at least. Style! Eye Fashions was a relatively small company compared to the competition. Returned frames wouldn't cause financial problems, but no one looked good when they missed the mark on designs or sales.

POSITIVE EMPHASIS AND BAD NEWS

As a professional business person, you will sometimes have to communicate bad news to customers or clients. No one likes to send or receive bad news, but there are ways that you can make readers feel better about the information that you send them. Generally, readers respond more favourably to descriptions of events that are depicted positively rather than negatively. One strategy is to put a **positive emphasis** on the discussion while also remaining clear about the unfavourable news.

One example of this occurs in Figure 9, which is a sample message declining an offer of employment. In the first paragraph, the writer thanks his reader for inviting him to apply to

LO 3 Understand and apply methods for presenting negative information as positively as possible, while still presenting it clearly and ethically

Positive emphasis: A writing strategy that emphasizes positive news and downplays negative information

---

Hi Marianne,

First of all, I would like to thank you for thinking of me for the position that you are trying to fill within First Financial right now. The projects that your team is working on are quite exciting.

Given my current position on my team, however, and the timing of the contract that you are trying to fill (eight months, with no possibility for extension) I don't think that it makes sense for me to pursue this position at this time.

Thank you again for thinking of me, and I hope you will keep me in mind for future openings in your organization because I find the collegial work environment and the interesting projects very attractive. You have a great team, and I hope to have the opportunity to work with you in the future.

Best Regards,

Paul

Paul Li
Senior Analyst
Epsilon Zeta Accounting
Phone: 613-123-4567
Fax: 613-234-5678
pli@eza.ca

Figure 9 Sample email that uses positive emphasis to decline an offer of employment.

her organization's open position. In the second paragraph, he notes the two reasons that underlie his decision to decline the offer. In the third paragraph he expresses his continuing interest in the organization and seeks to maintain the goodwill of his reader by remaining positive and appreciative of the opportunity he was offered. Although he sends bad news to his reader, he states his refusal as positively as possible. The writer uses three strategies in this message to present negative information in a positive way:

1. He uses positive language as often as he can.
2. He links the negative information (his refusal) to a reason.
3. He de-emphasizes the negative point and states it briefly.

Use Positive Language

Be sensitive to word choices and avoid words that state negatives or have negative connotations. Figure 10 reproduces the sentence from Figure 9 that contains the refusal, which uses some negative language that could be improved.

Link Negative Information to a Reason or Reader Motivator

Readers can accept negative news more easily if they know the reason for it. If you can include a reason that clarifies the negative, do so. Similarly, if you can, show readers how the negative might benefit them. Of course, make sure readers would agree that your suggestion is an actual benefit to them. In the revised example, the writer gives two reasons in advance of stating his refusal:

> "Given my current position and the fact that you are offering an eight-month contract with no possibility of extension, I would like to wait until you have a permanent position so that I could join the team permanently."

The writer identifies the eight-month month contract as the main reason for his refusal and when that detail is linked to his continued enthusiasm for First Financial as a potential employer, the message is intended to motivate the reader to look for permanent positions to invite the writer to apply for in the future.

Negative: Given my current position and the fact that you are offering an eight-month contract with no possibility of extension, I don't think it makes sense for me to pursue this position at this time.

Better: Given my current position and the fact that you are offering an eight-month contract with no possibility of extension, it makes more sense for me to remain in my current situation.

Better yet: Given my current position and the fact that you are offering an eight-month contract with no possibility of extension, I would like to wait until you have a permanent position so that I could join the team permanently.

Figure 10 Negative language revised to be more positive and include the reader's viewpoint.

Table 1 Avoid using several of these negative words in one message

Afraid	Fault	Lacking	Problem
Anxious	Fear	Loss	Reject
Bad	Hesitate	Mistake	Sorry
Delay	Ignore	Missing	Terrible
Difficulty	Impossible	Neglect	Unfortunately
Dissatisfied	Inadequate	Never	Unpleasant
Error	Incomplete	No	Unreasonable
Except	Inconvenient	Not	Unsure
Fail	Injury	Objection	Wrong

De-emphasize the Negative and State It Briefly

Using positive language doesn't mean omitting negatives. Sometimes you have bad news that readers must know. However, you can present the negatives clearly and simply without emphasizing the negative aspects, as the revisions in Figure 10 illustrate.

Table 1 lists words that communicate a pessimistic viewpoint. Sometimes we write without realizing that we have used these words, resulting in an overly pessimistic account of the subject matter. For example, Figure 11 presents two messages, one where the writer conveys disaster through repeated negative words, whereas the other conveys the same point more positively.

You can also de-emphasize the negative by placing it in the middle of a paragraph. Locating it at the beginning or end of a message or paragraph makes it stand out because the start and the end are points of emphasis (see emphasis in Case 3 of this module).

Dear Mrs. Graves, According to our records, your dog, Finn, has sadly missed his annual wellness examination and appropriate vaccines. Unfortunately, this province has a terribly high incidence of diseases such as rabies and distemper, so we urge you not to neglect your pet's welfare and good health any longer. If you fail to schedule an appointment promptly, your delay may compromise his health and the health of your whole household. We are certain that you are anxious to avoid this possibility of injury and death, so we urge you to address this problem immediately.	Dear Mrs. Graves, According to our records your dog, Finn, is due for his annual wellness examination and yearly vaccine boosters. Given the high incidence of diseases such as rabies and distemper in this province, it is important that Finn's immunization remains current. Regular vaccinations and a yearly inspection will protect your pet by helping him maintain a strong resistance to disease. Please call us at (230) 123-4567 to schedule an appointment. We look forward to seeing you and Finn soon.

Figure 11 The highlighted text emphasizes the use of negative phrases that convey a pessimistic impression to readers.

Exercise 3: Revising for Positive Emphasis

Rewrite the following sentences to state the negatives as positively as possible. As you revise, keep your readers in mind and work to build goodwill with them.

1. I am afraid that your payment reached us too late, so we will have to charge you a 10 percent late fee.

2. Because your file was incomplete, we were unable to consider your application.

3. Unfortunately, due to the hideousness of this frame line, most of our clients sent them back for a refund.

4. If you are dissatisfied with the resolution of your claim, do not hesitate to contact our customer service line.

5. I'm so sorry to be three days late responding to your request. I had to wait for our legal department to get back to me. According to our lawyers, there's nothing we can do about your injuries or lost work time. We recommend that in future you carefully read and follow all usage instructions.

ANALYSIS: RETURNED EYEGLASS FRAMES AND POSITIVE EMPHASIS

LO 1 Analyze communication situations and create appropriate written responses to them

When Toula Stephanos begins her report on her trip to promote the fall line, she plans to emphasize the positive outcomes—in particular, the popularity of the Cool Dudz and MyFrames lines. She will also need to report the somewhat high rate of return of the Casanova line, but she decides to phrase these returns as positively as possible. She knows that readers respond more favourably to positive than negative descriptions of events, so she will use that approach. She considers the options and decides to use positive language, to link negative information to a reason, and to de-emphasize any clear negative points. She also decides there may be one or two trivial negative points that she could omit from the report altogether. First she considers the range of choices available to talk about her trip positively. She jots down two points that she will have to make (Figure 12).

Point 1: Higher than average return rate of Casanova frames

Negative: Sales of the Casanova line failed to meet our expectations.

Better: Sales of the Casanova line were smaller than expected.

Better yet: Although returns on the Casanova line were generally higher than expected, six clients also ordered additional frames from this line.

Point 2: Low sales on Hectic frame lines

Negative: Unfortunately, sales of the Hectic line are also disappointing, missing sales targets by 50 percent.

Better: Sales of the Hectic line achieved 50 percent of targets.

Better Yet: Hectic line sales started slowly, but we expect them to build in the last quarter.

Figure 12 Toula revises two points to make them more positive.

> Reason: Several clients suggested that the Hectic designs are too contemporary for their patients.
>
> Reader benefit: This feedback from these initial sales of the Hectic line is invaluable because it suggests we may need a more conservative line of eyeglass frames at Style!.

Figure 13 Toula links the negatives to a reason or reader benefit.

Her first draft of both points is too negative, she decides, so she revises to give them more positive emphasis. Figure 12 shows several examples of how to change negatives into positives.

Second, Toula knows that her boss will want to know why the frame lines didn't sell as anticipated, so she reflects on her conversations with clients for clues. She knows that if she can explain why the frames were returned her boss will be more willing to accept this bad news. She also considers whether there are any ways that the company might benefit from knowledge about why the frames are being returned. Figure 13 presents the reason and the benefit that Toula develops for her report.

If the Negative is Trivial, Leave It Out

As Toula scans the data in Table 2, she notices that none of her clients who returned Casanova frames ordered any additional frames from this line. She jots this point down for inclusion in the report but then thinks further about it. She realizes that if she mentions

Table 2 Sales and merchandise return figures for July/August 2015

Office and Location	Casanova		Cool Dudz		MyFrames		Hectic	
	Order	Return	Order	Return	Order	Return	Order	Return
Ngô Brandon, MB	2	5	7	0	6	0	3	1
Vemulakonda Brandon, MB	0	7	9	1	7	1	4	0
Polizzi Portage, MB	3	1	5	0	5	0	1	2
Lemanski Winnipeg, MB	0	7	9	0	9	0	7	0
Lopez Winnipeg, MB	0	10	10	0	10	0	3	2
Vogler Winnipeg, MB	0	9	12	0	7	1	3	0
Ilioviciu Flin Flon, MB	3	0	2	0	3	0	2	1
Bhathal Prince Albert, SK	5	0	6	0	5	0	3	0
Blanchard North Battleford, SK	0	5	7	0	5	1	5	0
Shah Swift Current, SK	0	8	6	1	8	1	4	1
Krizek Saskatoon, SK	2	0	2	0	12	0	7	0
Quansah Saskatoon, SK	0	10	15	0	5	0	0	0
Brown Regina, SK	1	9	6	1	7	1	4	1
Nemcova Regina, SK	0	12	15	0	7	0	5	0
Pereida Regina, SK	0	4	9	1	8	1	7	1
Totals (Sales and Returns)	**16**	**79**	**130**	**4**	**104**	**6**	**58**	**9**

Negative Point 1: None of the clients who returned Casanova frames ordered additional frames from this line.

Better: Leave it out.

Negative Point 2: Clients who buy five or fewer frames from a particular line pay 25 percent more than if they bulk ordered (took six or more frames).

Better: Clients who bulk order (buy six or more frames from a particular line) save 25 percent over smaller orders.

Figure 14 If a negative is trivial, leave it out.

LO 5 Read source texts carefully and use knowledge gained from them to create appropriate professional documents

this point, she will draw her readers' attention to it. She decides that emphasizing this point is probably not necessary; her boss, Gaston Papineau, will probably look closely at the return data so he will see this point for himself. If not, it probably isn't that important; she decides, after thinking further, to omit it from her report. Figure 14 presents two examples where writers could omit the negative point because it is unimportant.

Professional Communication Assignments

3. Write a Status Report on Toula Stephanos's Sales Trip

Assume the role of Toula Stephanos and write a status report for her sales trip to optometrists' offices in Manitoba and Saskatchewan. Use appropriate sales and return figures from Table 2, as well as any other relevant information from Tables 3 and 4. Address your status report to her manager, Gaston Papineau, and in your summary of accomplishments, report the poor sales along with the new sales. Use positive emphasis where possible without glossing over the negatives

of the situation. Use the discussion in this module to help you write a report that will create a positive impression of Toula Stephanos and demonstrate that she is earning her sales bonus for 2015.

Audience: Gaston Papineau, Toula's manager

Purpose: To inform him of the high rate of returns on two lines of eyeglass frames that he helped design while maintaining his goodwill

Genre: Status report

Table 3 List prices for assorted frame lines 2015

Casanova	Cool Dudz	MyFrames	Hectic
111 Advantage $119	121 Sick $87	221 Enchanté $110	071 Pic-man $78
112 Outré $134	122 Wow $96	222 Absolute $125	072 Bongo $88
113 Oh la la! $159	123 Play $104	223 Mystical $135	073 Corsica $99
114 Nonpareil $189	124 Just $110	224 ZsaZsa $155	074 Retreat $99

Table 4 Toula's notes on doctor comments for top three returns

Optometrists	Frame line	Comments
I. Nemcova (Regina, SK)	Casanova (12 pair)	"Patients tried frames, chose something else. Frames display well but fit or proportion is not right."
R. Quansah (Saskatoon, SK)	Casanova (10 pair)	"Clients refused them, saying 'Not me.' Styles don't suit our clients."
J. Lopez (Winnipeg, MB)	Casanova (10 pair)	"I couldn't find a face shape that these styles flattered. Neither could Brenda (our frame salesperson)."

Based on the extensive return rate of several of Style! Eye Fashions' newest frame lines, Style! has to reduce expenses, including the planned trip of its top salesperson to Milan for Fashion Week. Writing as Gaston Papineau, draft an email to Toula Stephanos informing her that her planned trip to Italy has been cancelled. Present this news as positively as possible, using the discussion in this module to help you draft a message that will maintain Toula's commitment to her job and goodwill toward the company.

Audience: Toula Stephanos, top salesperson for Style! Eye Fashions

Purpose: To explain why Style! Eye Fashions cannot send her to Milan, Italy, for Fashion Week this year while maintaining her positive attitude and goodwill toward the company

Genre: Email conveying bad news

Case 3★★ The Arva Springs Promotional Event: Coherence, Emphasis, and Conciseness

Jayson Morito was feeling great. He had just finished a huge product promotion that was extremely successful. He stretched out his legs and clasped his hands behind his head, smiling broadly up at Dorian Alvarez, his boss. Dorian had stuck his head in the door a few minutes ago to chat. Dorian agreed that Jayson should be feeling good about this latest success. He explained that corporate was quite pleased with its success. Apparently Arva Springs' president, Jonas Crosby, called raving about how ecstatic they were about everything. That kind of feedback might even lead to a job offer here at Toronto Promotions when he graduated.

In fact, this was exactly what Jayson was working toward. Dorian pointed out that

Steve Skjold/Alamy

Jayson had worked 80 hours a week for the last month getting the details right on that event. Jayson had been working since April as an intern at Toronto Promotions, Ltd., in connection with his program at the Ryerson University School of Business Management. In addition to the Arva Springs Brewery promotion, he had also worked on events for the Toronto Marlboroughs hockey team and the Toronto Bobcats soccer team. He enjoyed putting the theory from his classes into action at Toronto Promotions. Jayson responded that he loved putting such events together and that he would love to do it 24/7.

Putting the events on was the fun part of the job. Dorian pulled a document out of the stack of paper he was carrying and placed it on Jayson's desk, asking him to draft another version of the report. The smile faded from Jayson's face as he saw the red circles and slashes on the page.

Dorian explained that while the event was fantastic, the report was difficult to follow because of its organization. Jayson kept changing topics, Dorian noted. He went on to explain that Jayson's writing could be more cohesive and concise. He pointed out that the president of Toronto Promotions, Albert Barker, would definitely read the report so Jayson

**Reprot on the Arva Springs Honey Cream Ail Promotional Event
at the Caribbé Festival**

On Saturday, July 5, Toronto Promotions kicked off the Arva Springs Honey Cream Ale promotional event at the Carribé Festival with an 14-hour extravaganza, featuring live performances, giveaways, free samples to anyone over 19, and a "surprise" visit by two players from the Toronto Marlies. Tomas Giordano and Alexi Poporov wowed the crowd with their appearance, and they spent more than 45 minutes talking to fans, signing autographs, and sampling the new honey cream ale. *Purple Hurricane* performed some of their most popular songs, and so did Alina Markova, and Toronto's newest hip hop sensations, *The Boardwalk Poets*. Their performances were scheduled to start at 7 p.m., and they run until quite a bit past midnight. We also arranged to give away baseball caps, t-shirts and beach balls with Arva Springs Honey Cream Ale name and logo on them.

Everyone really like the beer. We gave it out in 2 oz. plastic cups, made of recycle plastic. For underage drinkers we had soft drinks like grape or orange soda and some coke, so they weren't left out. We gave out wristbands to all 19 year olds and older. If they didn't have a wristband, they got pop. We set up the tent on the west side of the CN grounds, which festival organizers assigned to us, luckily had a very popular rib restaurant tent on one side and snack foods vendor on the other side, so we had high traffic in front of and through our tent from the patrons visiting the other tents. The music also attracted lots of fans and their friends. The beer ran out before 9, but luckily we arranged for a backup truck from Arva Springs, so disaster was avoided.

Dashini estimated from the number of gallons of beer and soft drinks we gave out that we had about 7000 people through our tent in those fourteen hours. Oh, yeah, we limited people to five samples of beer. A lot of peoples came and stayed, listening to music, dancing, and talking. It would have been better if we had a few more boxes of hats and t-shirts to give away since we had so many visitors. We only gave out about 2000 freebies, so only 1/3 of visitors got something. But they did get the beer if they wanted it and were old enough to drink it. The people from Arva Springs Brewery, Mo and Carson, were really happy with how the event went and so we were happy too. The spoken word hour went really good too. It was before the musical acts, at 3 o'clock it started. Actually, a couple of *The Boardwalk Poets*—Transom and B.T.—read some new stuff at it, that they later did to music during their set. Everyone thought it was really cool. A lot of people came with something to recite, which surprised me. This means that they came to the Caribbé Festival with our tent as one of their event destinations. We should definitely do this again at similar kind of event.

Jayson Morito
Events Organizer

Figure 15 Jayson Morito's report.

would want his report to make as positive an impression on Barker as the feedback he was getting from the event itself.

Jayson saw immediately that Dorian's evaluation was accurate. He did jump around from one topic to another. He concluded that Dorian was right: he should have revised it before he submitted it.

COHESION, EMPHASIS, AND CONCISENESS IN BUSINESS AND PROFESSIONAL COMMUNICATION

Cohesion in writing grows out of how your prose "flows" to readers. For readers, "flow" or cohesion comes when the topic in one sentence is connected to the topic in the next sentence. There are two ways to do this:

LO 4 Apply techniques for improving cohesion, concision, and emphasis

1. Organize the paragraph around a central topic that all of the sentences relate to.
2. Repeat the subject matter from the end of one sentence at the beginning of the next sentence.

Organize the Paragraphs Around a Central Topic

Examine the message in Figure 16. It is written as one long paragraph, but the sentences contain several complex ideas that make the message difficult to follow. When the message is divided into paragraphs, each organized around a central point, the message becomes much clearer and easier to follow.

In Figure 17, the message has been revised to make the ideas clearer. First, it was divided into paragraphs. The first sentence of each paragraph acts as a topic sentence, introducing its main focus. Each sentence after the topic sentence then contributes some aspect of a logical discussion to the paragraph:

1. Paragraph 1 announces the central topic of the whole message—the "updated data request form and specification sheet."
2. Paragraph 2 explains that the writer requires an updated data request form to re-run an earlier project.

	To:	Larry
Send	**Subject:**	Please send a new data request form

Hi Larry,

We can certainly re-run this portion of your previous request following these new specifications, but you will have to submit a new data request form, which will be treated as a continuation of your previous request in that we will use as much of the code and documentation from your previous request as possible. This will minimize the time required for your request. Please see the attached sample Data Request Form that I've filled out for this re-run, based on your previous request and the information you provided in your email. I have also created a draft specification sheet (also attached). Make any changes to these documents once you review them to make sure they accurately reflect the information you are interested in receiving. It should take 2–4 hours of work. The cost will be $274–548 (excluding taxes). We will just bill you for the actual number to a maximum of 4 hours. You will receive an updated cost estimate if the new specifications result in significant changes. Once we hear from you we will extract your data. Likely the report will reach you in 2 weeks (10 business days) but first we need the form plus your approval. Please let me know if you have any questions or concerns about this information.

Have a great afternoon,
Carmen

Figure 16 A message presented as one long paragraph may be unclear and difficult to understand.

Figure 17 To clarify how ideas are related, use the strategy of repeating topics within the sentences in a paragraph.

3. Paragraph 3 emphasizes that the writer has attached copies of the two forms that must be resubmitted to expedite the request.

4. Paragraph 4 addresses the cost (in time and money) of the request.

5. Paragraph 5 outlines the reader's next steps and the estimated time required to complete the request.

Each paragraph in Figure 17 has the main topic highlighted in a different colour so that you can see how it is elaborated from sentence to sentence.

Let's take a look at how paragraph 2 in Figure 17 is organized. Sentence a is the topic sentence: the writer responds to the reader's recent request to re-run the data using new specifications. The additional two sentences elaborate the context for the new request: in sentence b, how to request it, and in sentence c, how the writer will handle the new request in light of the previous request.

Overall, the message in Figure 17 is organized around these topics:

1. Paragraph 2 is organized around the topic of "your previous request," and some version of this phrase appears in each sentence (highlighted in the figure).

2. In paragraph 3 the central topic is "this information."

3. In paragraph 4 the central topic is "cost."

4. In paragraph 5 the central topic is "request form and your approval," which links the ideas in the paragraph together.

Repeat the Subject Matter from the End of One Sentence at the Beginning of the Next

Using linking strategies in Figure 17 can improve cohesion. In this type of cohesion, the idea at the end of one sentence is picked up to begin the next sentence. The repetition serves to show readers clearly how the ideas connect.

Figure 18 illustrates how this end-to-start linking can be done. The coloured highlighting indicates the relationship between the ideas and their location in each sentence. Note that in the paragraphs of the revised letter each sentence is structured in a particular way:

Old or known information at the start + new or unknown information at the end: "Your request to re-run the data extraction using these new specifications [old] + can certainly be done [new]."

Send	To:	Larry
	Subject:	Please send a new data request form

Hi Larry,

[1] Please find attached an updated Data Request Form and Specification Sheet.

[2] [a] Your request to re-run the data extraction using these new specifications can certainly be done. [b] To do this, we require you to submit a new data request form, but we will approach this activity as a continuation of your previous request. [c] As much as possible of the code and documentation from your previous request will be used to minimize the time required to process this new request.

[3] A new Data Request Form for this re-run is attached, completed based on your previous request and the new information provided in your email. Also based on this information, I have created a draft specification sheet (also attached). Please review both documents and make any changes necessary so that they accurately reflect the information you are interested in receiving.

[4] Based on this current specification sheet, I estimate that this re-run will take 2–4 hours of work. This time translates to a cost of $274–548 (excluding taxes). The bill will cover the actual number of hours required to complete your request up to a maximum of 4 hours. If the scope of this follow-up request changes, I will ask you to approve an updated cost estimate for the current specification sheet.

[5] Once we have received your signed request form and your approval of the specification sheet and cost estimate for this work, we will proceed with extracting your data. Your updated report should arrive within 2 weeks (10 business days) of the form and approval reaching us.

[6] Please let me know if you have any questions or concerns about this information.

Have a great afternoon,
Carmen

Figure 18 The coloured highlighting indicates the relationship between the ideas and their location in the sentence.

In sentence a, the new information from the end of the previous sentence ("can be done") is repeated at the start of the next sentence:

"To do this [now old], + we require you to submit . . . of your previous request [new]."

Sentence c then takes the topic "your previous request" and opens the next sentence with a reference to the previous request:

"As much as possible of the code and documentation from your previous request [old] + will be used to minimize the time required to process this new request [new]."

In paragraph 3, sentence a, the topic of " new request" is repeated at the beginning of the sentence, with the addition of "Data" and "Form" to highlight for readers how the new paragraph links to the previous one. The paragraph goes on to explain to readers that they need to review and approve the attached form.

"A new Data Request Form [old] + based on your previous request and the new information provided in your email [new]."

In sentence b, the writer summarizes "your previous request and the new information provided in your email" as "this information" at the beginning:

"Also based on this information [old] + I have created a draft specification sheet [new]."

Sentence c condenses the references to "Data Request Form" and "draft specification sheet" in the previous two sentences into "both documents" and outlines instructions for the reader to "review and make any changes." Paragraph 4 then addresses the issue of costs of the data re-run based on the new specifications and the time the new request will take to process.

Exercise 4: Revising for Cohesion

Using the pattern of end-to-start linking, revise these paragraphs to improve their cohesion.

1. Sales in the fourth quarter made up for the slow start in the first and second quarters. Our promotional efforts in the second and third quarters were mainly responsible for the 110 percent increase in November and December. Television advertising, mass mailings by mail and newspaper with discount coupons, and displays in distributing stores were our main promotional efforts. In addition, we gave free samples away to further promote our new products. Our outstanding results for the fourth quarter indicate these efforts were very successful.

2. None of us knows when illness, catastrophe, or plain bad luck might cause us to lose our comfortable homes. Many clients that Quispamsis House serve never expected to find themselves homeless either. But if we all work together to provide a reliable safety net that provides temporary and longer-term shelter for members of our community who need it, we can be sure that such services will be available should the unthinkable happen and we find ourselves in need of just this service. We are our brothers' and sisters' keepers and if we all do our part by making a cash donation or volunteering our time, we can help build and maintain a safe, caring community in the town of Quispamsis. Help Quispamsis House help those who need a hand up, not just a handout.

Emphasis

In cohesion, the first few words of a sentence are important because they announce the topic. The topic of the sentence gives readers a firm base from which to understand the rest of the sentence. The end of a sentence is equally important. Because readers remember the information they find at the end of the sentence, give important points and ideas emphasis by placing them at the end. Use the ends of your sentences to introduce:

- New information or difficult technical terms
- Complex phrases and clauses

Here are three ways to give your sentence endings more impact:

1. End sentences concisely.
2. Shift unimportant phrases to the start.
3. Shift new information to the end.

End Sentences Concisely
Trim excess words away so that sentences end with emphasis. For example, doesn't everyone who lives in Quispamsis know it is a town? Probably, so in the following sentence we could delete the unnecessary phrase "in the town of":

Wordy: If we all do our part by making a cash donation or volunteering our time, we can build and maintain a safe, caring community in *the town of* Quispamsis.

Shorter: If we all do our part by making a cash donation or volunteering our time, we can build and maintain a safe, caring community in Quispamsis.

Wordy: Their performances were scheduled to start at 7 P.M., and they ran until *quite a bit past midnight*.

Shorter: Their performances were scheduled to start at 7 P.M., and they ran until *3 A.M.*

Shift Unimportant Information to the Start
In the following sentences, the information at the end of the sentence creates a weak conclusion because it is unimportant. The revised version moves the qualifier to the start and ends with emphasis.

Original: Canvassing the riding for Gina Marconi, the Green Party candidate in Prince Albert North, was unsuccessful *despite our best effort*.

Revised: *Despite our best effort*, canvassing the riding for Gina Marconi, the Green Party candidate in Prince Albert North, was unsuccessful.

Original: We are going to need a new strategy *if we want to convert more people than we did when we were canvassing last month*.

Revised: *If we want to convert more people than we did when we were canvassing last month*, we are going to need a new strategy.

Shift New Information to the End
In the following example, the main idea is buried in the middle of the sentence. Shifting it to the end allows readers to recognize that it is the essential point.

Original: We are going to need *a new strategy* to reach the sparse population.

Revised: To reach the sparse population, we are going to need *a new strategy*.

Original: It's hard to build sympathy among *voters who are farmers and potash miners* when banning pesticides and chemical fertilizers makes up a central plank of your party's platform.

Revised: When banning pesticides and chemical fertilizers makes up a central plank in your party's platform, it's hard to build sympathy among *voters who are farmers and potash miners*.

Exercise 5: Revising for Emphasis

Rewrite the following sentences to place the most important information into a position of emphasis. Shorten or rewrite sentences as well to improve coherence and clarity.

1. Response to our new fall fashion line has been encouraging, believe it or not. All of our customers have ordered a broad range of sizes and styles from the casual line, and eight out of 10 have ordered a range of sizes in the business professional line, which exceeds projected targets. We believe that the partnership with Scoundrel Gold and Silver is partially responsible for the surge in orders because the buttons and fastenings that we purchased from them have increased our new styles' interest and appeal across the board with so many of our customers. Though the partnership resulted in increases in garment pricing, we are finding that customers are more than willing to pay a little extra for elegant styles and tailored finishing.

2. Our good news story of the year was receiving the $25,000 grant from the United Way, which allowed the shelter to stay open until midnight every night through the coldest part of the winter from December 15 until March 15. Being able to stay open those extra three hours each evening resulted in a 35 percent increase in clients who visited the shelter last winter. We are proud to note that not a single citizen from Cuddy's Cove or Totem Bay died from exposure last winter, even though we had nighttime temperatures that were 10 percent colder than those measured during the previous five years. We believe that this improvement is directly related to our extended hours at the shelter as well as our outreach work with local and regional law enforcement agents.

Conciseness

Conciseness refers to using the fewest words necessary to express your ideas clearly. When writing a first draft, ignore ideas about conciseness and focus on getting down what you want to say. When you are happy with your draft, then worry about conciseness. Read through the draft carefully and delete any words that you don't need. Use these principles to help you see and remove unnecessary words:

- Cut words that add nothing to the meaning.
- Delete words that repeat other words.
- Use a word in place of a phrase.
- State negatives positively.

Cut Words That Add Nothing to the Meaning   Words such as "really" and "very" can increase your sentence length without adding much to your meaning—they add empty calories. These words also add length without meaning:

- Kind of
- Basically
- Sort of
- Generally
- Usually
- Virtually
- Particularly
- Various

If you find you have used these words in a passage, delete them and tighten up the flow of your prose. For example,

Original: In *virtually* all cases, customers chose a *particularly* speedy delivery of their *various* orders.

Revised: In most cases, customers chose overnight delivery.

Delete Words That Repeat Other Words

We have habits of speech in English that encourage us to double up words for emphasis. The following lists some of the doubles that add length to a sentence; note that both words mean the same thing:

- First and foremost
- Here and now
- Any and all
- Various and sundry
- True and accurate
- Fear and trepidation
- Hopes and dreams
- Basic and fundamental
- Short and concise
- Surprising and unexpected

It is easy to revise this type of wordiness by deleting one of the extra words, as demonstrated in the following example:

Original: *First and foremost,* I request that you submit a *true and accurate* account of the *basic and fundamental* experiment that yielded such *surprising and unexpected* results.

Revised: First, I request that you submit an accurate account of the basic experiment that yielded such surprising results.

Even better: First, I request an accurate account of the experiment that gave such surprising results.

Use a Word in Place of a Phrase

This strategy is more challenging that the earlier ones because it requires that you reread your prose alertly, looking for places where you can distil your ideas into a few words. Draw on your vocabulary and creativity to make your writing more concise. Here are some examples:

Original: We *are seeking* a *highly-motivated* and creative person who *is capable of* working independently to prepare the *complete layout and design of the* book.

Revised: We seek a motivated and creative person who can work independently to prepare the book's layout and design. (25 words reduced to 18)

Original: *The people I have found whom I can be of the most assistance to are* individuals with $250,000 in investable assets or the potential *to have* $250,000 in investable assets, *have* a mortgage, and *have some* goals *they wish* to achieve.

Revised: I find that I can most assist individuals with $250,000 in investable assets (or the potential for $250,000 in investable assets), a mortgage, and goals to achieve. (41 words reduced to 29)

State Negatives Positively

Using negatives adds extra words and slows reader comprehension. For example, how many times do you need to read the following sentence to understand it? "Your ideas do not lack sparkle or shine, nor is your meaning unclear, but your spelling is without that precision and correctness that must thoroughly impress your readers." Readers must slow down to follow double negatives and translate them into positives.

With its negatives stated in the positive, the sentence reads, "Your ideas sparkle and shine and your meaning is clear, but your spelling lacks the precision and correctness to fully impress your readers" (28 words to 23). The sentence is still wordy: "Your ideas sparkle and your meaning is clear, but your poor spelling mars your readers' admiration" (28 words to 16). Note that the phrases in this example that state something negative are *not* revised to be positive. Only revise phrases that use negatives unnecessarily, such as "If your application is not complete, it will not be funded." Instead, say, "Only complete applications will be funded." It says the same thing clearly and concisely.

Exercise 6: Remove Wordiness

Revise the following passages to make them clearer and more concise.

1. It is in the best interests of all and sundry that a true and accurate account of those events is widely circulated. It helps no one if fiction and fable misinforms the general public and innocent readers misunderstand the true state of business affairs at our organization. A press release will not be amiss to set the record straight. Although our President and CEO is not present and available, this does not mean that first and foremost he will not contact us and explain his recent actions in light of the accountant's report that was carefully evaluated and assessed.

2. Profits in the third quarter were not unrewarding. Consequently, the CFO was not unhappy to approve a one-time bonus of 15 percent for all employees who work more than 25 hours a week. In point of fact, he also approved a one-time bonus of 10 percent for employees who work less than 25 hours a week. All employees should therefore check their forthcoming paycheque to ensure that they do not go unrewarded for their not inconsiderable efforts over the third quarter of this fiscal year.

3. Our recommendations are not insubstantial in fact. There are three of them. We suggest that all volunteers receive copies of the organizational newsletter delivered to their home addresses to inform them of what is happening at the museum. This should improve the sense of disconnect volunteers feel with the current paid staff. Second, we suggest that the newsletter editor does not fail to initiate a staff profile in each issue that features both paid and volunteer members to increase the visibility and profile of all members of the organization. Third, we urge the board of directors to consider the starting up of a small staff rewards and recognition program to ensure that hardworking volunteers, as well as paid staff, do not go unnoticed in their exemplary efforts to improve the service and morale of the museum organization. We believe that these three initiatives, if not implemented in an untimely fashion, could go a long way toward resolving the staff–volunteer issues that were the impetus for this report.

ANALYSIS: IMPROVING JAYSON'S STYLE

LO 5 Read source texts carefully and use knowledge gained from them to create appropriate professional documents

Cohesion in writing grows out of how your prose "flows" to readers. In Case 3, Jayson's draft felt disorganized to Dorian because of the topic changes from sentence to sentence. Readers experience a text as cohesive if the information in individual sentences is presented so that the topic talked about in one sentence is connected to the topic in the next sentence.

Figure 19 reproduces a sample paragraph from Jayson's report.

(1) The Arva Springs Honey Cream Ale promotional event was a resounding success. (2) Attendance peaked at 7,000 visitors over 14 hours. (3) We gave out 2,000 t-shirts, baseball caps, and inflatable beach balls stamped with the Arva Springs Honey Cream Ale name and logo. (4) Musical performers entertained the crowd. (5) Celebrity visitors signed autographs and chatted with fans. (6) We gave away 10,000 litres of product to legal-aged drinkers.

Figure 19 A sample paragraph from Jayson's draft report that is not cohesive.

(1) The Arva Springs Honey Cream Ale promotional event welcomed 7,000 visitors over 14 hours. (2) These visitors took home 2,000 t-shirts, baseball caps, and inflatable beach balls stamped with the Arva brand. (3) Arva Springs Honey Cream Ale also gave away more than 10,000 litres of product to legal-aged drinkers. (4) While legal drinkers enjoyed the new beverage, under-age visitors were served a variety of soft drinks. (5) Other entertainments featured at the promotion were a spoken word hour, musical performers, and celebrity guests.

Figure 20 A revision of the sample paragraph to improve cohesion.

This paragraph seems disorganized because each sentence contains new information at the beginning and ending of each sentence. As readers, we reel from the constant shifts in topic as we try to organize and process each piece of information. If the information is arranged and presented differently, we begin to see connections between the ideas. Note that in Figure 20 end-to-start linking strategies have been used to highlight how one idea is related to the next across the five sentences.

Jayson realized that he could also improve his use of emphasis in the draft report. To use emphasis effectively, examine the final phrase or clause in a sentence to determine whether it contains an important idea. If it does, then the sentence doesn't need revision. But if it ends with a trivial phrase or clause, reorganize the sentence to emphasize the central point. As Jayson got to work improving the style of his report, he decided to add more detail about some of the participants. He drafted the paragraph in Figure 21 and then underlined the final phrases in each sentence to assess their impact.

He realized that the end of each sentence needed some revision to highlight his main ideas. Sentence 1 could be improved, he decided, if he shifted the unimportant information to the start: "At the event, I interviewed three guests." He reviewed sentence 2 and decided that it could be more concise: "Fifteen-year-old Terry said he came with three friends and they were having a sweet time." After reviewing sentence 3, he saw that its ending was

[1] I interviewed three guests at the event. [2] Terry, who said he was 15, says he came with three other friends and they were having a really sweet time even if they can't score beer free samples, which they were really hoping to. [3] I asked Joanne why she came and she say she loves a party when there is music and drinking. [4] Plus she wanted to read some of her work but she decided not to because she was scared when everyone was looking at her. [5] I talked to Gil who said he was hoping to meet some of the band members or some other celebrity person.

Figure 21 Jayson examined the phrases at the end of sentences to determine their impact.

weak and repetitious: "I asked Joanne why she came and she said she loves a party." Next he considered whether to combine sentences 3 and 4. Ultimately he decided the point was probably better in its own sentence, and he shifted the main point to the end: "She said she wanted to read a poem but the crowd intimidated her." Jayson decided sentence 5 could also be improved by moving the main point to the end: "I talked to Gil, who said he hoped to meet a celebrity or band member."

Finally Jayson looked through his draft for phrases and words that he could delete to make it more concise.

> Profession Communication Assignments

5. Rewrite Jayson's Report

Use the discussion in this module on plain language (including paragraph organization and transitions), positive emphasis, and elements of style, including cohesion, emphasis, and conciseness, to rewrite Jayson's report. Aim to present the account of the promotional event as professionally as possible, so reword some of the casual and colloquial expressions that Jayson has used. Think of this report as additional evidence toward a possible job offer at the end of the internship.

Audience: Dorian Alvarez (Jayson's boss), Albert Barker (president of Toronto Promotions)

Purpose: To describe the main events at the promotion and to demonstrate Jayson's ability and competence

Genre: Informational report

6. Write a Report on a Meeting or Event That You Organized Recently

Report on an event or meeting that you have planned or attended recently. Direct the one- to two-page report to your supervisor. Use the information in this module to help you write a clear, concise, and cohesive account of the event that you choose. Use the report as a way to demonstrate your competence and ability as an employee so that you are building goodwill as well as making your supervisor look good.

Audience: Your supervisor

Purpose: To describe the event and to demonstrate your competence and ability as an employee

Genre: Informational report

MODULE SUMMARY

- Business writing should be clear, concise, positive, and accessible to a broad range of readers.
- Plain language emphasizes short, direct sentences, words that most people use in their day-to-day lives, and organizing messages to satisfy your reader's needs.
- Positive language and approaches build goodwill and credibility toward you and your communications.
- Connect your sentences so that readers can follow your thoughts with minimal effort.
- Write concisely so that the words that you do write stand out.

Module 4

Professional Writing in an Electronic Environment

Bikeriderlondon/Shutterstock

LEARNING OUTCOMES

LO 1 Differentiate between when to use online/electronic communications and when to use print-only communications

LO 2 Apply the conventions of business email to your writing

LO 3 Assess business communications for personal privacy as well as the privacy of the people whose information you handle

LO 4 Develop a writing style appropriate for online business communication

GETTING STARTED

The digitization of text communication has revolutionized how we interact with one another. Online instant message (IM) systems, social media, and text messaging on mobile devices created new ways to communicate using text. Mobile technologies like smartphones and tablet computers expanded the reach of email as a communication technology. Facebook, Twitter, and LinkedIn extend communication to the web and encourage people to interact using technologies that combine voice, text, and image (including video calling on cell phones). The electronic communication landscape changes quickly. How should you interact with it as a professional in a work environment?

Jeff Metzger/Shutterstock

One key component of your interactions will come through your social media pages. Consider this: when you apply for your next job, your potential employer may visit your Facebook or LinkedIn pages to evaluate your character. What level of writing will they find there? What pictures will they view? This new development—that employers can view webpages that were not designed for them—highlights a key aspect of electronic communications: electronic publication and distribution spreads quickly and widely. Electronic communications circle the globe in seconds. Email, especially work email, may be forwarded to your boss's inbox even though you didn't write the message for him or her to read. In this module, you'll learn more about how to use new technologies for your own advantage while avoiding the problems they can cause.

This module outlines the basics of using digital communication media effectively and professionally. In the first case, Melania Wong needs to create an effective email message to persuade sales and marketing associates to try out her new software application. In the second case, Bart Chung and Emma Gilbert brainstorm the details of an annual retreat event for analysts in their division of the Canadian Tourism Association. Their challenge: create an email invitation to the event that will excite the attendees and motivate them to read a report they might otherwise only skim. In Case 3, Mansur Jain, owner of Centre Cycle Centre, is looking for ways to get customers to write appropriate reviews of products on his company blog.

GOOD BUSINESS EMAIL MESSAGES: THE BASICS

LO 1 Differentiate between when to use online/electronic communications and when to use print-only communications

In business or large organizations, writing a good email requires more thought and preparation than writing in a personal or informal social context. Unlike texting, which many people first used in a nonbusiness context, email grew out of organizational needs for military researchers to communicate with each other in the late 1960s. Its origins in organizational

| **Send** | **To:** | Rachel McGillivary |
| | **Subject:** | My participation in SEBC meetings |

Hi Rachel,

I hope things have been going well with you.

I wanted to touch base with you about the working group meetings that I have been attending as a volunteer with the South Edmonton Business Community (SEBC) organization. I have found the meetings to be very interesting, especially for the purpose of creating the demographic profile of south Edmonton for marketing purposes. The last couple of meetings, however, I have felt like I didn't have as much to contribute because of the nature of the topics.

I was wondering if you felt it was still a good investment of my time to attend these meetings. I am still more than happy to volunteer with the South Edmonton Business Community organization. At the same time, I'm wondering if the work of actually establishing your mission, values, and direction for the coming years isn't best left to those of you in the organization who really know it best.

Please let me know what you think,
Jerry

Figure 1 Example email message.

communication show up in the headers for emails that prompt writers for memo-like information: "To"; "CC"; "BCC"; and "Subject" information. Texts and tweets do not prompt writers for that information because they were created to serve different communication purposes. Figure 1 is an example of a well-written email.

Emails include some or all of these elements:

- **"To":** The person or group the message is sent to
- **"From":** The person or group sending the message
- **"Subject":** The topic of the message
- **"CC":** People who get a copy of the message
- **"BCC":** People who get a copy even though the people in the "To" and "CC" lines cannot tell a copy was sent to them
- The **message** itself
- Any **attachments** sent with the message

The "To" Line

If you are replying to someone else's message, the "To" line will fill in automatically. You should also consider whom else you might include in the conversation. For example, if a topic comes up in an email that you think affects another person in the organization, consider adding that person to the "To" line. They will get a copy of the message, and because you have sent it to them directly (rather than adding them to the "CC" line) they are more likely to respond.

In cases where you are beginning an email conversation, or "thread," choose whom to include in your "To" line carefully. In many cases, this may be obvious because you are asking a specific person something you know they can answer or comment on. For some other situations, such as when you are not sure whom to consult about a topic, you may need to

- Your opinion [Opinion about what?]
- toolkit [What kind of toolkit? For what purpose?]
- See attached [What is attached?]
- numbers [Budget numbers? Attendees at seminar?]
- draft [Of what document?]
- (no subject) [This is automatically inserted if you do not include a subject]

Figure 2 Poor subject lines.

ask others in your organization whom to send the message to. In addition, some messages may need to go to several people. For example, a draft of a new process for handling the budget may need feedback from several members of your team. You should probably include all the people you would like comments from in the "To" line.

The "From" Line

Usually a message that originates from your account will be marked as coming from you. In some cases, however, you might want to set up a separate email account for a project or workgroup. Messages sent from this account would show the group name in the "From" line. This technique allows several people to manage communications on a project—they could all share access to that account. If one person is out of the office or moves on to another project, the account continues uninterrupted.

The "Subject" Line

The subject of the message often determines how quickly readers open the message. In Figure 1, Jerry writes a specific subject line: "My participation in SEBC meetings." It communicates the topic of the message clearly and concisely. A less informative subject line that Jerry might have used is "Your opinion, please." Rachel would be unable to judge from this subject line what Jerry is writing about or how important the topic is. She would need to open the message to find out whether she needs to reply immediately or leave it until after lunch. Figure 2 lists some other poor subject lines.

These subject lines are too short and too vague. Readers cannot tell what the message is about. In many cases, the lack of information may cause readers to ignore the message and not respond. Good subject lines indicate what the message is about. Figure 3 lists some examples of subject lines that give readers a good idea of the main point of the message.

- Upcoming seminars in March and April
- Canadian Web Hosting can build your mobile app or website
- Please rate your recent interaction with Information Systems
- This afternoon's meeting times
- Technical question regarding SBUD

Figure 3 Good subject lines.

They all inform readers of the specific topic of the message and summarize it in a few words. Readers can judge the importance of the message as well as its subject matter.

The "CC" Line

Traditional memos within organizations included the CC: line. Originally "CC" referred to "carbon copy," a reference to carbon paper, which enabled business communicators to make immediate copies of their messages, both for storing and for sharing with one or two people. In an electronic environment, however, this copy feature expands almost infinitely.

Use the CC: line to communicate the message to people not directly affected by it but who might need to be aware of it. For example, when you write an email to an instructor on behalf of a group of students asking for clarification on an assignment, you should copy the other members of the group so that they know the message has been sent. This keeps the entire group involved and limits misunderstandings about exactly what you asked the instructor. In turn, when the instructor responds, everyone in the group will receive the reply. Note the social function of using the CC: line—in this case it keeps communication channels within the group open.

In other cases, however, you may want to use the CC: line to ensure that the person to whom you send the email understands that other people within the company are aware of the situation that is discussed in the email message. By using the CC: line in this way, you bring other people into the virtual conversation. That act changes the nature of what is said and how it is said because others are there to witness it. If you think that the topic of the email is going to lead to disagreements about how to proceed on a project, then using the CC: line to invite others into the conversation might help keep the communications professional.

The "BCC" Line

The BCC: line refers to "blind carbon copy" (see Figure 4). This means that the people who receive your email do not know whom else it was sent to. Use this line to send multiple

Send	To:	H. Brodie
	From:	R. Graves
	CC:	roger.graves@universityofalberta.ca
	BCC:	[not listed]

Thank you for registering for the Writing Across the Curriculum Reading Group on Teaching and Evaluating Writing. Sufficient numbers of people have registered for the reading group that we have opened a second session. This second group will meet in Telus 145 at the identical dates and times of the first group.

Since you are part of the second group, we are requesting that you join us in Telus Building Room 145 from 3:30 to 5:00 p.m. on Thursday, October 31, Nov. 7, Nov. 21, and Nov. 28.

If you would like to get started preparing for the reading group before our first meeting, please contact my administrative assistant, Jane Bennet, at jbennet4@universityofalberta.ca about picking up the text (John Bean's *Engaging Ideas*) or receiving it through campus mail (please email your campus mail address). We look forward to meeting you and talking with you about teaching writing over the next several weeks.

Figure 4 Appropriate use of the BCC address line.

email messages without displaying the addresses of all the people who received it. By using BCC:, you can protect the email privacy of individuals in the group. If you are circulating a newsletter at work to dozens of people, use the BCC: line to avoid filling the top of the email message with email addresses. You can also use the BCC: line to send a copy of the message to your other email address without revealing that address. This allows you to make sure your message really did get sent.

Resist the urge to use the BCC: line to send messages to coworkers without letting them know that you sent the message to their supervisor, for example. Unless you have a very good reason to hide the fact that others will also receive copies of the message, this practice will create distrust when it becomes known.

The Message Space

Email messages should start with a salutation if you are directing the message to someone in particular. Using "Dear Ms. Lemay," for example, is formal; using "Hi Odette," on the other hand, would be informal and conversational. Using just a first name suggests that you know the person you are emailing fairly well.

The body of the email should be direct and concise. Although email messages offer the ability to extend to just about any length, only rarely should you write an extensive message. Keep the message to the topic you identified in the subject line. Say what you have to say about that topic, and then end the message. If you need to communicate with the same person about a different topic, consider creating a second email message with a different subject line. Sending separate messages helps recipients deal with issues separately and file the messages so they can be found easily later, if necessary; such practices help colleagues manage their email workflow.

Figure 5 is a personal message that uses nonstandard spelling and informal salutation and closing. Avoid sending messages at work using this level of informality. Always keep in mind that workplace communication can circulate beyond the individual to whom you sent it; if you always use a professional tone and language, you will demonstrate your abilities as a competent and professional employee. Figure 6 presents a short email that uses a more appropriate and professional tone.

| Send | To: | Donna, Oscar, Jordan |
| | Subject: | Vegas idea |

Hey Guys,

Would u want to go to this? Sounds cool and based on that I think u guys liked the illusionist movie I thought u might want to go?

The deal expires tonight tho . . .

Doing okay. Got my antibiotics + pain killers and just icing my face from wisdom teeth extraction.

E

Figure 5 Informal message that is not appropriate for professional communication.

	To:	Robert Graves
Send	Subject:	Change of address confirmation

Dear Mr. Graves:

Please accept this email as confirmation of receipt of the completed "Change of Address" form, which we received on February 04, 2015. We have now completed the process of changing your address (all three accounts) as you requested. All future communications will be sent to your new address.

If you require any further information, please let us know.

Many thanks,
Omar Saludin

Figure 6 Maintain an appropriate tone for professional email messages.

Endings for email messages should mirror the introductory salutation. If you begin the message informally, then end it informally: use "Hi Pete" with "Talk to you soon" and "Dear Ms. Lemay" with "Best wishes," for example.

Attachments

Consider attaching a file when you need to communicate about complicated or extensive topics. These topics might include a report or a draft of a letter or document. In your email, refer the reader to the document and explain what you need from them—comments about the style or the accuracy of the figures in it, for example. Use the email message as the cover letter in which you explain what is in the attached document. However, avoid sending large files (over 1 megabyte). Most text files will be well under this limit.

Case 1★ Getting Coworkers to Respond to Your Email Messages

After a lot of trial and error, the new Sales & Marketing Support system application was ready to go. Melania Wong, a junior employee in the Information Systems division of Architectural Ecosystems Products, had spent almost a year developing and perfecting the pilot project. The system was a digital tool that offered various kinds of help to the sales force: sales projection documents; reports based on actual sales in real time; and trip accounting software, among other features. The value in those features came mainly from centralizing already existing information into one web-based interface. The system featured a social media feature, Sales Buddy (SBUD). SBUD, in essence, created an internal Twitter feed: texts from any sales or marketing employee worldwide would be fed into this online space, and members could post questions, strategies, information they gained about competitors, and successes. As a result of feedback from the 40 sales and marketing specialists who had volunteered to participate in the pilot trial of the system, the finished system was ready to launch.

LO 2 Apply the conventions of business email to your writing

Send	To:	SalesForce@AESystems.com
	Subject:	A favour
	CC:	Reid Simpson, Technical Systems Manager, Information Systems Division; Prashant Sharma, Manager Information Systems; Hyun Kim, Vice President, Sales

Sales Associates,

I am writing to request your help with a project. I am a relatively new employee in the Information Systems Division of AEProducts. I have enjoyed my first year and like working for the company. Although it is a large company with many people working throughout the world, it seems very open and welcoming to me. One of my main responsibilities for the coming year will be to develop a new system. It will be a virtual interaction and communication electronic chat system, web-enabled, and compliant with SSI standards for network systems, including the IEEE 802 standards for wireless networks. When we have a prototype of the system ready to test, it would be great if some of you would consider using it to help me find ways to improve it.

Thanks for reading this far and I hope to hear from some of you if it isn't too much trouble.

Warmly,
Mel

Figure 7 Melania's first recruiting email for the SBUD project.

The next step, one that Melania Wong knew would be difficult, was to write a company-wide email to promote SBUD. Melania had written an earlier email a year ago to recruit the 40 sales and marketing specialists that eventually took part in the pilot study (see Figure 7 for a copy of this email). At first, only 11 people had signed up. To get the rest of the recruits for the pilot study she had to ask people she knew in the company for suggestions. She knew that sales and marketing people were busy and worked under a lot of pressure. They also were very smart readers of marketing material. But even those facts could not explain why so few had replied to her original email.

Her task was clear: Review the earlier email and draft a new message that would get better results. The success of the entire year-long project depended on this.

ANALYSIS: MELANIA REVISITS HER UNSUCCESSFUL RECRUITING EMAIL

Melania rereads her earlier draft of the recruiting email. After the months that have passed since she wrote the draft, she can easily place herself in the position of reader, which she had had difficulty doing when she first wrote it. Immediately, she notices the generic listserv in the "To" line. She feels her eyes wavering as she reads because she recognizes that it resembles those batch emails she receives daily that are usually irrelevant to her job responsibilities or interests. She understands that this choice depersonalizes the message for the recipient.

CZQS2000/STS/Gettyimages

Next she reviews the "From" line and sees her own name and email address. This seems like a good choice because recipients can quickly see that the message is from her, not a generic or group address with no clear human sender.

She rereads the subject line, "A favour," and grimaces. She realizes that readers cannot tell the subject of the message beyond the fact that she is asking them to do something for her. Questions flood her mind: What is the favour for? Is the favour personal? Reflecting on her past year's experience, she admits that she herself would not jump to read this email when it's clear the writer is going to ask her to add one more activity to her already over-filled schedule. The subject is too vague, she decides. It also does not help readers know whether the message is important.

She sees that she copied her boss, his boss, and the head of sales at AESystems on her original message. She decides that copying them on the message was a good decision, and she considers whether she should add anyone else for the next mailing.

Next, she contemplates the possible use of a BCC: in a subsequent message. If she uses the BCC: function, she can address each recipient individually without filling the first screen of the message with all those individual email addresses. She also wonders whether she should worry about publicizing all those employee email addresses or whether they are readily available throughout AESystems—something she could ask Reid, her boss.

Then she examines the content of the original message. She is shocked to realize that the first four lines of the message are totally about her: Who she is, how she feels, what she is doing. The next point she notices is that only three sentences discuss the project itself, and she had used so much technical jargon that her readers probably didn't understand the subject matter or what she wanted them to do.

Finally, Melania reviews her concluding paragraph and closing, deciding that the deferential tone and weak request would be unlikely to motivate even herself to participate. She sees that there are many areas where she can improve the recruiting message. She also feels that her critique has given her some good ideas as to how to write the message to publicize the launch of SBUD as a useful application for the company sales force.

Professional Communication Assignments

1. Revise Melania Wong's Initial Email

Use the details in the case to revise the initial email (Figure 7), as Melania Wong, to recruit volunteers to work on the pilot project. Remember that she wants to show them that the end product will help them increase their sales and market AE products more effectively. Keep in mind that most readers of this email do not understand technical language related to computer applications.

Audience: Sales and marketing professions within the company

Purpose: To persuade readers to participate in piloting the proposed new software application

Genre: Persuasive and informative email message

2. Write Melania Wong's Email Announcing the SBUD Application

Use the details in the case to write a new email from Melania Wong to the sales and marketing agents in the company. The message needs to be concise but also persuasive. It should be formal because Melania does not know many of these agents. It also should have an informative subject line so that the agents will open and read the message. Consider copying the message to other, more senior people in the organization to encourage the agents to open the message.

Audience: Sales and marketing professionals within the company

Purpose: To persuade readers to use the proposed new software application

Genre: Persuasive and informative email message

TONE, LEVELS OF FORMALITY, AND PRIVACY IN ELECTRONIC COMMUNICATION

LO 3 Assess business communications for personal privacy as well as the privacy of the people whose information you handle

Electronic communication differs from printed versions of memos and letters in several particularly important ways. Electronic communications can be

- Distributed widely
- Shared quickly
- Copied effortlessly
- Forwarded indiscriminately

These characteristics mean that you, as a writer, must choose your message carefully. If you have a message that you do not want circulated widely, consider sending a paper copy of the memo or conveying the message in person or through a phone call. Similarly, if you need to communicate information that should not be shared until after a particular time period passes, consider alternative ways of sharing that message.

Text Messaging and Chat

"Work appropriate" is a phrase that can be applied as fruitfully to clothing as it can to the language you use at work. In professional contexts, employees usually are expected to behave according to rules and norms that the company sets. There is a wide range of formality between companies, with some being famous for their informality (WestJet encourages their flight attendants to tell jokes) and others being famous for their lack of it (Air Canada). Politeness helps people get along by creating ways to converse that show respect for the other person. In online exchanges, professionals need to observe a set of rules that reflect the business culture of the organization that employs them. In Figure 8, Paul uses a formal style for his message. Texting as part of building and maintaining work relationships demands different kinds of language use than the texting you do as part of your social life.

To: Marianne

Subject: Position you have open on your team

Send

Dear Marianne: ——————————————————————— Formal greeting

First of all, I would like to thank you for thinking of me for the positions that you are trying to fill within First Financial. The projects that your team is working on are quite exciting.

Formal words: "positions," not "jobs"

Given my current position on my team, however, and the timing of the contract that you are trying to fill (eight months, with no possibility for extension), I believe it makes more sense for me to wait and apply when you have a full-time position at a later date.

I hope you will keep me in mind for future openings in your area. It is very much an area I would like to work in in the future. You have a great team, and I hope to have the opportunity to work with you in the future.

No contractions: "you are," not "you're"

Best regards,
Paul

Figure 8 A professional tone in a letter or email.

Electronic Mail

Readers make judgments about writers based on the correctness and clarity of the message. In professional settings, you are judged by how you express yourself even in something as simple as an email message. At the very least, you should always proofread before you click "send." Even if email can be an informal method of communication for many people in their personal lives, it is also an important means of communication in business, where it is generally neither informal nor personal. It is fast and direct. You can ask a question and receive a response within minutes. You can dash off an explanation to a customer that resolves the problem quickly and efficiently.

LO 4 Develop a writing style appropriate for online business communication

Of course, the quickness and directness of email can also create problems. If you react emotionally to a word or phrase in the original message, you might send off a **flaming** retort that could embarrass you later or even get you fired. A message written and sent too quickly can encourage you to say what you really think rather than what you should have said. Let's look at some tips for negotiating email in the business and professional world.

Flaming: A response to an email that is emotional and verbally abusive

1. Email is not always private.
2. Humour rarely travels well electronically.
3. When a message reaches you that makes you angry or defensive, do not respond immediately.
4. Use standard edited English (or French) when writing email in a professional or business setting.
5. Before you send, reread carefully to catch errors.

Email Is Not Always Private Employee email is not always private. Supervisors at all levels can legally access and read any message that you compose and send from a business or professional account, particularly if you use a device that belongs to the company.

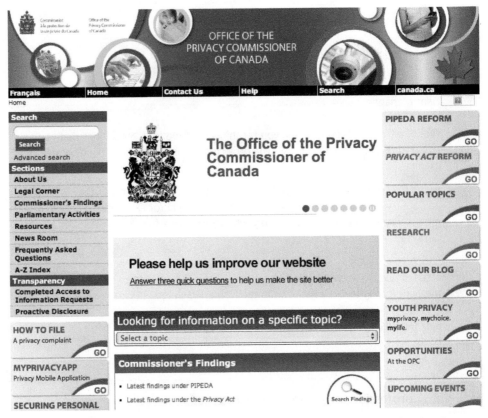

Figure 9 The Privacy Commissioner of Canada's website is an authoritative guide to privacy issues for individuals and organizations.

Source: http://www.priv.gc.ca/index_e.asp, Office of the Privacy Commissioner of Canada.

For this reason, you should not use work email (or the equivalent) to transact personal business or to make comments about your colleagues, coworkers, or organization that you would not want your boss or some other member of the organization to read.

Instead, use your personal (not company-issued) smartphone to check and respond to personal email, texts, and chats. At some organizations, employee email is routinely monitored; at others supervisors rarely review it. Don't take the chance with your career. Free email accounts are available from Yahoo!, Hotmail, Gmail, and others, and many internet providers also offer email accounts as part of their services, so use one of these types of email accounts for your personal communications. Reserve your work email for matters related to work, and don't use work computers to view your personal email accounts.

Humour Rarely Travels Well Electronically　Be careful about making jokes online in a business or professional environment. The humour does not always travel safely across the electronic divide. Some people circulate and forward jokes electronically through email (see Figure 10), but you should ask friends and family not to send such messages to your work account. Given the lack of privacy and workplace discrimination laws, you can be held responsible for sending or receiving inappropriate material online.

Email icons (emoticons): Symbols that are used to convey emotions within email and text messages

A variety of **email icons (emoticons)** have evolved to help writers convey emotion electronically (see Figure 11). The number of icons available in any instant messaging program can quickly become overwhelming. If you know your reader well and you share similar status levels at work, you can probably safely use the occasional emoticon. If you are writing to someone of a higher status level, avoid using emoticons. They can make you look unprofessional.

Do Not Respond Immediately to an Inflammatory Message　If you receive a message that makes you angry or defensive, by all means, write the response you'd love to send back, but instead of sending it, click the "discard" button. *Never send that inflammatory*

Send	To:	Shawna, Apurv, Tate, Lucy
	Subject:	Alternatives to foul language

Dear Employees:

It has been brought to management's attention that some individuals throughout the company have been using foul language during the course of normal conversation with their co-workers.

Due to complaints received from some employees who may be easily offended, this type of language will no longer be tolerated.

We do, however, realize the critical importance of being able to accurately express your feelings when communicating with co-workers.

Therefore, a list of 18 new and Innovative 'TRY SAYING' phrases have been provided so that proper exchange of ideas and information can continue in an effective manner.

<u>Number 1</u>
TRY SAYING: *I think you could use more training.*
INSTEAD OF: You don't know what the f___ you're doing.

<u>Number 2</u>
TRY SAYING: *She's an aggressive go-getter.*
INSTEAD OF: She's a f___ing bit__.

<u>Number 3</u>
TRY SAYING: *Perhaps I can work late.*
INSTEAD OF: And when the f___ do you expect me to do this?

Figure 10 Do not forward inappropriate messages like this one.

Figure 11 Avoid emoticons in professional email exchanges.

Source: Matthew Cole/Fotolia

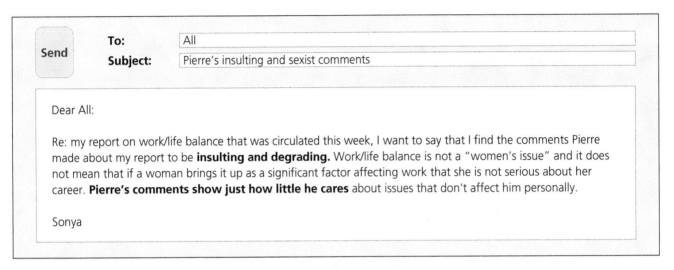

| Send | To: | All |
| | Subject: | Pierre's insulting and sexist comments |

Dear All:

Re: my report on work/life balance that was circulated this week, I want to say that I find the comments Pierre made about my report to be **insulting and degrading.** Work/life balance is not a "women's issue" and it does not mean that if a woman brings it up as a significant factor affecting work that she is not serious about her career. **Pierre's comments show just how little he cares** about issues that don't affect him personally.

Sonya

Figure 12 Avoid writing emotional and accusatory email messages.

reply back. These types of unconsidered responses usually make you look unprofessional and mean-spirited, especially if your reply is then circulated widely around the organization. Often the message doesn't actually need a reply. If you do have to respond, wait 24 hours so that you can carefully think through what you should say. Take the time to compose a response that is logical, carefully argued, and avoids using inflammatory language in return. Always aim to be calm and professional in your replies.

Do not write an email like the example in Figure 12! If you receive or are the target of an email like this, do not respond to it immediately, and perhaps do not respond to it at all through email.

Use Standard Edited English in Business and Professional Email   Your friends may not mind phonetic spelling or abbreviations when you invite them out for dinner, but your coworkers will not appreciate receiving an email such as in Figure 13 because of the time they may have to take to decipher it. Use standard edited English in all professional electronic communication to make your message as clear and easy to understand as possible (see Figure 14). Demonstrate your competence and strong literacy skills by always using standard edited English when you write in any kind of business or professional situation, whatever the medium. If you are unsure about a point of grammar, consult a handbook or someone whose knowledge of English grammar is solid and trustworthy.

Reread Carefully to Catch Errors Before You Send   Proofread your text before you click "send." Too many people skip the review and send off a message with letters missing or words misspelled. If your email program does not have a spell checker, then copy and

| Send | To: | salesvp@healthsolutions.com |
| | Subject: | ready for lift-off |

Okie, thanks! I'm thinking to reply tonight and see if spacey has time to meet up this week for coffee, and ask her a few questions, to make sure this ptential foray away from work isn't a disaster like the last one (if possible!) . . . Then, get that cover letter + updated resume off before I fly to montreal :)

Figure 13 Do not use texting language in work emails.

| Send | To: | Frank |
| | Subject: | Pysiotherapist position you might be interested in |

Dear Frank:

Hope you are doing well. We will be posting a position within my team for a physiotherapist specialist. It's an advanced position and I immediately thought of you. If you like, I will send the job posting along as soon as it is available. Just let me know if that's okay.

Figure 14 An example of appropriate use of Standard English in email.

paste your text into a word processing file and turn on the spell check feature to catch obvious errors. Never rely entirely on spell checking programs to find your errors. Instead, read your message carefully to help you catch mistakes.

Case 2★★ Communicating to Create Anticipation and Excitement

"Okay, we have the date, the venue, the food, a schedule of activities, and manager approval of our plan," summarized Bart Chung. "What we are missing is the invitation to the branch retreat."

Emma Gilbert, the other analyst assigned to plan the retreat, agreed that it was a good time to start publicizing the retreat. Bart and Emma had been tasked with organizing the branch retreat at the Canadian Tourism Association, where the junior and senior associates gathered yearly to take stock of the previous year's work and to set out their plan for the short and long term. Although it was intended to be a team-building exercise that inspired the group to work cohesively for another year, it often turned out to be dull and uninspiring. Emma and Bart had set as a main goal in their preparations that all attendees would enjoy themselves this year. To that end, they had reserved the Hockey Hall of Fame in downtown Toronto as the location, and they had planned games and contests with prizes to share information and encourage everyone to develop and contribute ideas for the strategic plan.

Emma volunteered to draft a copy of the email and send it to Bart for editing before distributing it. Bart offered to brainstorm a list of information it should contain to make the drafting easier. They created a list of information they needed:

- The date: December 4
- The time: Coffee and breakfast at 8:30 and festivities full on at 9 A.M.
- Location: The Hockey Hall of Fame (the address plus a map link)
- Dress: Wear your favourite team gear

Bart mentioned that perhaps not everyone would have a hockey jersey and wondered if they should allow people to wear other sports

The venue: Hockey Hall of Fame.
Source: Ritu Jethani/123RF

paraphernalia. After a few minutes of discussion, they decided that the venue should limit the gear to hockey, since it should be possible for anyone to borrow a jersey, T-shirt, or ball cap if they didn't actually own one. T-shirts with a team logo aren't expensive, Emma pointed out. Bart conceded her point and added that it would also be important to create excitement for this retreat in the message. From his point of view, most employees dreaded these events, especially after last year's event.

"Well, I don't think anyone will be bored at our meeting," said Emma. "At least, I sure hope they aren't. With all of these activities, everyone should be able to keep their eyes open."

In preparation for the retreat, all members of the branch were supposed to read the annual report, circulated one month earlier, and to familiarize themselves with the central accomplishments of the branch during the past year. Usually, no one did more than flip through it briefly. To encourage their coworkers to read the report more carefully, Bart and Emma had decided to stage a contest with trophies and prizes. They planned to divide the unit into three or four teams of people who would earn points by answering a series of questions based on the contents of the annual report. Trophies would be awarded to the two teams with the highest scores, and the individuals with the two highest personal scores would receive hockey-themed prizes. Emma and Bart had decided that it would only be fair to warn their colleagues in the invitation that they would benefit from taking more than a cursory glance at the report this year. They didn't want to give them too much information. They did want them to read the report but not necessarily know *why* they should read the report. They decided that they should at least hint at why attendees should do more than skim it.

Next they debated the extent to which the catered lunch was a selling feature that should be highlighted in the invitation. The Stepping Stone Café, a local foods restaurant near the Hockey Hall of Fame, had recently revamped its menu, and Bart had arranged for the chef to prepare gourmet lunch boxes based on some of its most popular new offerings. They decided that including a brief mention in the invitation was appropriate.

Finally, they discussed whether the invitation should appear in the body of the email message or as an attachment. Emma argued that an attachment would allow them to design the page layout to ensure its visual appeal, but Bart pointed out that if the invitation included live links to a map and the Hockey Hall of Fame website it couldn't be in an attachment. They decided that an in-text message would make sure everyone could access the invitation from their cell phones and prevent them from printing out multiple pages for the invitation.

After a few more minutes of discussion, Bart and Emma agreed that they had covered what seemed to be the obvious details that should be included in the message. Bart passed his notes across the desk to Emma and then the two of them turned to her computer to get started drafting the invitation.

ANALYSIS: CREATING EXCITEMENT AMONG EMMA AND BART'S COWORKERS

Before they began writing, Emma and Bart discussed their readers for a few minutes. Bart made several suggestions of possible approaches that would catch their readers' interest about the branch retreat and how the email might increase their enthusiasm for what, in the past, had been a long dull meeting. Emma also pointed out that they would need to use a **formal tone** in the email, because it was going to go to the branch manager, their own manager, and the senior analysts in the branch, not just the other junior analysts whom they knew quite well. Although some of their readers were good friends, others they did not know that well. Bart agreed, noting that they weren't just dashing off an informal message to friends; the tone should be professional to build their credibility in the organization. Emma pointed out that in many cases their readers would make judgments about the writers' competence based on this message.

Formal tone: In writing, the use of language to convey a respectful and serious approach to business communications

Professional Communication Assignments

3. Write the Invitation to the Branch Retreat

Use the details in the case to draft the invitation, as Emma Gilbert or Bart Chung, to the other employees of the branch at the Canadian Tourism Association to the annual retreat. Remember that you want to stir up excitement among your coworkers for the day-long event, so try to persuade readers to read the annual report, to wear some hockey-related gear, and to look forward to an enjoyable and interesting meeting. As you write your invitation, incorporate the discussion from this module to help you draft a message that is appropriate to the business context. Where appropriate, use visual aids (this might include an electronic map to the site and maybe an image from the Hockey Hall of Fame website) and include links that will give readers more information about various aspects of the meeting (e.g., links to the café website or the Hockey Hall of Fame website). Remember that your message should take into account the difference in status between you and many of the senior employees at the branch.

Audience: The branch manager, the unit manager, junior and senior analysts at the branch

Purpose: To ignite interest and excitement in fellow employees for the upcoming annual branch retreat; to demonstrate Emma and Bart's ability and competence as employees at Canadian Tourism Association

Genre: Persuasive and informative email message

4. Write an Email to Bart and Emma's Boss Requesting Budget Increase for Annual Retreat

Bart Chung totaled up the projected expenses for CTA's annual retreat and realized that he and Emma were $200 over their allotted $1000. After reviewing the costs for food and coffee, the facility reservation, and other expenses, he realized that the only area they could reasonably reduce their costs was in the prize budget. He and Emma discussed alternatives and decided they could make some tacky trophies with plastic goblets and spray paint, but they also wanted two or three good prizes such as restaurant certificates. They decided to ask their boss for an additional $100 so they could purchase two $50 gift certificates for their grand prize winners. Write the memo to Bart's boss, Michael Banner, asking for a $100 increase to the CTA retreat budget to buy prizes.

Audience: Michael Banner, manager of data analysts at CTA

Purpose: To convince Michael Banner to approve the budget increase

Genre: Persuasive message

PUBLISHING ON THE WEB: TWITTER, BLOGS, FACEBOOK, AND LINKEDIN

Handling Other People's Private Information

LO 3 Assess business communications for personal privacy as well as the privacy of the people whose information you handle

One special aspect of writing in electronic environments involves handling the personal information of customers and clients. In addition to two federal laws, all provinces and territories in Canada enforce laws governing how personal information—much of it collected electronically—is stored. Links to these laws can be found on the website of the Office of the Privacy Commissioner of Canada (www.priv.gc.ca/index_e.asp).

When you communicate as an employee of a business or government organization, you need to be aware that strict rules apply to the use of personal information. For example, do not send email messages with someone's confidential information in it (social security number, birth date, credit card information) outside the business's secure intranet. Regular email is not secure, so unintended readers might gain access to this information and compromise that individual's privacy. If you handle this kind of information, always lock your screen when you leave your desk so that coworkers or visitors do not gain access to it while you are away. Do not store personal information on a portable memory stick that could easily be lost or left on another computer.

You will probably find yourself communicating regularly with clients and potential customers over email. In one-to-one communications, you may choose to write and

kbuntu/Fotolia

attach copies of documents to messages to explain a procedure, share a proposal, or supply a graphic image. To take advantage of this feature of email, become familiar with how to create attachments. Word processing documents can easily be attached to email messages, but the default file format can only be read by someone with the same word processing software on their device. Unless you know what kind of software your recipient has, choose a file format that is more generally supported. For example, when a new version of Microsoft Word™ was issued, anyone without the latest version could not open the new .docx (document) file format. To ensure that your word processing attachments are widely available, save them as .rtf (rich text format) files or, better still, to .pdf (portable document format) files. Although all of these file formats can be posted to a website for people to download, you might consider using an .htm (hypertext) file instead, if that is your most likely use of them.

Though email may be the primary method for communicating with coworkers and clients online, other electronic tools work better for extended and repeated communications. Many companies have websites, of course, but new technologies for social networking also provide opportunities for online publication such as Twitter, Facebook, LinkedIn, and blogs.

Online publication tools such as these provide a variety of ways to communicate with potential customers and clients. Although it's unlikely that you will do the design work for these pages, you may be asked to write copy for them. When you write for web publication, keep these principles in mind:

- Shorten your message; create separate, printable files for longer messages
- Write short paragraphs
- Use visuals where possible
- Write short (12 to 20 words on average), simple sentences
- Use bullets for lists
- Add links to other pages

Several practical realities of electronic communication explain these principles. First, messages may be read primarily on portable devices such as cell phones. Longer documents and documents with long paragraphs demand that readers keep scrolling. Paragraphing is, to some extent, a visual phenomenon. The act of breaking texts into paragraphs gives readers clues about how the ideas within the paragraphs are related. However, when readers cannot see the paragraph breaks, they can no longer visually determine the point of the paragraph.

People reading on electronic devices have less patience for reading longer texts. To help them read and process information more quickly, write shorter sentences (12 to 20 words). Also, write mostly simple sentences—that is, that contain one main clause (main subject plus a main verb). Use dependent phrases sparingly. If you have an opportunity to include a visual, take it.

Weblogs

Like most new technologies, weblogs (blogs) are an evolving genre. They range from personal (catexpert.blogspot.com) to political (www.macleans.ca/rss-feeds) and beyond (see Figure 15). If you are an aspiring journalist, writing your own blog offers you an opportunity to write and publish as a way into the profession. This also holds true for the fields of public relations and marketing communications.

Writing style for blogs tends to have an **informal tone**, even in "professional" blogs sponsored by major media outlets such as *Maclean's*. You'll find words like "sucks," nicknames for political figures ("Sarko" for former French President Sarkozy), contractions ("How's" for "How is"), rhetorical questions ("You know what?"), and other kinds of language meant to mimic conversation between people. Sentence lengths tend to average under 20 words, and paragraphs tend to be shorter—five lines or fewer. In keeping with the conversational style, the tone is often personal: writers talk about their feelings, what is outside their windows, or their personal reactions to events. If you write a blog for work, keep these stylistic characteristics in mind.

Informal tone: Written communications that employ conversational, relaxed, colloquial language

Figure 15 The Canadian Blog Awards site provides a useful way to find good blogs.

Source: Elan Morgan, Canadian Weblog Awards, 2014. www.canadianweblogawards.com

Case 3★★ Centre Cycle Centre's Weblog for Returning Customers

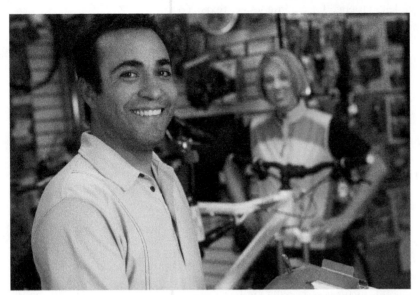

Bikeriderlondon/shutterstock

Centre Cycle Centre, or C^3 ("sea cubed," as the locals said it) was established in 1935 and had long been the top merchant for local cycling enthusiasts. The business had been sold a couple of times since the original owners parted with it, but the brand remained strong locally. Cycling clubs, a store-specific discount card, and charitable donations to just about every fundraising event all helped to keep C^3 in the public eye. Big box stores on the edge of town had managed to cut into the sales of low-end products, but Centre Cycle's devoted following and focus on high-end equipment helped them stay profitable.

The most recent buyer of the business, Mansur Jain, knew all of this when he made the purchase. But even though Windsor was not growing, he saw an opportunity to increase sales by developing a website for the store. Work on the site had started modestly two years ago, and so far sales had indeed gone up. Building the site and maintaining it had proven to take more time than he had thought,

Dusan Zidar/Fotolia

but by hiring a company to host and program the site he had avoided the computer head-aches that often cripple internet marketing efforts.

All the same, he felt that sales could be increased. He was surprised to learn that in-store customers used the site frequently, and in talking with them he often heard the complaint that although the information on the site was good, it could be better written. A recent example involved what cyclists called a trainer—a machine to hold your bike so that the back wheel spins and you can ride the bike indoors during the winter. The current text on the website had been largely lifted from the manufacturer's site.

Mansur thought that the manufacturer's site, although not perfect, was good enough—he could include a link to it from the C^3 website. He decided that what he needed was an online journal or comments from customers about the products, perhaps a blog. That way, customers would stay on his site or come back to it, and that would make them more likely to purchase from him. He decided to ask the organizer of the Centre Cycle Riding Club, Cahya Pham, to see if one of the members would like to try out the trainer in exchange for writing something about it for the website.

ANALYSIS: PLANNING THE C^3 BLOG ENTRY

Cahya Pham decided to write the first blog entry for Mansur's page on the MySpinner trainer. The chance to try it out had been a powerful incentive for volunteering to write. Obvious angles to discuss would include how easy it was to install the bike on the trainer; how durable it was for regular use by multiple users, including Cahya's three teenaged sons; and how realistic the trainer was as an exercise option once the Windsor streets became icy and snow-covered. Having posted regular observations about the cycling culture in Windsor on a personal blog over the past year or two, Cahya was familiar with how to write a blog posting: Let your personality come through in your conversational tone; keep sentences and paragraphs short; add visuals from the manufacturer's website; make some interesting observations about the trainer that other cyclists will enjoy.

> Professional Communication Assignments

5. Write a Description of the Trainer as a Blog Entry for the Centre Cycle Website

Mansur Jain has asked you to write something you think the other members of the club as well as other cyclists would be interested in reading about cycling trainers generally, and the MySpinner ones specifically. He sells the complete MySpinner line, and as part of the deal with the manufac-turer he is able to sell them online across Canada as well. If the blog helps increase sales, he is willing to compensate the writers with free and discounted equipment. Using the writ-ing style principles described earlier in this module, write a blog entry about cycling trainers, focusing on the Minoura line for your examples and for pictures.

Audience: Current and potential customers of Centre Cycle Centre (C^3)

Purpose: To evaluate cycling trainers generally, Minoura trainers specifically, and to motivate readers to visit the blog site regularly

Genre: Evaluative blog posting

6. Write a Blog Entry Based on a Current Fashion Topic

Identify a current topic in fashion design and write a blog entry in a style appropriate for a fashion blog. Be sure to use an informal tone and language, contractions, rhetorical questions, conversational phrases, short sentences, and short paragraphs. Begin by reading several fashion blogs: try the *New York Times* site (http://runway.blogs.nytimes.com); Fashion Salad (www.apparelsearch.com/fashion/Fashion_Blogs.htm); Canadian Beauty (www.canadianbeauty.com); or final fashion (http://finalfashion.ca). Then write an entry in that style.

Audience: Friends and family members who are also interested in fashion

Purpose: To express your opinion and insight about the fashion topic that you chose and to motivate readers to return to your blog site regularly

Genre: Evaluative blog posting

MODULE SUMMARY

- Email messages should be concise, direct, and sent to the right people in the organization.

- Email messages should be professional in tone: use formal language, not slang, and avoid contractions and humour.

- Electronic communications at work are not private, and they may be forwarded and copied to others both inside and outside the organization without your knowledge.

- Blog posts, tweets, Facebook posts, and public comments on websites that are made from a company account must represent the organization well. Posts made from your own personal accounts enable you to decide how you want to be represented.

Module 5

Writing in Teams

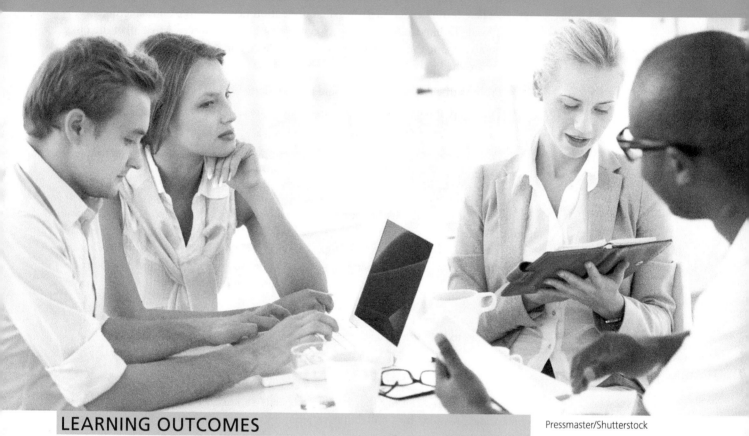

LEARNING OUTCOMES

LO 1   Identify the kinds of projects that are usually completed in teams

LO 2   Describe the two types of collaboration and their characteristics

LO 3   Identify activities teams can engage in to help promote their group's success

LO 4   Avoid behaviours that sabotage group success

LO 5   Develop four different strategies for resolving group conflict

GETTING STARTED

Although some instructors may discourage you from working with others on course material and assignments at school, you will find the attitude toward collaborating in the workplace is completely different. Employers welcome employees combining their talents to efficiently and effectively complete work projects. In fact, you will be viewed as a less desirable worker if you cannot work well with others. Take every opportunity while you are still in school to develop your interpersonal skills so that you can work positively and productively with others.

This module outlines tips and strategies that you can use to improve both your interpersonal skills and your productive abilities. It also provides opportunities for you to work with your classmates on discussion-based as well as document-based exercises and assignments.

WORKING AND WRITING IN GROUPS

LO 1 Identify the kinds of projects that are usually completed in teams

In the case that you will read shortly, the employees of an event planning group have been asked to organize and run a government-sponsored conference for academic researchers, scientists, and industry partners. The timeline for holding this conference is quite short, so a group of people are needed to gather the information necessary to plan the conference, a task that would be impossible for one person working alone. However, when all of the tasks are distributed among the group, the short timeline is not an issue.

These are the kinds of projects that are often done collaboratively:

- Projects that are too large or would take too long for one person to complete
- Projects that require expertise from different areas that no one person has
- Large projects that need to be completed quickly
- Projects that are especially important, so many people contribute; therefore no one person is responsible for whether the project succeeds or fails

Many large projects require team members to work and to write individually and collaboratively. If you have had bad experiences collaborating on school projects, with team members who did not complete their assigned tasks or did them poorly, you may hesitate at the prospect of contributing to a large, important work project. If you have had good collaborative working groups, then you also know that such group work can also be energizing and enjoyable: when everyone does their tasks well and on time, it is a recipe for success and possibly promotion.

In addition to doing your assigned task well and finishing it before the deadline, here are other ways to help the group succeed.

Request Knowledge and Opinions

Ask questions to figure out what the group needs to know. Figure 1 displays a list of brainstorming sessions by a collaborative group in their first meeting. The group begins with questions to identify the target audience for the event they are planning. By learning the characteristics and needs of their target attendees (as well as secondary groups

What do we need to know?

Who is going to come to this event?

What is our main and secondary demographic in this audience?

What kinds of activities do they enjoy?

What amenities are there in Penticton that our target audience might enjoy?

Who/what will attendees bring with them? (Children? Pets? Other?)

Will we need to arrange childcare? Pet care?

What age groups? Activities? Kind of care?

Figure 1 **What does the group need to know to get started on the project?**

who might attend), they can figure out what activities to include in the event as well as the additional arrangements that might be necessary. Once they thoroughly discuss the questions that they need to answer, they can divide up the list and assign tasks to committee members.

Offer Information and Opinions

Answer questions when they are asked. Another role that you can play in a group is to suggest answers when a group member asks a question. For example, one member of the group generated a list of types of people who might want to attend the event that they were planning. Two others logged onto a company laptop to check out the Chamber of Commerce website in Penticton, where the event would be held, to find out what activities and amenities were advertised in that region. When they noted the town's location on the shore of Lake Okanagan, several people suggested they look for water equipment rentals and boat tours to add to the list.

Summarize

Restate major points that are made. The role of summarizing in a group can be helpful for reviewing the highlights of the discussion and ensuring that all members agree on what topics have been covered. By restating major points, the group can assess its progress as well as review the direction of the discussion. Toward the end of the meeting, pull ideas together by reviewing notes, summarizing key points, and allowing group members to ask questions, point out problems, and such. At this point, everyone should focus on whether something important has been forgotten and evaluate the progress they've made toward their goals for the meeting as well as the larger project.

Review Decisions

The review of decisions can be important to ensure that everyone shares the same understanding about the plan. Often a review of key decisions can uncover misunderstanding or disagreement about the group's final position. The group can clear up any problems before proceeding.

Evaluate Decisions and Ideas

Compare group decisions. Evaluation of the group's process is important. It raises the issue of quality, which can head off potential problems with **groupthink**. Groupthink refers to a group process in which members rush to decide on an action without thoroughly discussing it. Often, the group stifles disagreement to avoid unpleasantness, but thoughtless agreement results in an inferior outcome. Step back from group decisions to evaluate whether they are, in fact, the best solution or the best action to take.

Groupthink: The tendency of group members to immediately agree with each other and not really evaluate an idea or direction

Measure decisions against group goals. An evaluator looks at decisions that have been made and assesses further whether these decisions are good ones that will contribute to the group accomplishing its goal(s). Thinking critically about group decisions will usually help the group to arrive at the best solutions.

Coordinate

Plan Work A group coordinator uses the decisions that the group makes to figure out how best to subdivide the work to accomplish the goal. It is a valuable contribution to the group to plan or work out in greater detail how something should be done. If one member of the group makes detailed notes about what needs to be done, the tasks can be assigned around the table and a workable plan can be developed for what to find out. Of course, planning work can also be done verbally with several members contributing.

Give Directions   Someone in the group should take the leadership role and supervise the division of responsibility for the work. The leader may sketch out a timeline for completing the various stages.

Figure out how all group members will contribute. The group who generated the list of questions in Figure 1 collaboratively decided who would research each topic. Everyone had a subject and knowledge of what in particular they needed to find out when they left the meeting.

MODELS OF COLLABORATION

There are two basic models for collaborating and writing collaboratively: hierarchical and dialogic. In **hierarchical collaboration**, one person assumes a leadership role and the rest of the team occupies subordinate reporting roles. Hierarchical collaboration takes place within a well-defined system of reporting and authority. The leader directs the meeting, gives instructions, and assigns deadlines. Members complete their tasks and report back to him or her.

In contrast, **dialogic collaboration** is characterized by the absence of a clear, single leader. Instead team members share the common goal of compiling the research and drafting the report. They act as peers and share the authority and decision-making process.

GROUP BEHAVIOURS THAT CREATE A SUCCESSFUL COLLABORATION

Encourage Participation

One goal of the team is to have everyone participate and contribute their ideas. You can encourage participation by demonstrating your openness to the ideas of others. Ask quieter team members what they are thinking and then respond positively and encouragingly to their ideas. As the discussion continues, give appropriate credit to team members for their ideas so that individuals feel good about being validated and appreciated.

Relieve Tension

Such activities as joking can help everyone relax and remember to enjoy themselves. If you feel tensions are high because of disagreement or heated discussion, consider suggesting that the group take a short break or engage in a fun activity for a few minutes to give everyone a breather and a chance to reset their emotions to a more relaxed level.

Check Feelings

It fosters group loyalty, helps resolve conflicts, and keeps the group functioning smoothly if you check occasionally to see how everyone is feeling about the decisions being made and the direction of discussion. You can encourage others to speak up about their feelings by sometimes sharing your own feelings about the group's activities.

Solve Interpersonal Problems

Sometimes interpersonal problems will develop between group members. Directly dealing with these problems by opening up discussion and suggesting ways to solve them can go a long way toward ensuring the continued smooth functioning of a group. Don't ignore or

- Respond to the speaker
- Give feedback (for literal meaning, emotional content, and/or both)
- Ask for more information
- State your own feelings

Figure 2 Active listening strategies.

discourage discussion of problems because they can escalate and prevent the group from successfully accomplishing its goals.

Listen Actively

Active listening signals to speakers that their ideas are being heard and understood. It involves showing group members that they are being taken seriously. Active listening refers not to just hearing the sounds coming from someone's mouth, but understanding and interpreting those sounds accurately. It means understanding the meaning of another person's comment as well as attending to the feelings that are being communicated along with the information. To be an active listener, respond to the speaker. This means making such comments as "Yes," "Uh-huh," "I see," "Interesting idea," "Okay," and so on to indicate your connection and interest. Remember to give feedback. Feedback can include paraphrasing what you believe the speaker said so that he or she can correct your understanding, if necessary.

Ask the speaker to elaborate on a point that is interesting or that you may not have understood. This shows the speaker that you are engaging fully with his or her ideas. Another method of listening actively is to share your feelings about what the speaker is saying. This demonstrates your response to what he or she is saying as well as how he or she is saying it.

Listening actively can help you reduce conflict in the group that results from miscommunication. Active listening allows you to hear and understand what others are saying. It provides a way to verify your understanding by foregrounding possible areas of misunderstanding. At the same time, active listening cannot solve all problems: it doesn't remove conflict when group members want divergent solutions or when one person has an interpersonal conflict with another person.

Case 1★★★ Organizing a Conference on Water Quality

"Our contact at Environment Canada is Douglas Gervais." Howard Kent looked up from the sheet of paper and glanced at his staff around the conference table. Gervais was supposed to be running this conference, but he was too oversubscribed to handle it, so he asked Mueller Kent Events to step in and take over. If Mueller Kent Events could do a stellar job putting this conference together, then they definitely would have a shot at signing other contracts, not only with Environment Canada, but other government bodies as well. Kent reminded everyone how important it was to get some government referrals. There had been a few lean times at Mueller Kent Events while Howard Kent and Rebekah

Mueller struggled to break into the events planning business in central Canada. The long-term picture was slowly looking brighter, but contacts with lucrative government offices had continued to elude them until now.

The conference was sponsored by Environment Canada and the Canadian Association on Water Quality. These two groups usually sponsored three symposia in regions across the country, but this year they also wanted to hold a three-day conference to bring together water quality researchers from around the globe to network with Canadian water quality experts.

"Here's our first timeline for this project." Kent distributed the handout that he'd been reading from around the table (see Figure 3, Items A and B). Item A in the outline listed contact information and a brief overview of water quality and the Canadian Association on Water Quality. Item B listed a deadline for the end of the week to have several ideas and options for the conference. By the end of next week Kent wanted a draft of the report to send to Douglas Gervais outlining the plan for the conference. Gervais wanted the call for abstracts distributed widely by the end of the month, all proposals due by the end of November, and the conference held in the middle of January. This was a tight turn-around for this kind of event planning.

Kent asked if anyone had been to one of these academic conferences before. One hand shot up: Linda Johnson. As an undergrad she helped a couple of professors plan a history conference. She had worked at the information booth, but also helped with some of the arrangements.

A. Contact
    Douglas Gervais, Environment Canada, 416-123-4567, dgervais@enviroca.fgc.ca

The Canadian Association on Water Quality (CAWQ) was established as a voluntary not-for-profit organization in 1967 as a collection of individuals from industry, government, and academia who were interested in water treatment and pollution control. Since that time, the organization has evolved to include engineers, scientists, and managers who are directly involved in issues surrounding water quality. The objectives of the CAWQ are to:

• Promote research on the scientific, technological, legal, and administrative aspects of water quality and of the control and treatment of water pollution
• Further the exchange of information and practical application of such research for the public benefit
• Promote the goals and objectives of the International Water Association (IWA)

(Source: www.cawq.ca/en/about.shtml)

B. Timeline
    Monday, Sept. 16, Organizational meeting:
    • Brainstorm relevant topics
    • Assign tasks
    Friday, Sept. 20, Research reports:
    • Email a copy of your research and recommendations to the other team members (as well as Howard Kent)
    • Read the reports you receive from other team members
    Monday, Sept. 23, Decision and drafting meeting:
    • Discuss team members' research findings and recommendations
    • As a group decide on a plan for the conference
    • Begin drafting longer report on plan for the conference for Howard Kent

Figure 3 Timeline for planning the First Canadian Conference on Water Quality.

Wednesday, Sept. 25, conference plan report:
- Email draft of team-written report to Howard Kent
- Revise based on feedback received from instructor

Friday, Sept. 27, Final draft of conference plan report:
- Submit final draft of conference plan report to Douglas Gervais

C. What we need to know

On Water Quality
- Names and contact info (institution, email, phone number) of water quality experts in Canada, U.S., outside of North America
- Brief/paragraph summary of person's research focus and interests
- Reasons why this person would make a good keynote speaker on water quality
- Need information on five or six researchers in Canada, four or five from the U.S., and two or three international researchers (i.e. outside of North America) (notes to self: remember gender of speaker, range of expertise, INTERESTING research topics)
- Recommendations about who to choose and why (up to five suggestions)
- Useful and relevant websites to start with:
  - www.cawq.ca
  - www.cawq.ca/en/links.shtml
  - www.earth.uwaterloo.ca/research/ucsigrc

Conference Locations
- Conference facilities in town that can handle 100–120 participants on January 15–17, 2015
- Hotel accommodations plus quotes for costs that can meet our needs for this conference (3, if possible)
- Restaurant facilities near the hotels/conference centre for lunch, dinner, conference banquet, plus cost estimates per person
- Costs for morning and afternoon beverage service for three days
- NB. Who has deals for large groups?

Professional Associations and Related Groups Who Might Be Interested
- Professional Associations in Canada, U.S., and internationally who should be interested in water quality and pollution issues
  - Need director or president name, contact info (request mailing list?)
- Activist Groups interested in environment, pollution, water quality
  - Director or president name, contact info (request mailing list?)
- Related academic disciplines? Science? Engineering? Humanities fields?
  - How to contact these people?
  - What are their professional associations?

Methods of Sharing Conference Information with General Public
- Generate a list of documents we could create, ideas for how to create them, how to disseminate them to the public
- Multimedia presentations based on conference presentations: list of ideas for different types of media, possible content, etc?
- General interest publications?
  - Ideas for how to publish them? Newspapers? Magazines?
- One or two innovative and off-the-wall methods of educating public re: pollution, water quality, etc.

Figure 3 (*continued*)

Chad McMichael noted the need for keynote speakers. Environment Canada usually invited two or three experts in the area to come and give a talk. McMichael suggested that they would need to know who the biggest people in Canada on water quality are. They might look for someone from outside of Canada, such as the United States or somewhere else where they do a lot of work in water quality.

Kent noted that Gervais had given him a list of water quality–related research centres in Canada to get them started. Gervais said there is also some excellent work being done internationally, and that he would like to invite at least one international speaker. That was the main focus for the keynote speakers: To recommend three or four international researchers doing innovative or interesting work. Gervais would write the call for abstracts and take care of choosing the papers for the program, but Kent's team would do the organizational stuff. Liz Ahmad noted that they would need a conference location and rooms, including hotel rooms for the speakers.

After a few more minutes of discussion and brainstorming, Kent had created a list of areas in which they needed more information. One of them was identifying the big names in water quality research in Canada and as well as several names of international researchers. They decided they would also look for a couple of important Americans as well as a couple of water quality researchers outside of North America.

Another area that they needed to research was possible locations for the conference as well as accommodations for conference participants and attendees. Gervais wanted a venue that would promote the involvement of the public and academics in related disciplines in the conference. Dane Smith suggested that they should also figure out what professional associations existed that might be interested in attending or contributing to a discussion of water quality. This might include farmers' groups, environmental activists, manufacturing associations, and so on.

A fourth area to consider was outcomes for the conference—how to publicize the information presented at the conference, how to move from an academic discussion to educating the general public on water quality and conservation, what kinds of documents and/ or media resources might be produced using information from the conference. Linda suggested that the local newspapers would report on some of what went on at the conference.

When they finished the list, Kent turned it over to the group to decide who would research which topic. After a minimum of wrangling, the topics were distributed satisfactorily. Kent began giving instructions: Each of them would write a short report on the outcomes of their research. "I want you to email a copy of your report to everyone by Friday afternoon so that we can review these before the meeting on Monday. Unfortunately, I have to fly to Moncton on Sunday night, so you will have to meet without me. I'd like you to pool your research and make decisions about where to go with this conference. When I get back here on Wednesday morning, I'd like the team to have assembled a draft of the report we'll send to Douglas Gervais. Any questions?"

Linda Johnson gathered up her notes (see Figure 3, Item C) and thought to herself that in the next few weeks she would become a mini-expert on water quality in Canada.

ANALYSIS: THE MUELLER KENT EVENTS PLANNING MEETING

Howard Kent has a tight timeline for organizing the First Canadian Conference on Water Quality. Four months is a short time for a conference to be organized and held. Kent's team needs to gather information and make decisions about how to run the conference in the next two weeks. When one part of the task is assigned to each person in Kent's group, the project becomes much more manageable. As a result, it is likely they will accomplish everything so that the conference turns out well.

Learning about and planning the conference requires the Kent team to work and to write individually and collaboratively. Chad generally enjoyed working alone; he had had bad experiences working with others, mostly at school. He had completed huge projects by himself when the other members of his group either didn't do their work or did it poorly. He had to admit, though, that working with Dane, Liz, and Linda had been largely a positive experience in the past. They did their jobs and did them well—a definite recipe for success where collaborative projects are concerned.

What Does the Group Need to Know?

The brainstorming session identified the four areas that Kent's group needed to research to develop a good game plan for the conference (The items under C in Figure 3). Each member of the work group contributed to this discussion with ideas, questions, and qualifications that resulted in detailed and relevant notes for them to work from on their individual tasks. Then Kent threw the discussion open to his team, inviting them to talk about what they knew about running or planning an academic conference. They each contributed new ideas that helped identify goals and areas of further research. In response to Kent's question about their prior experience with conferences, Chad provided useful information about keynote speakers, which helped the group to figure out what they need to learn about research in water quality, not only in Canada but around the world.

Linda made a relevant point when she noted that the conference will likely get media coverage that will advance Douglas Gervais's goal of educating the public. She thought further and noted that newspaper coverage might inform readers about the conference but wouldn't necessarily educate them about their role in maintaining water quality in their area, which was the real goal of the group's discussion at that point.

As the meeting drew to a close, Kent started to pull their ideas together, going over what needed to be done in what order going forward. Linda played the part of group coordinator. Part C of Figure 3 displays her detailed notes about what the researcher in each of the four areas should find out. Each group member can take her notes from the discussion and have a workable plan for what to find out, for example, about experts in water quality around the globe. Her efforts to coordinate are essential to mapping out a plan of work for each member of the group. After the group decided who would be responsible for each research area, Kent sketched out a timeline for completing the individual reports and then explained how the group should run Monday's meeting in his absence. He also outlined deadlines for the different stages of planning the conference.

This meeting is an example of *hierarchical collaboration,* with Howard Kent assuming the leadership role and his team of Linda Johnson, Dane Smith, Chad McMichael, and Liz Ahmad taking subordinate reporting roles. As leader, Kent directs the meeting, gives instructions, and assigns deadlines. Members complete their tasks and report back to him. Chad requests that Kent (and not his fellow team members) provide feedback to the individual reports the team will write.

In contrast, the Monday meeting where Linda, Dane, Chad and Liz get together to draft the conference planning report is an example of *dialogic collaboration.* They share the common goal of compiling their research and drafting the report. They act as peers and share the authority and decision-making process.

GROUP BEHAVIOURS THAT CAN SABOTAGE A GROUP'S PROCESS AND PRODUCT

Figure 4 describes a possible scenario for the Monday meeting when Chad, Linda, Dane, and Liz assemble their individual reports into a conference plan. As you read this scenario, note the interpersonal interactions among participants.

LO 4 Avoid behaviours that sabotage group success

"Okay, Chad," said Linda as the group sat down in Howard's office to assemble their plan for the conference. "I didn't get a copy of your report yet. Did you bring one with you?"

"Yeah," responded Chad, sliding a copy over to each person. "I wanted to hear from Howard before I sent you guys copies, but he didn't get back to me until late last night."

"I'd like to take a few minutes to read Chad's report before we get started," commented Dane as he started to read. The others followed his lead, except for Chad, who started checking his email on his BlackBerry. Even when they finished reading and started talking, he continued to type a message. "I'll be with you in a sec," he said, not looking up. Linda and Liz exchanged glances.

"Where should we start?" asked Liz. "I thought that maybe we should start with the location of the—"

"I'll start," interrupted Chad, as he clicked "send." "Since you've all just read my report, it will be fresh in your minds. I'm researching the guys who are experts on water quality, remember? Now, there's a guy in Sri Lanka who is doing some interesting work. We should include him as a keynote speaker. There's also a guy at the University of Waterloo who would be good. And I recommended that guy in Australia, as well. They have a huge groundwater research centre there so he's a good choice."

"Correct me if I'm wrong, but I thought we were going to choose one international person and one American?" commented Dane. "Not two international people."

"Well, I did the research on this," Chad said defensively. "Look, if you don't like what I recommend, then do it yourself!"

"Whoa," responded Dane. "That wasn't a criticism. I was just asking for more information about what your rationale is for doing something other than what we talked about last week. For all we know, you've made a good decision."

"Oh," said Chad. "Well, mostly it's because I thought these three guys were doing really interesting research. See, if you look at the second page, there's a table that compares their research projects." He proceeded to lead them through a brief overview of how he chose the three experts he was recommending. As he continued, his three colleagues began nodding their heads in agreement with his explanation.

Figure 4 Negative behaviours can undermine the group's chances of success.

In this meeting, Chad behaves in a way that is potentially alienating. First, he did not circulate his report to the group in advance the way Howard Kent had instructed them to. As a consequence, they had to skim the report quickly, causing some confusion and misreading without the chance to review it carefully and plan questions. Chad also checks his email while the group reads when he could review his report with them or be available for answering questions. When the group has finished the report and begins the meeting, Chad continues to finish his email, signalling that his message is more important than his coworkers' time. These three behaviours distance him from the group (withholding his work, engaging in a non-group-related activity, and continuing the activity when the meeting begins). This type of behaviour is called withdrawing, because Chad uses it to separate himself from the group.

Liz attempts to initiate a discussion of group procedure at this meeting, asking them where they would like to start, but Chad interrupts her. He ignores her question, rejecting the

Blocking: Disagreeing with everything the other members propose

Dominating: One person appoints him or herself leader and tells everyone else what to do

Withdrawing: Not participating in meetings. Remaining silent, or skipping work sessions

Clowning: Constant disruptive behaviour that distracts and slows group productivity

Figure 5 **Negative group behaviours.**

option of discussing group procedures, and begins to lead the group. He focuses group attention on his report. He summarizes his conclusions briefly without explaining them, apparently expecting everyone to agree instantly. Chad's behaviour as he assumes leadership is called *dominating*. Dominating refers to one person insisting on controlling the meeting and running the project. When Dane asks a question about his recommendations, Chad becomes defensive, interpreting the question as blocking or disagreeing with everything he said. He responds to what he perceives as blocking by withdrawing, refusing to discuss the issue further. See Figure 5 for a full list of negative behaviours that can undermine group success.

Fortunately, Dane does not react to Chad's negative emotions; instead he tries to clarify that he meant to ask for more information rather than to attack Chad's decisions. When this misunderstanding is cleared up, Chad begins to contribute to the meeting in a more productive way; he explains his ideas so that his coworkers can follow his thinking.

Conflict Resolution

Negative group behaviours can grow out of conflict in the group. Individuals may feel their ideas are not being heard and respond in negative ways, such as by clowning or withdrawing.

Colin Gray/Photonica/Getty Images

Either way, they cease to help the group. To forestall negative behaviours such as clowning or withdrawing, the group should address conflict up front. In Chad's case, he appears to have come to the meeting with some baggage: his past negative experience of working in groups at school, even though he has had positive experiences working with Dane, Liz, and Linda in the recent past. Perhaps the absence of Howard Kent to provide clear leadership caused Chad's anxiety. At any rate, his anxiety set up the conditions for a negative experience in this collaboration as well. Ironically, he could be the *cause* of the negative experience this time.

Four Ways to Deal with Conflict

LO 5 Develop four different strategies for resolving group conflict

1. *Check to see that everyone's information is correct.* "Correct me if I'm wrong, but I thought we were going to choose one international person and one American?" Dane heads off further conflict in the meeting by explaining that this question was not intended as disagreement, necessarily, but checking his own understanding of what they had agreed on earlier as a group. In fact, his understanding was correct, but the incident provided Chad with the chance to explain why he came to a different conclusion than the one originally agreed on. Once explained, the group understood Chad's rationale. They may disagree with it, but at least they understand it first.

2. *Make sure the people involved really disagree.* Often individuals will use different language to talk about the same thing so they think that they disagree when, in fact, they are on the same side. Exploring the point of disagreement further can reveal whether they do actually disagree. For example, when the group begins to discuss the list of possible locations for the conference, Chad argues that they should book rooms at the Hilton downtown even though it will cost a little more because the rooms are more comfortable and the coffee breaks are cheaper than the Ramada Inn near the airport. Liz explains that the extra cost of the rooms might discourage some attendance, but the participants would actually save on their trip to the airport over staying at the Ramada because the Hilton runs a free shuttle service. Linda eventually figures out that Liz agrees with Chad, although it sounds like she doesn't. The group can now move on to the next issue under discussion.

3. *Discover the needs that each person is trying to meet.* Sometimes conflict arises out of two people attempting to solve different problems that sound similar. Or people value different aspects of the problem so they work to make the others in the group agree that their view is a priority. If others in the group hold different values or priorities, conflict can arise over the order in which the group tackles different problems. If someone follows up to determine what needs each person is trying to meet in a conflict, the group may be able to re-establish priorities to minimize the conflict.

4. *Search for alternatives.* If people disagree on a particular solution, the group can take a creative approach to the issue and try to find alternatives that both sides can accept. For example, Chad thinks the three male keynote speakers that he's recommended are the best choices of those researchers he looked at, whereas Liz insists that at least one of their keynote speakers be a woman. After much discussion, Chad admits that he didn't search carefully through the options: he made his selection based on interesting projects rather than demographic characteristics. Dane suggests that Chad spend one hour looking carefully through the work of Canadian women researchers on water quality to see whether any of them have interesting projects going. Then he can choose one to add as a fourth option for Douglas Gervais to choose among. Chad agrees that this is a reasonable suggestion, and he is willing to spend one more hour doing a little more research. They find an alternative that both Chad and Liz can live with, putting the final decision about who to choose for keynote speakers in Douglas Gervais's hands.

1. Research Topics and Write Individual Reports

Form groups of four people to emulate the four members of the collaborative group at Mueller Kent Events. Have each member of the group assume the role of one of the employees named in Case 1. Decide amongst the group who will be responsible for collecting the information needed in each area. Although one person in the group will be responsible for deciding what information to include in his or her area, you can conduct the research collaboratively or individually. Use the internet or school library to find the information you need. If you are researching possible conference venues, research locations and prices as if you were going to hold the conference in your city. When the research is complete, each person in the group should write up a short report on the results of his or her research. The report should not only summarize the information, it should also include recommendations about what the group should do. For example, of the experts on water quality identified, which two or three would the writer recommend as keynote speakers for the conference and why? Use the notes included in the time-line handout (see Figure 3) to help you conduct your research and make decisions about what to include in your report.

Purpose: To report succinctly on your research on the area of conference planning assigned to you

Audience: The other members of your group, but ultimately, Douglas Gervais, the client at Environment Canada

Genre: Short report

2. Write a Collaborative Report to Plan the Conference

When the four members of your group have completed their individual reports, each member should email a copy of his or her report to the others. Before you come to class, make time to read and think about the reports submitted by your group members. When you come to class, spend 15 or 20 minutes discussing the research and recommendations made by each group member, and map out a plan for the conference that incorporates each group members' contributions. As a group, begin drafting the report that Howard Kent needs to send to Douglas Gervais, a water quality expert with Environment Canada and the president of the Canadian Association on Water Quality. Use the discussion in this module to help you work successfully as a team to draft this document. Each group should submit one report, containing the names of all the group members, to the course instructor.

Purpose: To combine group members' research into a coherent plan for running the conference

Audience: Your boss, Howard Kent, but ultimately Douglas Gervais, the client at Environment Canada

Genre: Short report

Case 2★★ Understanding Group Dynamics: Display-Works Prepares for a Client Conference Call

Bob looks around the conference table and decides to get started. Doreen over at Canadian Radiant Heat Specialists, their potential client, has agreed to a 15-minute call to answer questions about their Request for Proposals (RFP). They have to make the most of this opportunity.

Canadian Radiant Heat Specialists needs a sales display unit for the main North American construction trade show held in Las Vegas in March. The RFP notes that they want the display to provide an overview of their products, but also to focus mainly on their newest product, a radiant floor heating system that uses "hot water conveyed through flexible piping in the floors to heat the structure." Everyone looks at the RFP, focusing on the part of the description that most closely matches their own expertise. There are six participants: Brianna, the graphic artist in charge of the unit's design; Bram, the structural engineer in charge of its materials and construction; Amita, Bob's administrative assistant, who will manage the conference call; Luanne, chief writer, who will draft the proposal; Victor, the programmer and technical support wizard who will coordinate the electronic display; and, of course, Bob, the salesman at DisplayWorks, who has brought this team together to help prepare the proposal.

DisplayWorks manufactures custom trade show display units consisting of collapsible lightweight matrix-like structures with magnetic plastic panels that adhere to the structure. The plastic panels are often graphically rich. Some of the panels are fabric so brochure holders as well as laminated changeable content can be attached to them with Velcro. The client usually has up to six sales representatives at the trade show circulating around the booth and interacting with clients, distributing product information, and giving out branded and other types of promotional items. These trade show display units can cost between $25,000 and $50,000, and they are usually about eight metres long and two metres high. They can be disassembled fairly quickly and transported from one show to the next in lightweight plastic cases. DisplayWorks has created display units for a variety of different companies across North America.

Victor notes that they want a computer-controlled flat panel display and slideshow to present their product details and description, so he needs to know who is going to be running this booth. How technically savvy are they? Does he need to set up this show as an endless loop or should it be indexed so employees can locate a specific section to show a customer?

Brianna agrees and notes that presumably they would be producing the presentation on the flat screen. She wonders aloud about the kind of access to Radiant Heat's manufacturing process she and her group will have to create the video. Bob replies that he is unclear on whether Brianna's group is creating the video. The RFP isn't clear on that point. They both agree that this issue is something that needs to be cleared up at the start of the conversation, because production of the video will be time consuming and potentially costly.

Brianna nods and asks whether anyone knows the company colours. Amita said she visited Canadian Radiant Heat Specialists' website and made copies of their logo and homepage. They are using a kind of pumpkin and hunter green in their logo, she notes.

"Oh," interjects Brianna, raising an eyebrow. "That doesn't give us the best palette of colours to work with, but if we use variations of . . ." Her voice trails off as she begins jotting down notes in the margins around the company logo. Everyone watches her for a few seconds, waiting for her to finish her sentence, but she keeps writing and then turns the paper over and begins drawing on the back.

Bob shrugs and looks at the other members of the team. "Any more questions? What about you, Bram? You haven't said anything. Is the RFP that clear on their structural requirements?"

Bram acknowledges that he could use a little more clarity about the size and nature of the content they want to display. He points to the RFP and notes that in the second paragraph, it sounds as if they want posters and digital photos of their products, but on page two, they are also talking about having a selection of actual products on site to handle. He has questions about where they want to display and store those products—on site or in a secure location off site. Also, he needs to know if they want to display some of the products on the unit itself, which will affect the unit construction. The more weight placed on the unit, the better designed and braced it needs to be so it won't tip over. The conversation continues for several minutes with Bram explaining the technical aspects of unit construction and the others asking questions and making suggestions.

Luanne takes notes of the conversation. Amita asks Bram, Brianna, and everyone else to write down the actual questions that they want to ask because 15 minutes isn't very long. They need to ensure that they cover the most important questions first, and then if there's time left over, the ones of lesser importance. She asks them to rank order their questions and be as concise and clear as they can.

Bob decides that the group hasn't gotten very far in this discussion. He suggests that they try individually brainstorming a list of issues or problems that each person sees with this proposal from the perspective of the area that they will be responsible for in this project.

A groan comes from Bob's right. "Why can't we brainstorm as a group?" suggests Victor. "That way I don't have to write everything down twice."

"I already did that," laughs Bram, a bit smugly. "It was part of my preparation for this meeting to write down the questions that I have about this RFP. I would have thought the rest of you would have gotten prepared before coming too."

"Well, not all of us are single and can devote every waking moment to our job," retorts Brianna, glaring at Bram. "I did prepare, by the way. I just didn't write everything down because I can't drive and write at the same time."

"What about red lights?" jokes Luanne. "My boss at Jazco answered letters by scribbling in the margins while she waited at red lights."

Bob sees the discussion going off

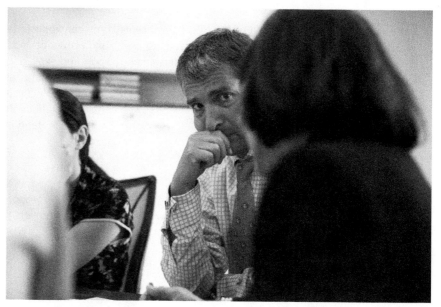

John Wildgoose/Stone/Getty Images

track, so he intervenes by pointing out that they are supposed to place the call to Doreen in less than 10 minutes and they aren't organized yet. Victor suggests rescheduling the conference call, and after some discussion, Bob asks Amita to try to reschedule the meeting for 11:30, giving the group an extra half-hour to organize themselves fully.

Bob then suggests that Bram check out the sketch that Brianna has just finished to see if he can foresee any possible structural problems with the design. Then he directs the rest of the group to brainstorm at least three questions that they have about the RFP. After a few minutes, he gestures for the writers to pass their questions forward to him, and then asks Brianna to present her ideas for the display unit. In 15 minutes, Brianna's initial idea is quickly modified with input from Bram and Victor into a workable model over which the team expresses general satisfaction. During this time, Amita returns, announcing that the meeting has been successfully rescheduled for 11:45 A.M. While she was gone, Bob passed the group's questions over to Luanne, who reviewed them, rewrote two or three to make them clearer and more pointed, and then rank ordered them according to complexity and importance. She now reads the questions aloud, noting who she has assigned to read them during the conference call. Victor and Brianna each add follow-up questions to the ones they were assigned. Luanne drafts a schedule on the whiteboard of the order in which each person will speak, how much time they can allot to each question, and what else they should ask if they finish up a bit early.

"Terrific work, everyone," announces Bob with satisfaction. They have a workable plan and a few minutes to practise their execution before placing the call.

▷ Professional Communication Assignments

3. Analyze the Group Dynamics in Case 2
Using the discussion in this module on working and writing in teams, analyze the meeting in Case 2 to describe what is happening and why. Write a short report in which you present the following:

▪ Your analysis, including theoretical concepts from this module

▪ Evidence from the case

▪ Your interpretation of what happened

▪ Why you believe it might have happened

▪ How specific parts of the situation were or were not handled well

Include suggestions about how particular interactions might have been handled more effectively.

Purpose: To demonstrate you understand the concepts in this module and can apply them to a situation to analyze the group dynamics with an eye to understanding and improving them

Audience: Write the analysis for your instructor and classmates

Genre: Critical analysis essay or report

4. Analyze a Transcript of a Meeting That You Attended

Attend and record a meeting and produce a transcript of the group dynamics. Be sure to secure permission to record the meeting in advance. Using the transcript that you created, analyze the group interactions and write a short report presenting that analysis. Use the discussion in this module to help you formulate theoretical concepts that you can apply to the interactions documented in the meeting transcript. Include evidence from the transcript to support and explain your analysis. Also evaluate the quality of the interactions, assess whether specific interactions were handled effectively, and make specific suggestions as to how the various situations might have been handled more effectively. Hand in the meeting transcript along with your analysis.

Purpose: To demonstrate you understand the concepts in this module and can apply them to a situation to analyze the group dynamics with an eye to understanding and improving them

Audience: Write the analysis for your instructor and classmates

Genre: Critical analysis essay or report

MODULE SUMMARY

- Use collaboration to complete large, complex tasks
- Help groups succeed by requesting knowledge and opinions, summarizing, evaluating decisions and ideas, and coordinating the group
- Use one of two models of collaboration: Hierarchical (structured, with a well-defined system of reporting and authority) or dialogical (shared authority and decision making)
- Group behaviours that create successful collaboration include encouraging participation, checking feelings, and listening actively
- Group behaviours that can sabotage a group's process and product include blocking, dominating, withdrawing, and clowning
- Conflicts can be resolved by checking to see that everyone's information is correct; making sure the people involved really disagree; discovering the needs that each person is trying to meet; and searching for alternatives

Module 6
Communicating Across Cultures

Konstantin Chagin/Shutterstock

LEARNING OUTCOMES

LO 1 Differentiate between national identity and cultural identity

LO 2 Understand the importance of multiculturalism to Canadian political policy and identify the implications of this policy for business communications

LO 3 Identify the components of cultural and business practices of intercultural business communication

LO 4 Recognize that many people have multiple and shifting senses of their own cultural identity—they can be members of more than one cultural group

LO 5 Adjust written documents to communicate well with audiences from a variety of cultural groups

GETTING STARTED

Canada is composed of many subcultures from First Nations and immigrants from across the world. As a business communicator writing to other people within Canada, you will write and speak to people who have different backgrounds from your own. As a business communicator writing to others outside Canada, you will need to be even more aware of cultural differences. The bottom line: How well you communicate across cultures will greatly determine how far you advance in your career.

Take every opportunity that comes your way to seek out information about cultural groups you are not familiar with. Even informal exchanges around a campfire can count as much as formal business meetings in conference rooms. Whenever you have a chance to meet someone who has a different background from your own, take that opportunity to learn more about them and how they see the world. You will find some of these individuals have ideas and experiences that may differ radically from your own, but you will also find that you share common ground, perhaps in surprising areas. When you feel comfortable working with people from diverse backgrounds you can work more effectively and do a better job of understanding them and meeting their needs. The more you learn about the lives of other people, the greater your understanding and acceptance will be of the variation that exists among people's ideas and assumptions

When you talk to people whose backgrounds differ from yours, pay particular attention to **politeness, formality, and social interaction** practices. These are the ways in which they interact with other people. For example, when they address you or someone else, do they use honorifics—for example, Mr. Brown, Ms. Yusaf? Do they use first names from an initial greeting? Do they shake hands or incline the head in acknowledgement? Your knowledge of these practices is a prerequisite for building effective business communication practices.

In the first case in this module, you will meet Lauren Toews, a newly promoted commercial banking officer. In this new job she oversees client accounts, over 40 percent of whom are from Southeast Asia. The **cultural values** and ways of doing business that she encounters provide challenges not only for her, but also for the people who need to do business with her. Specifically, she needs to learn more about the cultural backgrounds of her clients if she is to work well with them, and her clients need to understand her beliefs and values. In the second case, Daniel McMahon faces a common problem: he needs to reach beyond the borders of Canada to build his business, but he doesn't know enough about how to interact with people from a culture distinctly different from his own. At the same time, it is important to understand McMahon's cultural background in order to determine ways to interact with a white, middle-class, Canadian businessman. By researching other cultures—in this case, India—you will become familiar with the resources that exist to help individuals and companies succeed internationally. Both these cases require you to learn more about other cultures and subcultures and to adjust your writing and communication strategies to these readers.

COMMUNICATING ACROSS CULTURES

Business in Canada crosses cultural borders every day. **Multiculturalism** is the most obvious sign of these borders: Canada operates with two official languages and promotes the use of many other languages. This alone suggests the reality of the many cultures that form our Canadian culture. But Canadian business also relies heavily on trade with other nations. Some of these other nations share aspects of their culture with some parts of Canada. For example, we can group these nations by languages shared with large groups within Canada:

- French-speaking nations around the world
- English-speaking nations
- Mandarin- and Cantonese-speaking nations

Politeness, formality, and social interaction: Social rituals people engage in to demonstrate their relationship to each other and to interact smoothly

Cultural values: The beliefs people have about what is important in their society, including rules for speaking, interacting, and deferring to others

LO 1 Differentiate between national identity and cultural identity

LO 2 Understand the importance of multiculturalism to Canadian political policy and identify the implications of this policy for business communications

Multiculturalism: The political policy adopted in Canada that values multiple cultural groups rather than one dominant culture

- Hindi- and Urdu-speaking nations
- Spanish-speaking nations

As a student of business communication, you may bring to the classroom knowledge of more than one language or cultural group. This knowledge can be an important asset for you as a communicator because it gives you real insight into another cultural group.

What Constitutes Another Cultural Group?

Culture refers to social practices and objects that unite a group of people. Cultures can be identified many ways, including.

- The language used by members
- Objects produced by members of the culture
- Activities members engage in
- Beliefs and assumptions about how to understand the world
- Geographical or national borders
- Politeness and social interaction rituals

In many ways Canadians have an advantage in understanding variations in culture. Our history of the equitable and generally peaceful union of English and French culture and language in Canada ensures our awareness of cultural differences in a way that is not available to citizens of other countries. We accept the premise that to be Canadian means to perhaps not understand one another (unless we are bilingual) and to share different visions of Canadian history and culture. We are historically more comfortable with and accepting of cultural difference: during the mid-1970s some provincial governments promoted heritage language instruction for immigrant children in Canada to help them maintain linguistic and cultural connections with their birth country.

Canada officially adopted multiculturalism as a policy in 1971.[1] Today it remains a fundamental part of our society.

> Multiculturalism begins with the idea that all citizens are equal. A fundamental part of this is that citizens have the right to keep their identity and in fact should be proud of their heritage. If they are proud and feel that their heritage is welcomed, they become more self-confident and more open to others, too. The end result of this process is a country that enjoys racial harmony and understanding across the cultures.

The attitudes enshrined in this multicultural policy mean that generally our citizens tend to view "foreign" cultures as bringing positive ideas and experiences that enrich Canadian culture. As a policy, multiculturalism gives citizens advantages because recent advances in technology have made international communications more important than ever. Canadians who speak many languages and understand many cultures make it easier for Canada to participate globally in areas of education, trade, and diplomacy.[2] However, challenges such as recognizing educational credentials from abroad mean that the ideals enshrined in policy are sometimes difficult to realize every day.

---

[1] Adapted from Canadian Multiculturalism: An Inclusive Citizenship, http://www.cic.gc.ca/english/multiculturalism/citizenship.asp
[2] www.cic.gc.ca/english/multiculturalism/citizenship.asp (October 23, 2013).

As you can see from these statements, communicating across cultures is important both within Canada and with people living and working across the globe.

Communicating Across Cultures Within Canada

Many businesses operating in Canada find it profitable to reach out to customers by adapting their communications to the languages of their customers. Communicating with other cultural groups involves more than translating from English or French to another language. Writers must also demonstrate knowledge and sensitivity to the cultural values of the group they are communicating with. One way for students to do that is to visit the websites affiliated or associated with these cultural groups.

One large cultural group within Canada is the Chinese community. To learn more about Chinese groups within Canada, consider visiting these pages:

- www.chinesebusiness.org
- www.ccbc.com
- www.ccnc.ca/index.php

The Chinese Business Chamber of Canada, for example, runs a one-day course on learning about how to conduct commerce with Chinese businesses, both located in China and owned by members of the Chinese community in Canada. They emphasize the importance of having a sophisticated understanding of the variations in cultural practices and etiquette among sub-groups. Among the topics they cover are cultural knowledge and etiquette. They begin with an overview of best practices in business communication, including appropriate business writing style. Model documents serve to provide examples for participants to work from on their own writing projects. But in addition to the standard business communication knowledge you might expect, they have also added discussions of cultural etiquette that are specific to Canadian business practices. Finally, they introduce students to the typical ways Canadian people tend to conduct business meetings, including how to follow-up with meeting participants. A full description of the course is available by going to http://www.chinesebusiness.ca, selecting Business Training Centre, and clicking on International Trade Workshops.

As you can see, there is much to learn that goes beyond simple translation.

Exercise 1: Prepare a Presentation on Chinese Culture and Business Practices

Visit the sites listed previously for information about Chinese culture and business practices. Prepare a short (10-slide) presentation to give to your class. Focus on only one or two aspects—for example, Guanxi or deal-making—in your presentation. Alternatively, pick another culture and prepare a presentation on one or two aspects of that culture.

Within Canada, you can see this kind of hybrid or complex identity in the example of the First Nations Bank. Among the core values of the First Nations Bank are these statements:

- We are a leader in the provision of financial services to Aboriginal People and an advocate for the growth of the Aboriginal economy and the economic well-being of Aboriginal People.

About CCAB   Events   Member Directory   Programs   Awards   Research

Upcoming Events

Oct 2014 Aboriginal Business Luncheon DETAILS

Nov 2014 Aboriginal Hot Topic Series: Toronto DETAILS

Progressive Aboriginal Relations (PAR)

PAR is a certification program that confirms corporate performance in Aboriginal relations at the Bronze, Silver or Gold level. LEARN MORE

Progressive Aboriginal RELATIONS

Canadian Council for Aboriginal Business

Become A Member

The Canadian Council for Aboriginal Business (CCAB) is a member based organization driving business opportunities and advancing corporate social responsibility for the Aboriginal community. CCAB offers unique programs and services that help facilitate sustainable relations between First Nation, Inuit, and Métis people and the Canadian business sector. LEARN MORE

JP Gladu's Financial Post Blog

President and CEO, JP Gladu attracts attention. Read More

Promise and Prosperity

Read the 2014 Ontario Aboriginal Business Survey. LEARN MORE

Promise and Prosperity

CCAB Celebrating 30 Years

► 00:00 —————————— 00:00 ◄━

Source: https://www.ccab.com

■ The Bank was conceived and developed by Aboriginal People, for Aboriginal People and regards itself as an important step toward Aboriginal economic self-sufficiency.[3]

These statements emphasize the need to speak to the cultural values of the audience: in this case, economic well-being and economic self-sufficiency are two of these values.

Recently, First Nations Bank has become over 90 percent owned by aboriginal shareholders. In articles written for aboriginal readers, such as the one in Figure 1, the writing shifts in perspective to connect with aboriginal readers of the *Globe and Mail* newspaper.

Exercise 2: Identify Some of the Cultural Values Expressed

Read the Globe and Mail newspaper article reprinted in Figure 1 and write a paragraph in which you identify three of the cultural values that aboriginal readers would identify with. Focus on Martell's responses to the questions. Then write another paragraph in which you identify the business values discussed, for example, "drive for business."

---

[3]First Nations Bank of Canada, The Aboriginal Bank, http://www.fnbc.ca/about-us/about-the-bank/. Accessed October 23, 2013.

How Canada's other national bank is expanding

Keith Martell runs Canada's other national bank, the First Nations Bank of Canada, whose mainly aboriginal clientele extends from the Yukon to Northern Quebec. With more than $300-million in assets, it is the only chartered bank with a head office in Saskatchewan, where it started 13 years ago. Based in a province - where more than 15 per cent of the population is aboriginal - and projected to climb much higher - Mr. Martell has insight into the economic plight, and potential, of native Canadians. His bank has just expanded into Nunavut, opening a full-service branch in Iqaluit in partnership with an Inuit group.

Has the aboriginal population participated in the Saskatchewan boom? I think so. We do a lot of banking for first nations governments, which deliver primary social programs in many of these communities. You look at some of these remote reserves, and you can have 80-per-cent unemployment. But we did see a noticeable change in some social assistance budgets - they were beginning to decrease because more people were working out [of their communities] There were more individuals with . . . [earning]capacity.

But you have a long way to go? Definitely, but the other positive is that the median age of the First Nations population is still 18-19 years. So we have the same aging demographics of the employed work force, just like any other part of Canada, but we have this young growing engine that is ready to be engaged. The success will be in engaging them.

Don't you desperately need to get people to stay in school? I'm a chartered accountant, born in a first nations community in Northern Saskatchewan. Clearly, education does a lot. Every aboriginal person I know who has achieved an education is self-sufficient and functioning quite well.

I talk to companies looking for a strategy and they say "We go to the high schools and we don't see aboriginal people there. We go to universities and they are not there." I say you should spend all your effort and time getting to children in Grades 4, 5, and 6.

But they need to see there is a future for them, so they don't make the bad decisions you make once you become a teenager. If you can make them understand there is a future, they don't do things like having children when they are still children. They don't quit school early or take the easy route. They stay with it.

How did you get the education bug? My mother is not aboriginal and her family was all teachers, so she made sure we were getting education. My dad is Cree and went through residential schools - and one of the negative legacies of residential schools was that it lowered the importance of education for a lot of those folks. That's because it wasn't a very positive experience.

But he still understood the importance of education and he gave me my drive to work in business. He's always been a businessman and our family on that side goes back to the fur-trading days as traders and outfitters for the Hudson Bay Co. So I got my drive for business from the aboriginal side.

Does that really fit with the image we get? I regularly hear people say to me, "Aboriginal people don't have a history as being involved in business, and it's interesting that you have a bank." And I say aboriginal people actually ran the economy of this country for about 300 years.

When I talk to our young people, a lot of them don't know that history. That's really sad. I am of Cree background and the Cree stretch from the shores of James Bay all the way into Northeastern B.C. They actually didn't dominate those areas throughout history - they moved with the fur trade. They were traders and they settled into this area. They were sort of the first imperialists - bad word, I know - because they ran out and started business going in these regions before the Europeans even got here.

So how do you connect with this tradition? Just through little things. In the 1990s, we weren't getting people working at the McDonald's and other fast food outlets. These aren't lifelong jobs but they are first jobs and they teach you how to work. At that time we would go down to local franchises, and even into neighbourhoods that are predominantly aboriginal, and you wouldn't see one aboriginal person across the counter.

Figure 1 This newspaper article from the *Globe and Mail* on the First Nations bank speaks from the perspective of aboriginal Canadians.

Source: "How Canada's other national bank is expanding" by Gordon Pitts, *Globe & Mail*, July 4, 2010. The Globe and Mail Inc. All Rights Reserved.

Case 1★★ Banking and Culture

Lauren Toews knew what she was getting into when she accepted this transfer to the Central Region Commercial Banking centre in Toronto: a big step up the corporate ladder—two steps, actually. Her last position with the bank had been as a branch manager in Guelph, Ontario. She enjoyed it—meeting customers in the branch, helping them negotiate the forms and requirements that the bank had for securing a loan. Managing the staff had taken most of her time, and although it had its challenges she did enjoy helping her team develop.

But this was a new week, and it presented new challenges. Commercial banking took place out of a large office building in an industrial park in the north suburbs of Toronto. Customers sometimes came in to the office, but more often than not Lauren would meet with them at their businesses. There were several advantages of this arrangement: she got out of the office, she ate lunch at a variety of interesting restaurants, and she got a first-hand look at how their businesses were doing. It was one thing to look at balance sheets and financial reports; it was another thing entirely to see how much inventory was on site and how many customers were in the stores.

John Slater/The Image Bank/Getty Images

But the biggest and most pressing challenge facing Lauren was cultural: 40 percent of her accounts were companies run by people who had emigrated from China and Southeast Asia (Thailand, Vietnam, and the Philippines). Most of these clients spoke passable English, and all had employees or relatives that spoke good English. She knew that language would not present an insurmountable problem. Instead, she was more concerned with understanding their ways of doing business.

Lauren's visit to the Thai Noodle Pot highlighted the need for her to learn more as she talked with Anand Shinawatra, the owner of the restaurant. Mr. Shinawatra began their conversation by noting that Lauren was new to her job, and then he asked Lauren if she was married. Surprised, Lauren said she was married. Mr. Shinawatra asked her if her husband objected to her having lunch with him. She replied that her husband knew that having lunch with clients was part of the job. Mr. Shinawatra then asked what her husband did for a living. Lauren replied that he was a lawyer at a big law firm downtown. Mr. Shinawatra noted that lawyers make a lot of money and then speculated that the two of them must make a lot of money—even more since Lauren's promotion. This then led him to the thought that Lauren could stay home and start a family if she wanted to, and he was truly puzzled that she had not chosen to do this.

Lauren was speechless for a few seconds, wondering how to shift this discussion away from her personal life. But then she remembered why she was there and asked Mr. Shinawatra how things were going at the restaurant. She remarked that the soup was wonderful. She couldn't identify the seasoning—the sour flavour—and asked him what it was. He smiled and told her that it was the tamarind, an important ingredient in many Thai dishes. That led to more questions about food and how the business was progressing.

As she reflected on the lunch later, Lauren was surprised that Mr. Shinawatra seemed to be excessively polite, on the one hand, while asking what she thought of as personal questions about her life and recent promotion—a little too personal for her. She wondered if he meant anything by it, but she also recognized that she needed to learn more about Thai culture if she was going to be able to understand him.

Professional Communication Assignments

1. Analyze Thai Culture to Understand Human Behaviour

Visit the following link to read about Thai society and culture: www.kwintessential.co.uk/resources/global-etiquette/thailand-country-profile.html.

Write a paragraph analyzing how what you learned about Thai culture applies to Lauren's experience and, drawing on what you know about Canadian culture, explain potential reasons for Lauren's reaction to Mr. Shinawatra. What aspects of Thai culture and social interactions would explain his personal questions?

Audience: Your instructor and classmates

Purpose: To demonstrate your research into Thai culture and your analytical abilities in applying this research to Lauren Toews's experience

Genre: Critical analysis report

2. Reference Notes on Thai Culture for Lauren's Replacement

Starting with the URL provided, do some research on Thai culture. Visit two or three other websites to gather information about Chinese or Filipino culture. Prepare a page of notes on Thai, Chinese, or Filipino culture and how you think these cultural attitudes and expectations would affect a business relationship that employees at the bank might have with customers from these cultures. Writing as Lauren

Toews, draft notes for the next person who will hold this job so that they can quickly learn more about your customers' backgrounds. The notes should include advice about working successfully with them. These notes should be typed and organized neatly so that when you move on to another job in the bank you can pass them along to your replacement or share them with other bank employees.

Audience: Another bank employee who will replace Lauren

Purpose: To summarize and present important details about Thai, Chinese, or Filipino culture and to suggest ways that they might affect business relationships so that readers (from the bank) can learn quickly and easily from them

Genre: Briefing notes

Communicating Across Cultures Outside Canada

LO 3 Identify the components of cultural and business practices of intercultural business communication

Each country has unique cultural characteristics, but in the interests of classifying types of cultures, we can find categories of similarity. For example, one way to identify international business opportunities is to classify countries according to the nature of their economies:

- A fully developed, fast-paced market (Canada, Germany, the United States)
- A developing market with rapid growth (China, India)
- A developing market with marginal growth (some countries in Africa)

  (*Source:* "A step-by-step guide to exporting: Identifying your target market" http://www.tradecommissioner.gc.ca/eng/step4.jsp)

A country's type of economy affects the cultural practices and expectations of those individuals who conduct business there. For example, fast-paced, competitive economies and their societies value directness; business people from such countries see time as money, and their social practices promote productivity and profitability. They want to make a deal; if the deal is ongoing and beneficial, they may cultivate the personal relationship. Even non-profit business in these economies is affected by culture, so while it may not prize profit to the same extent as private enterprises, it still values directness and efficiency in communication and action. In contrast, **relationship-based economies** value social interaction among people. Business people from affluent, relationship-based countries insist on building a personal relationship before discussing business details. They value trust and reliability first, and they establish these attributes before the deal is struck.

Relationship-based economies: Economies that value personal relationships and trust as a precondition for business relationships

The Step-by-Step Guide to Exporting, a Foreign Affairs and International Trade Department document, offers this good advice to communicating with potential customers in other cultures:

> The usual Western business practice is to negotiate a transaction and then construct a buyer-seller relationship around it. In the business cultures of many countries, however, this process is reversed. One starts out by building a personal relationship with a prospective customer and, once that relationship has been established and everyone is comfortable with it, the actual business negotiations can begin.

> While the ultimate goal of all parties is to sign a contract, the immediate objective in a relationship-based business culture is to establish the personal connections. Your non-Canadian counterparts often see this as a necessary precondition for serious negotiations. (*Source:* Foreign Affairs and International Trade Canada. Accessed October 23, 2013. http://www.tradecommissioner.gc.ca/eng/pdf.jsp?did=100278&fn=guide-exporting.pdf)

High-Context Countries/Cultures	Low-Context Countries/Cultures
Asian countries such as China, Japan, Korea, Thailand, Vietnam	North American countries such as Canada, U.S.A., Mexico
Arab countries such as Iran, Iraq, Afghanistan	European countries, including the U.K., Australia, New Zealand
South American countries such as Argentina, Brazil, Chile, Ecuador, Colombia	

Figure 2 Countries/cultures typically designated as high- and low-context communicators.

This quotation highlights the possibility for cultural misunderstanding whenever people from varying cultural backgrounds assemble to do business. Canadian businesspeople may be frustrated at the slow pace of the deal as their counterpart seeks first to establish a comfortable relationship. Individuals from competitive cultures can view relationship building as wasting time and money. In contrast, a businessperson from Argentina may view Canadian impatience as rude and untrustworthy, undermining the goal of creating a solid working relationship.

Once you identify the kind of economy that your business partner works in, you can make decisions about the implications for your communication strategies. Many stereotypes abound in discussions of intercultural communication. For example, Asian countries such as China and Japan have been described as **high-context cultures**, whereas North American countries (primarily Canada and the United States) are designated **low-context cultures**. The phrases *high* and *low context* refer to the degree to which the context around a statement affects its meaning (see Figure 2). A *low-context* statement is stated directly and does not depend on outside information for meaning. For example, "I am angry because you did not answer my email right away" is low context because the message is complete and unequivocally stated. In contrast, a *high-context* statement may not signal the speaker's emotion at all; instead it communicates through contextual clues—for example, "Have you had the chance to check your email recently?" Couched as a question, this statement subtly directs attention toward the intended meaning: "If so, did you get my message? If so, why have you not answered it?"

High-context cultures: Cultures that communicate through indirection and suggestions

Low-context cultures: Cultures that state directly what the speaker wants to communicate

Traditional intercultural communication advice has stereotyped Asian communication as high context and warned business writers to be aware and pay attention to the alternate meanings that any statement by an Asian businessperson might have. In fact, the recent boom in Chinese capitalism means that this advice may be a sweeping generalization. Although the use of high- and low-context statements may have some cultural basis, individuals within the same culture also use these contrasting styles of communication. Michelle LeBaron offers this advice to individuals with a preference for low-context communication who are working with high-context speakers[4]:

- Nonverbal messages and gestures may be as important as what is said
- Status and identity may be communicated nonverbally and require appropriate acknowledgement
- Face-saving and tact may be important, and need to be balanced with the desire to communicate fully and frankly

---

[4]LeBaron, Michelle. "Communication Tools for Understanding Cultural Differences." Beyond Intractability. Eds. Guy Burgess and Heidi Burgess. Conflict Research Consortium, University of Colorado, Boulder. Posted: June 2003. http://www.beyondintractability.org/essay/communication_tools/

- Building a good relationship can contribute to effectiveness over time
- Indirect routes and creative thinking are important alternatives to problem solving when blocks are encountered

In contrast, she offers this advice to high-context communicators working with low-context speakers:

- Things can be taken at face value rather than as representative of layers of meaning
- Roles and functions may be decoupled from status and identity
- Efficiency and effectiveness may be served by a sustained focus on tasks
- Direct questions and observations are not necessarily meant to offend, but to clarify and advance shared goals
- Indirect cues may not be enough to get the other's attention

There are other important aspects to consider when communicating with people whose backgrounds vary from your own, including issues of power, distance, hierarchy, and gender. In his research into cultural differences, Geert Hofestede developed the **power distance index** as one way to categorize cultural expectations between workers and their managers. A high power distance culture expects managers and bosses to display their rank and for workers to seek direction from higher up and to take the blame if a problem develops. In contrast, in low power distance cultures, managers and bosses treat workers with respect. Workers work on important projects, and if a problem develops, the manager takes the blame. Parallels have been drawn between high power distance cultures and totalitarian politics and low power distance culture and liberal democratic politics.[5] Examples of high power distance cultures include Russia, China, India, and Arabic-speaking countries. Low power distance cultures include Japan, Australia, and Canada[6].

Another issue that can affect intercultural communication is **hierarchy**, which is related to the power distance index. The more hierarchical a culture, the more individuals perceive social and status differences between themselves and others. For example, Mexican culture is "steeply hierarchical. Persons can rank high on the social ladder by reason of family lineage, power, education, and wealth."[7] In a steeply hierarchical culture, higher status individuals expect to be treated with deference by those they consider to have less status. In contrast, American and Canadian culture has a flatter hierarchical structure because the cultures emphasize the equality of all citizens. Novinger notes that Americans or Canadians who address high-status Mexicans too informally can offend by ignoring their status or not "maintaining a proper distance." Similarly, if they treat someone with less status than themselves as an equal, they can "confuse or embarrass the person because they perceive a clear status difference."[8]

A third area in which misunderstanding can occur in intercultural communication in business is **gender relations**. Cultural expectations differ from culture to culture about appropriate roles for men and women in society and in business. When expectations conflict about the appropriate role of men or women, misunderstandings can easily occur. For example, in cultures where men and women are viewed as more or less socially equal, the gender of those people negotiating a deal doesn't particularly matter. However, in cultures where one gender has greater value than another or where women are prohibited from interacting publicly or professionally, expectations can prevent or undermine successful communication. For example, Lauren Toews wonders initially whether Mr. Shinawatra feels he can ask her personal questions because she is a woman. She considers whether he would still ask about her marital status and desire for children if she were a man. In this

Power distance index: A measure of the cultural expectations between managers and workers

Hierarchy: The degree to which social relations are managed from the top or elite members of society down through managers to the workers

Gender relations: Expectations about the appropriate role of men or women

---

[5]www.kwintessential.co.uk/intercultural/power-distance-index.html
[6]http://demoblography.blogspot.com/2008/01/geert-hofestede-and-intercultural.html
[7]Tracy Novinger 2008, http://culturespan.blogspot.ca/search/label/Mexico
[8]http://culturespan.blogspot.ca/search/label/Mexico

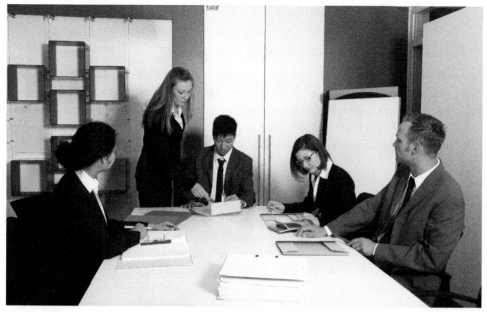

Christine Langer-Pueschel/Shutterstock

case, her sensitivity to gender bias (which arises from *her* cultural experience) results in her assessing whether his questions offend her.

Of course, gender bias is not confined to specific cultures or societies. It operates on individual levels as well. Individual attitudes about gender can also interfere with successful communication. Although you have limited control over how elements like gender or hierarchy may affect the responses of people of different cultural backgrounds toward you, you can control your own reactions and responses. By intentionally pursuing chances to meet people with various cultural backgrounds, you can expand your own areas of experience and knowledge so that you can do your part to facilitate the interaction. By becoming sensitive to, recognizing ways in which, and learning about how cultural practices differ, you can become more adept at interacting effectively with individuals you will meet in your work or personal life.

LEARNING TO COMMUNICATE ACROSS CULTURES

In Case 2 in this module, Daniel McMahon faces some of the most basic challenges for business people starting out on a cross-cultural venture in India: an almost complete lack of knowledge of Indian business practices, a lack of understanding of how critical it is for him to conduct meetings, and a lack of understanding of the amount of time the venture would consume. He did not, however, have to face one of the most basic challenges of communication across cultures: working in a language that he did not speak, because English is the language of business in India.

LO 4 Recognize that many people have multiple and shifting senses of their own cultural identity—they can be members of more than one cultural group

Language

One of the most obvious markers of culture is language. By recognizing both French and English as national languages in Canada, our country makes a political statement about the relative importance of these languages, both to each other and in comparison to the languages of other immigrant groups and First Nations groups. As a business communicator, you will want to respect the values and culture of the person or group to whom you are writing. How can you communicate your respect? Try one of these strategies:

- Offer a salutation (such as "Nee Hau Ma," which is Mandarin for "How are you?") in the language of the person you are writing to

- Offer to provide a translation or summary in the language of the person you are writing to
- Limit your use of idiomatic words and phrases ("That's life"; "that's my word")

If at all possible, communicate in the language of the people you are writing to. If you are giving a presentation to a group whose English skills are not strong, consider presenting a slideshow that summarizes your talk in their language or that uses their language on the slides. This will help them confirm their understanding of what you have said in English, and it will also demonstrate that you respect their language.

Politeness, Formality, and Social Interaction Practices

Different cultures often have different ways of greeting people, different ways of introducing new people to a group, and different rules for interacting. In some residential areas of North America, politeness exchanges include saying "Hello" or "Hi" to people you walk past on the street. In a downtown business area, however, you are not expected to say hello to others unless you know them or have some business to conduct with them. At work, you might say "Hi" to a coworker but "Hello" to a superior (issues of hierarchy).

When you are writing to clients from a culture outside Canada, assume a formal tone at first. Write "Dear Ms. Yousova" rather than beginning with "Dear Ingrid." After you have talked with the other person several times or exchanged several emails, you can gain a sense of how formal they expect you to be with them by studying their letters and emails.

Politeness and social interaction differences are particularly important when meeting people for the first time. In preparation for the summer Olympics in China, Beijing residents were advised to avoid asking foreigners about their age, religious beliefs, politics, or occupations. They were also warned not to ask foreigners about their health, love life, or marriages. These are all perfectly acceptable topics of conversation in Beijing, but Westerners might find them too intrusive for casual conversation with a new acquaintance.

Oral Communication Practices

Oral communication practices vary significantly throughout the world. One general rule is to observe others in the culture closely. A second rule is to research the culture before you interact with people of that culture so that you have at least some general knowledge that you can draw on as you try to piece together rules for how you should behave. You should try to determine these kinds of practices:

- Who opens and closes conversations?
- How do people determine who speaks next?
- Who may interrupt and how does this happen?
- How is silence used (e.g., to communicate respect)?
- Is humour appropriate or disrespectful?

Business Practices

As you might expect, business practices around the world differ dramatically depending on how different the culture is from Canadian culture. The list of information that you should acquire about a target culture should include:

- Language(s) spoken
- Politeness (how to greet business partners, how to say no in a polite way, how to thank your business partners)
- What nonverbal actions communicate (which gestures are offensive, how close you should stand to other people)

Figure 3 Consult country-specific sources on business protocol.

The best way to learn about the different practices in a particular country is to consult one or several of the internet resources listed in Figure 3.

COMMUNICATING IN A CHANGING WORLD

Guidelines about cultures are just that: guidelines. For example, typical business communication advice about China will tell you that China is a "collectivist" culture—that is, Chinese people tend to work as a group. More recent commentators, however, suggest that this may no longer be accurate. Business owners in China combine elements of Chinese culture, such as collectivism and harmony, with elements drawn from Western culture, such as ambition and individualism.[9] Wei Wang describes this mixture of cultures:

> But in my years of experience in both the West and China, I have realized that, although Chinese individuals have a strong tendency to relate to each other, they do not necessarily work together towards a shared goal. In fact, on the contrary, the Chinese are much less collectivist than Westerners. For instance, inside Sino-Western joint ventures, I have found that, while Westerners debate vigorously among themselves about the best way to get something done, local employees neither communicate well with Western personnel nor discuss business issues adequately among themselves. When they do talk among themselves, they talk a lot about personal matters, and when they act, they tend to follow their own rules rather than those of the group. (Wei Wang, *The China Executive: Marrying Western and Chinese Strengths to Generate Profitability from Your Investment in China*, 2006, p. 20)

In essence, this new research suggests that you need to have a complex understanding of people from other cultures. Of course, you need to learn as much as you can about politeness rituals (greetings, gifts, salutations, and so on)—that hasn't changed. However, you also need to recognize the complexity of people: many people are a mix of traditional values characteristic of their regional or national culture along with values from global influences

LO 5 Adjust written documents to communicate well with audiences from a variety of cultural groups

[9]Spence, R. (2008, July 21). Nuggets from 'best in show' papers. *National Post*, FP4.

(for example, American culture as depicted in movies or advertising). Individuals are also a mix of business values and cultural values outside of their business roles.

We encourage you to learn more about other cultural traditions, both within and outside Canada, and to apply what you learn from your research to your communications. This module has introduced you to a range of topics from social interactions and politeness rituals to business practices. We hope that you will extend the start you have made here by learning more about cultures outside your own. The more we all learn about the different cultural groups in our country, the richer we all will be.

Exercise 3: Test Your Knowledge of Business Etiquette

To test your knowledge, take one of the international business etiquette quizzes at www.international-business-etiquette.com/besite/culture.htm.

Exercise 4: Summarize Best Practices

Using the information in Figure 4, summarize the basic advice you would give to a colleague traveling to India to begin the process of signing a contract with an Indian company.

Relationships and Communication
- Indians primarily do business with people they already know and have known for a long time.
- Mutual trust and respect are the foundations of relationships.
- To build credibility, get someone else to introduce you.

Business Meeting Etiquette
- Allow up to two months lead time to set up appointments.
- Confirm your appointment a week or two in advance and again the day before the meeting. Remain flexible and prepare for last-minute rescheduling of meetings.
- Arrange meetings in late morning or early afternoon
- Arrive on time: punctuality is important.
- Share an agenda and supplementary materials and charts before the meeting.

Dress Etiquette
- Men should wear dark business suits and dress conservatively; in hot areas, less formal wear is acceptable.
- Women should dress in suits or conservative dresses.

Titles
- Address business peers using titles such as Professor, Doctor, and Engineer.
- If someone does not have a professional title, use the honorific title "Sir" or "Madam."
- Do not use someone's first name without their title unless they specifically invite you to address them by their name only.

Business Cards
- Offer your card with your right hand after the initial handshake and greeting.
- Business cards in English are acceptable.
- Hand your card in such a way that the recipient can read it as they accept it.

Figure 4 Advice about cultural practices in India, intended to help travellers conducting business in that country.

Case 2★★ AccountSoft and the Patel Group

Daniel McMahon, president of Account-Soft (a small but quickly growing accounting software company), considered the options: he was going to travel to Mumbai to meet Narendra Kulkarni of the Kulkarni Group to negotiate a deal to handle the customer relations side of his new product, or he was going to develop and manage it in-house. He didn't really like either option, but they were the only two he had.

uniquely india/Getty Images

AccountSoft's new software package, Accountant's Advantage, represented the next generation of programming for the financial services industry in Canada. One of its big advantages was that it could directly link up with (online, in real time) a client's financial records from the major brokerages, including i*TRADE and TDWaterhouse. The software could also download trading records from those sources and, with a few clicks of the mouse, save accountants huge amounts of time trying to reconcile trades and calculate the resulting taxes. The future of his company depended on this new product.

But his company's margins were also being pressured. He had to save on costs, especially support costs such as customer service call centres. It was this potential savings that led him to investigate the Kulkarni Group. He had seen a presentation by one of their North American sales representatives at a recent technology conference in Mississauga, ON, and their name came up in one or two technology trade magazines he read. They were leaders in providing customer services for smaller companies like his. In fact, they could do it for half the cost.

McMahon liked what he had read on the website, and from talking to the sales representative he felt like the Kulkarni Group would make a good match. However, he also got the feeling that he really needed to visit their operations centre in Mumbai, India, to meet with their management. He wanted to meet the people who might make or break his business before he committed to signing a contract with them. It turned out that the Kulkarni Group also wanted to meet McMahon before they went forward. Adding AccountSoft would demand a significant investment on their part. They, too, wanted to know whom they were dealing with.

McMahon didn't have much time to prepare for the trip, and what time he did have would be spent working out production schedules and timelines for the first release of Accountant's Advantage. But he knew next to nothing about India. He called Pravnay Khera, one of the few programmers he had on staff who was Canadian but also was connected to the Indian community through his parents.

He told Pravnay that he was planning a trip to Mumbai in three weeks to work out a deal with the Kulkarni Group. Pravnay agreed that this was the right move financially, but noted that they did business differently over there. For example, he mentioned that they probably would not want to sign a contract immediately. He explained that they would want to meet Daniel and make a judgment about him first. Then they would accept his spoken word as enough of a commitment. McMahon wondered aloud if maybe Pravnay should be going on the trip, but Pravnay pointed out that they would not deal with him because he was not the company president. McMahon would have to go. Pravnay offered to put together a memo with some tips and pointers in it, together with some websites where McMahon could find more information. He felt that a tip sheet might alert McMahon to the most obvious cultural differences. McMahon was interested in having this document and asked Pravnay to draft it as soon as possible. He also asked Pravnay to include links to specific websites where he could learn more.

Professional Communication Assignments

3. Write the Memo for Daniel McMahon

Daniel McMahon asked Pravnay Khera to write a memo outlining some tips and general information on how to conduct himself when he visits India in a few weeks. Write a one- or two-page memo in which you outline the most general kinds of things he should know, such as the value of an oral agreement over a written one. Use the websites on cross-cultural knowledge identified in this module as your sources of information. If you know anyone with previous knowledge, consider interviewing him or her and including that information in your memo.

Audience: Your boss, Daniel McMahon

Purpose: To orient Daniel McMahon to the important ways in which doing business in India differ from a Canadian context to help him achieve success in his business venture

Genre: Email memo

4. Advise McMahon to Postpone the Trip

One of the key components of successful business relationships with Indian businessmen is that they know who you are—that is, they either have a personal history of working with you or a mutual friend has introduced you. In this case, Daniel McMahon seems to be too eager to embark on this trip. Write a memo to him advising him to postpone the trip until he can do more planning and perhaps find a mutual friend or businessperson who already does business with the Kulkarni Group to write a letter of introduction.

Audience: Your boss, Daniel McMahon

Purpose: To persuade your boss to postpone his business trip to India so that he can establish a relationship with his Indian counterparts before appearing in person

Genre: Email message

MODULE SUMMARY

- Business communication must take into account subcultures within Canada as well as cultures outside of Canada
- Businesses in Canada adapt their communications to the multiple cultures and languages of their customers
- Communicators can reduce miscommunication by identifying whether the people they are writing to belong to a high-context culture (where much explanation and relationship building is necessary) or low-context cultures (which require more explanation through texts and contracts)
- Cultural tendencies as well as individual tendencies employ context to make meaning in communication
- Key aspects of intercultural communication include hierarchy, power distance relationships, gender dynamics, politeness, formality, and social interaction practices

Module 7

Positive and Informative Messages: Writing Letters, Memos, and Emails

Odua Images/Shutterstock

LEARNING OUTCOMES

LO 1 Analyze a writing situation to decide whether a letter or a memo is the appropriate genre of document to send

LO 2 Differentiate between the purposes and ways of organizing positive and informative messages

LO 3 Organize positive messages appropriately to build goodwill with readers

LO 4 Adapt positive and persuasive messages to motivate readers to perform actions the writer wants them to do

GETTING STARTED

Letters and memorandums (aka memos) are the oil that makes the modern corporate machine work. In fact, they are arguably the most essential tools for getting work done in the modern business world. The memo came into existence when the invention of the type-writer made it easy to communicate through paper. That ability to communicate through easily duplicated paper messages enabled corporations to grow to sizes that were previously unheard of. One hundred years later, the invention of the computer and the internet

Organizations exchange information through letters or memos, whether electronic (email) or print form. Print memos communicate important information among employees within the same organization, whereas printed letters communicate information between individuals at different organizations. For example, the human resources manager of a medium-sized financial services organization might draft a memo to inform all employees of the new guidelines for submitting trip reports. When asking to correct an error in his boss' disability policy, an administrative assistant might send a print letter to ensure a paper trail to document the solution. Communicators in business generally use email for brief or informal transactions, but for communicating formal and important information or inquiries, they might send a print letter across town by courier.

Figure 1 What distinguishes a memo from a letter?

spawned a new genre: email messages. The ability to communicate through electronic messages in turn helped develop work arrangements that span the globe.

The generic conventions of formatting a letter or memo are easy to learn. It is also fairly easy to decide when to write a letter and when to write a memo (see Figure 1). However, organizing and presenting your message within the genre can be a major challenge. There are three different kinds of messages that you will find yourself writing frequently: positive messages, negative messages, and persuasive messages. Positive messages deliver good news to readers, or at least neutral information. Negative messages deliver bad news to readers. Writers of bad news messages want to manage readers' emotions and maintain goodwill toward the organization. Persuasive messages present complex information that readers may react to with mixed emotions. This type of message requires writers to manage reader emotion or motivate readers to act when they might not particularly want to. In this module, you will read several examples of messages that deliver good news or information. It also outlines patterns of organization that you can use or adapt to the different writing situations that you encounter.

CHOOSING THE MESSAGE TO FIT YOUR SITUATION

LO 1 Analyze a writing situation to decide whether a letter or a memo is the appropriate genre of document to send

Rhetorical situation: The context in which a writing or speaking event takes place, including information about the audience, purpose, and message

Writing situations are not usually labelled as positive or negative (see Figure 2). Instead you must analyze the **rhetorical situation** to determine what kind of message or response fits best. The main focus of your analysis should be your readers. Examine the situation from

Informative messages: If you expect readers to respond neutrally to the information you communicate, the message is informative.

Positive messages: If you expect readers to be happy about the information you communicate, the message is positive.

Negative messages: If you expect readers to be angry or disappointed by the information you communicate, the message is negative.

Persuasive messages: If you expect readers to be resistant or opposed to your message, it is a persuasive one.

Figure 2 Different types of messages.

their viewpoint to decide how they will respond to your communication: Will they be happy to hear your news? Indifferent? Disappointed? Angry?

For example, if you were the administrative assistant in a medium-sized business that sponsored an academic award at the local community college, you might find yourself having to write to both successful and unsuccessful applicants for the award. Some of your readers should be pleased to hear that they have won. Therefore, this letter is a positive message. You will use the organizational pattern outlined in the next section of this module to develop your message. In contrast, when you write to unsuccessful applicants, your news is rejection, so you expect your readers to be disappointed or even angry at losing. To develop a bad newsletter to losing applicants, you will use a different organizational pattern.

To decide what type of message best fits your rhetorical situation, learn to distinguish one type of message from another. Use the checklist in Figure 3 to decide which pattern to use.

For example, as you start to draft the letter to the successful award applicants, you might review the checklist in Figure 3 to determine that you are writing a positive message (sharing good news) as well as an informative message (informing the reader of details about accepting the award). You also know, based on your analysis, that you should format the messages as letters because they are going outside the organization.

Ask the question	Choose an answer	Our recommendation
What is the main reason for my communication?	☐ To share good news	• Use the **positive and informative** message pattern outlined in Figure 4.
	☐ To communicate important information	• Use the **positive and informative** message pattern outlined in Figure 4.
	☐ To communicate bad news	• Use the **negative** message pattern.
	☐ To argue a particular point with which readers may not agree	• Use the **persuasive** message pattern.
What are the elements that I must include in this message?	☐ My situation lacks some elements from the pattern	• Omit those elements listed in the pattern. • Discuss the elements you do have in the order recommended in the pattern.
	☐ My situation has elements from more than one pattern	• Use the pattern that fits best with your **main** reason for communication. • Adapt elements from other patterns as necessary.
Should I format my message as a memo or letter?	☐ I am writing to someone who works for my organization	• Use a **memo** format.
	☐ I am writing to someone who works for a different organization	• Use a **letter** format.

Figure 3 Use this checklist to analyze your message.

HOW TO WRITE POSITIVE AND INFORMATIVE MESSAGES

LO 2 Differentiate between the purposes and ways of organizing positive and informative messages

Like most business and professional communications, positive and informative messages usually have more than one main purpose. They generally aim to

- Inform or share good news
- Have recipients read the message, understand it, and respond positively to it
- Downplay any negative elements

Simultaneously positive and informative messages have several secondary purposes:

- To have the reader think well of the writer and his or her organization
- To reduce or end further correspondence on this subject

Figure 4 is an example of a positive and informative message. Note the information that it contains and how it organizes and presents this information.

The annotations in Figure 4 show how to organize a positive or informative message. If we examine the annotations, we quickly note that the sample letter could be improved on to make a more effective positive and informative message. For example, the negative elements in the message are not stated as positively as they could be.

Exercise 1: State Negative Elements as Positively as Possible

Rewrite the negative sentences reproduced from Figure 4 so that the points are stated as positively as possible, while remaining clear and comprehensible.

1. Please note that your vehicle has been rated for personal use only, which does not include a commute to work.

2. We have confirmed that the vehicle is not modified or customized in any way, nor is it used for commercial purposes such as delivery, courier, etc.

3. If these conditions should change, please advise our office as soon as possible to ensure that your coverage is not negatively impacted.

4. Other than those drivers already listed on the policy, we understand that no one else is using the vehicle on a regular basis.

5. If you do have additional drivers in the household not currently listed, please contact our office to discuss.

MOTIVATING YOUR READER

The sample informative and positive letter in Figure 4 provides excellent additional details to the readers. The writer, Vivian, also includes one motivator to the readers, Horace and Bertha Baxtrom, when she requests a copy of the new vehicle ownership to ensure her records are complete. Of course, the Baxtroms want her information about their insurance requirements to be complete. To continue the topic of complete insurance records, Vivian reports that the policy currently lists Horace as the principal vehicle driver. She invites the Baxtroms to inform her if there are more possible operators of the vehicle than are listed on their current policy. For example, if one of Horace and Bertha's family members has moved home (perhaps their son, while he helps out on the farm over the summer), they should

ROBERTS & MANJIT INSURANCE/BENEFITS/FINANCIAL SERVICES

January 4, 2015

Horace & Bertha Baxstrom
10,972 S. Qu'Appelle No. 157,
R.R.# 4
Mclean, SK S0G 3E0

Dear Horace and Bertha:

As per your request, we confirm that we have advised Southern Prairie Mutual to process the following change to your policy #0867143 effective January 4, 2015.

Add coverage on the 2015 Toyota Tundra as follows:

> Liability - $100000000 limit
> All Perils - $500 deductible
> Rental Vehicle coverage (SPCF #12/89)
> Waiver of Depreciation (SPCF #26)
> Claims Protection

Please note your vehicle has been rated for personal use only, which does not include a commute to work. We have confirmed that the vehicle is not modified or customized in any way, nor is it used for commercial purposes such as delivery, courier, etc. If these conditions should change, please notify our office as soon as possible to ensure that your coverage is not negatively impacted.

To complete our files we would appreciate receiving a copy of the Ownership, which may be faxed, mailed, or scanned and emailed to our office. We have the registered owner and principal driver of the vehicle listed as Horace Baxstrom. Other than those drivers already listed on the policy, we understand that no one else is using the vehicle on a regular basis. If you do have additional drivers in the household not currently listed, please contact our office to discuss.

Enclosed are liability slips for your use. The documents amending your policy will follow from Southern Prairie Mutual in the next few weeks. Please review these, as it is important that all the information be correct.

Should you have any questions or if we can be of further assistance, please contact me at (123) 456-7890 or vivian.pierugi@romanjit.com. Thank you for continuing to entrust your insurance needs to Roberts & Manjit.

Sincerely,

Vivian Pierugi

Vivian Pierugi, CAIB
Insurance Advisor

---

**Callouts:**

1. Briefly present the main points and share any good news.

2. Add details, and include all information that Horace and Bertha need.

3. Include any negative elements, but state them as positively as possible.

4. Add details to show readers how they benefit (in other words, reader motivation).

5. Add goodwill ending.

Figure 4 Sample informative and positive message.

notify Vivian so that she can make changes to their records. If their son crashes the new truck and it turns out he has been a regular driver of the vehicle over the summer but was never listed on the insurance policy, Horace and Bertha may find the insurance adjustor unwilling to process their claim. Vivian uses this argument as a motivator to prompt the Baxtroms to update their coverage details.

To decide whether you need to motivate your reader to accept your information, consider the following questions:

■ Should you manage readers' responses toward the information or your organization? If you want readers to respond positively, include reasons why they should do so.

■ Does your message present a new organizational policy? Often new policies are obvious as to how they benefit the organization; how they benefit the individual employee is often less obvious. Highlight for readers how the new policy or change in an existing policy benefits them as well.

CONCLUDING POSITIVE AND INFORMATIVE MESSAGES

LO 3 Organize positive messages appropriately to build goodwill with readers

Concluding a short positive or informative message gracefully can be a challenge. Some people fall back on the weak and negative invitation, "If you have any questions, please don't hesitate to call." Avoid this type of closing for two reasons: one, it invites readers to create more work for you (calling you with questions when your message should have answered them clearly), and it introduces a negative into an otherwise positive situation ("do *not* hesitate"). Alternatives are to just stop or to use a goodwill closing that addresses readers directly. To build **goodwill**, close by referring to the business relationship that you have with your reader (rather than personal aspects).

Goodwill: A positive disposition that the reader has towards you as the writer or your organization

In Figure 4, Vivian Perugi uses a variation on "If you have any questions, please call" but her approach is successful because she phrases the invitation positively. It is feasible that her letter might prompt questions or notification of changes to the existing policy records. Her conclusion also includes a direct effort at building goodwill with readers by thanking them for their business.

Exercise 2: How Effective Are These Closings?

Evaluate the quality of the following brief endings for a positive or informative message. If you decide it is a poor conclusion, discuss ways to make it better.

1. Please don't be afraid to email me back if I've missed explaining something.
2. I'm really sorry that I won't be able to make it to the banquet, but when I return from my trip to Europe, I will definitely contact you to arrange to pick up my award.
3. I do hope we have the opportunity to meet at the banquet in May so that we can discuss further the ways in which Roberts and Manjit Insurance may contribute to the development of your knowledge of insurance and finance through our internship program.
4. Thanks for your consideration.
5. Together we can stem the growing disaster that the unchecked spread of the pine beetle represents to the timber reserves of this province.

Case 1★★ Congratulations, You Have Won a Lily's Choice Award

Dirk Pelham realized he wasn't done for the day the moment Lilian Fung, owner of the Lilian Fung Collection, Inc., swept into the room brandishing a stack of file folders several centimetres thick. She asked him to draft letters notifying the three winners of this year's Lily's Choice Awards. She placed the folders on his table and began searching in the large bag that hung from her shoulder.

Kzenon/Shutterstock

Dirk picked up the top folder and looked through its contents. He had noticed the competition information on the company website. There was a description of the award there, along with the contest rules and information about how the winners of the award would be decided.

Lilian explained that the company contacts the fashion program directors at post-secondary schools around the country every fall and invites their students to send in their designs. Students submit a portfolio of women's fashion designs, and she selects three students as "Young Designers to Watch" through her Lily's Choice Awards (see Figure 5). Every year they got more submissions. This year they got 25 applicants; in the first year they started with just five. The contest was starting to catch on.

The three winners were in the green file folder on top. The rest were the other submissions. From her bag Lilian pulled out several pages of handwritten notes with her comments on the designs and her criteria for selection. Dirk's job was to make one or two specific references to the work in each letter using the notes. She advised him to look through the designs before drafting the letters. Lilian pointed out that the designs in the second folder were particularly exciting, but warned Dirk not to spend too much time browsing through the entries. She wanted the notification letters in the mail by early next week.

Dirk was unclear, though, about when she wanted to see the letters: was Monday okay or did she want to read a draft sooner? Lilian replied that he should draft the first one and email it to her. She could look at it in the airport on Friday evening. Once Dirk got her feedback, he could draft the other letters.

Dirk said this sounded pretty straightforward. Lilian noted that in addition to knowing why they won, the winners also needed details about the award presentation ceremony. The awards were usually given out at each school's formal awards banquet at the end of term. Lilian asked Dirk to contact the program directors at the three winners' schools for banquet details. He would also need to arrange for one of Lilian Fung's representatives to attend.

Once Lilian left his office, Dirk began reviewing the winning student design portfolios with interest. He knew that the kind of recognition that came from a Lily's Choice award could really jump-start a young designer's career. He was also interested in picking up some cutting edge ideas for his own work.

After a few minutes, he set aside the design folders to begin the task of writing the letters. He would take them home with him tonight to study them more closely. He needed to check the Lilian Fung website for details about the awards and then make some phone calls for details on how and when the awards would be made.

Before drafting the letter to contest winners, Dirk analyzes his writing situation. He quickly identifies his main reasons for communication—to share good news and relay important information about receiving the award. Next he reviews the pattern outlined for writing positive and informative messages to determine which elements are relevant to his situation. As he jots down his ideas related to the analysis, he decides that, at least initially, there are no negative elements to receiving the award, unless the recipients are unable to attend the banquet ceremony. Next he makes a list of the information that must appear in the letter; as he brainstorms the letter's contents, he realizes that the challenge of this message will be ensuring readers have all of the details they need to collect the award (whether or not they can attend the banquet) and how to start arrangements for the winners' internships.

Suddenly Dirk realizes that an important component of this message is to ensure that recipients are motivated to contact him about setting up the internship part of their awards. Although he knows that if he were to win such an award he would be banging on doors to set up his internship, he also recognizes that different personality types might be nervous about contacting Lilian Fung Collection, so this means he should analyze his readers' needs to determine the most effective means of prompting them to act.

Exercise 3: Motivating Readers to Attend an Awards Event

1. Generate a list of needs that readers might have in connection with their education and the winning of an award. Here are three to get you started:
   - Being a successful student
   - Distinguishing themselves from other students
   - Earning income

2. Add at least three or four more needs to the list that you think are relevant to the reader.

3. Expand the three that look most useful to you into two or three sentences of explanation that you might be able to use in a notification letter that will motivate your readers to attend an awards program event. Remember to choose reasons that your readers will find motivating.

Professional Communication Assignments

1. Congratulations on Winning a Lily's Choice Award

Using the details presented in Figures 5 through 8, write a draft of Dirk Pelham's letter for Lilian Fung in which you inform one of the winners that s/he has won a Lily's Choice Award for innovative women's fashion designs. Make sure that your letter includes any information the recipient needs to accept the award as well as Lilian Fung's feedback about the designs. If necessary, reread the discussion on writing positive and informative messages to review the important aspects of writing this kind of message and for pointers on how to organize and draft your message.

Audience: The three recent winners of the Lily's Choice Award

Purpose: To inform readers that they have won the award, which includes a cash prize and a six-month internship working at Lilian Fung Collections, Inc.; to provide details on where and when they will receive the award (and what to do if they cannot attend the awards banquet); and to motivate them to contact Lilian about arranging their internship

Genre: Business letter (on company letterhead)

Lilian Fung invites all fourth-year students enrolled full time in an accredited Canadian school of fashion apparel design program to submit a portfolio of between three and five designs of women's casual or work apparel for consideration for a Lily's Choice Award. The awards include a $1,000 cash prize, a commemorative brass plaque, and an opportunity to work for six months as a paid intern at Lilian Fung Collection in their Toronto studio. Deadline for submissions: Nov. 30 (yearly).

Figure 5 Lily's Choice Award description.

Scheduled for May 7, 6:00 P.M. to 8:00 P.M. at Fondini's Bistro, west campus (211 Spadina Rd)

Attendance by representative from Lilian Fung Collection is now confirmed.

Send name and email address of representative [check this with Lilian?] to Anne Bechaumé, program administrative assistant (fshninfo@ryerson.ca), no later than April 15.

Figure 6 Dirk's notes on details regarding one of the school program awards banquets.

Rashana Develani, Apt. 807, 439 High Tech Rd, Richmond Hill, ON (905-123-4567)

Harcourt Van Sittart, 325 Queen St., Oakville, ON (905-234-5678)

Lami McTier, 22 Littlebottom Cresc., East York, ON (416-345-6789)

Figure 7 Lily's Choice Award recipients.

Rashana: Fascinating use of beading to add upscale elegance to casual weekender design. Textured fabric combination is quite arresting.

Harcourt: Flamboyant pantsuit design will give the working woman options. Stunning use of merino wool.

Lami: Functional yet elegant approach to basic jeans and t-shirt combination. This combination demonstrates understanding of contemporary women's need for style and comfort.

Figure 8 Lilian Fung's commentary on Lily's Choice Award winners' designs.

2. Accepting the Award and Requesting Additional Information

Imagine that you are one of the three recipients of a Lily's Choice Award (Rashana Develani, Harcourt Van Sittart, or Lami McTier), and draft a letter to Lilian Fung, the president of Lilian Fung Collection, thanking her for the award and notifying her of whether you are able to attend the awards banquet on May 7 to receive your award. In your letter, also request further information about Lilian Fung Collection's internship program, a position that you have been offered as part of the award. Include information about your availability to accept the internship as well as your particular interests and goals for the internship. Use the information in this module about writing positive and informative messages to help you structure and draft your letter.

Audience: Lilian Fung, the president of Lilian Fung Collections, Inc., who has just notified you that you have won an award sponsored by her company

Purpose: To accept the award and request additional information about the details of the internship that you will receive as part of the award

Genre: Positive and informative email message

Figure 9 is a sample letter written to inform a client of the details associated with a corporate move. As you read it, attend to how the message is structured, starting with the complete contact information for Jasper Moving & Storage. The message itself establishes a positive first impression by thanking the reader for his business and repeats the agreed-on dates for his move. The writer formats the letter using bold headings and white space to highlight the information of central interest to Dr. Savage: the dates for his move and important details associated with those dates. This formatting allows readers to scan quickly to check the details.

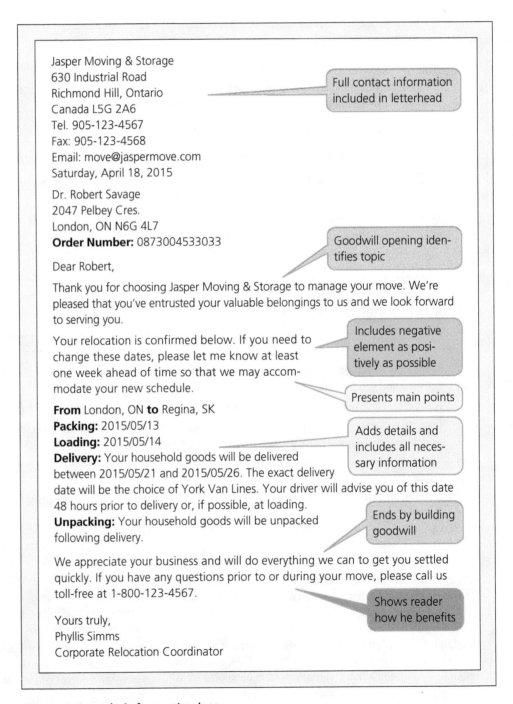

Figure 9 Sample informative letter.

Exercise 4: Analyze a Positive and Informative Message

Analyze the sample letter in Figure 10 to answer the following questions:

1. What pattern or organizational structure does this letter use?
2. How effectively does this letter present important details?
3. What suggestions can you make for changes in formatting to improve its presentation of information?
4. What stylistic changes can you make to move important details to positions of emphasis?
5. How could you rewrite the goodwill ending to improve its use of positive emphasis?

Dear Cardmember,

Welcome to a new world where all those exotic locations on your bucket list seem much closer. You are packed and ready for an adventure that only CanadianCredit® FlyFreePlus® Titanium Card can offer.

Your new Card membership works like this. For each $1.00 purchase charged to your Card, you earn 1 FlyFreePlus® Mile. But FlyFreePlus doesn't stop there. Once you have reached $10,000 in purchases each year, you will start earning 1.25 FlyFreePlus Miles for every additional $1.00 purchase. If you use this Card for spending every day, you earn FlyFreePlus Rewards more quickly.

But this Card isn't just about earning FlyFreePlus Miles. It also gives you Canadian Credit's global service, plus the warm welcome of 5,000 fine establishments in Canada and worldwide. Your unique Canadian Credit benefits include:

- No spending limit
- Travel assistance and insurance protection
- Our exclusive *NoMoreWaiting*® program

With FlyFreePlus, only your imagination can limit your travel options. Visit over 863 destinations in over 149 countries served by our member airlines. Whether it's short domestic flights or your round-the-world dream vacation, Canadian Credit FlyFreePlus Titanium Card has you covered. And your choices continue to multiply.

Redeem your miles online for hotel rooms, car rentals, or vacation packages. Reward yourself using hundreds of options for merchandise, gift cards, and FlyFreePlus experiences. Whether you pursue the heart-pounding excitement of heli-skiing in the Rockies or the quiet contemplation of an ocean fishing trip, Canadian Credit cards have something for you. For details on the FlyFreePlus program, please see flyfreeplus.com.

The enclosed Benefits Brochure will introduce you to all the nuances of your Titanium Card. If you have questions not answered in the brochure, do not hesitate to visit our website at canadiancredit.ca or contact us at 1-800-Can-Credit.

We appreciate you choosing the Canadian Credit FlyFreePlus Titanium Card. We strive to give you no less than the best possible service, whether you are in Toronto or Timbuktu. We do not believe you can find a better business partner than us.

Sincerely,
Devrim Karga
Director,
Consumer Card Marketing

Figure 10 Sample positive and informative letter.

Case 2★ Soliciting Customer Feedback

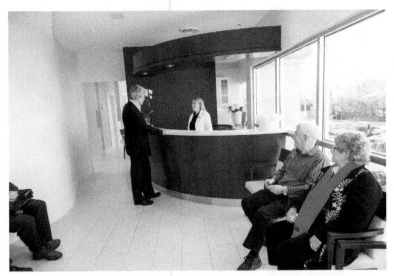

Stuart Westmorland/Image Source/
Getty Images

Filipa Dragovic, the customer relations manager for the Centre for Skin Research (CSR), was always looking for ways to improve the services that CSR offered to their clients. The Centre had thousands of clients in their database, but most came and went quietly. Most clients were nervous before their appointments and in no mood to fill out a form afterward. The problem she faced was getting some insight from these clients about their experiences as patients.

Jayson Jacks, an internship student working on a commerce degree, thought he could help. He was a marketing major, and getting this kind of feedback from clients was something that interested him. He had recently received a similar letter himself after his appointment at a physiotherapy clinic. That letter was short—just four paragraphs. The first paragraph talked about how the physiotherapy clinic was committed to providing the best health care possible. In the second paragraph they requested that Jayson complete a two-minute survey as part of improving their services. To encourage him they offered to enter him in a draw for a $100 gift certificate—something he found attractive because the odds of winning were much better than any lottery ticket he might buy. They ended the letter by thanking him and noting that any information he provided would be confidential. He noted that the chief physician of the clinic had signed the letter and thought that maybe Filipa might try to get their president, Dr. Mykyta Zelenko, to sign this letter.

Jayson brainstormed the following list of items that might be included in the letter:

- An incentive for returning the survey
- Some information about the online survey
- Some idea of what the questions would be about: info about wait times in the office, courtesy of the staff, cleanliness of facility, parking
- The url for the survey (http://www.csr.ca/survey)

One of the key aspects of the letter that Jayson responded to was that it was short. He read the letter in less than one minute, and he could do the survey from his phone while waiting for the bus just by clicking a few buttons. This project seemed like something he could handle.

≫ Professional Communication Assignments

3. Write a Letter to Get Clients to Respond to the Survey

Using the information in Case 2, write a short letter (fewer than 150 words) to the clients of the CSR. Use the structure outlined in the sample letter in Figure 10 and described in the letter Jayson received to organize your message.

Audience: Clients of the CSR who plan to continue using the Centre's services and have an interest in improving the services they receive

Purpose: Motivate them to visit the link in the letter and fill out the survey

Genre: Informative message sent as an email

4. Write Questions for the Online Survey

Write the sample questions that would be included on the survey mentioned in Jayson's letter. Use the issues identified by Jayson in the case and add other questions that you think would be useful for the administration of the clinic. Limit the survey to no more than seven questions and include no more than one open-ended question (a question where the respondent has to write out an answer rather than click a box).

Audience: Clients of the CSR who plan to continue using the Centre's services and have an interest in improving the services they receive

Purpose: Obtain information that can be used to improve the client experience

Genre: Short survey or questionnaire

MODULE SUMMARY

- Decide the best medium for the message that you have to send (email, print memo, letter).

- Analyze a situation to identify how best to pattern your message to accomplish your purpose.

- Organize positive and informative messages so that they present good news, include all necessary information, show readers how they benefit, and build goodwill.

- Motivate readers to respond to the requests made in informative and positive messages.

Module 8

Negative Messages: Writing Letters, Memos, and Emails

Andreas Saldavs/Shutterstock

LEARNING OUTCOMES

LO 1 Identify how to structure a negative message

LO 2 Read critically to identify important information and make inferences

LO 3 Develop the ability to write a good buffer to soften negative news

LO 4 Demonstrate how to structure a negative message to recipients who have more or less status within the organization than you do

GETTING STARTED

We've all received them—the rejection letter, the phone call informing you that you did not get the job, or any one of the many other bad news messages. Nobody likes getting them, but some are clearly easier to deal with than others. Why? There are ways to break bad news that can make the situation easier to deal with. In this module, we'll explore how to do that.

Negative messages deliver bad news to readers. Your goal in writing a negative message is to manage readers' emotions and responses to your message and to maintain their goodwill toward your organization. In this module, you will learn two ways of structuring a negative message to manage your readers' response, including using a buffer to open the message and giving a reason before your refusal. You will also learn how to structure your letter based on your relationship to the recipients, including coworkers, customers, and supervisors. Breaking bad news well can often mean the difference between maintaining clients and losing them, and between building relationships at work and finding yourself out of work.

HOW TO WRITE NEGATIVE MESSAGES

Negative messages are ones to which you expect your reader will respond with displeasure: they will be unhappy to hear the news you have to communicate. Figure 1 is a sample negative message sent to a school-aged child whose book order is delayed while the book club waits for it to be restocked. Although a short message, Figure 1 uses the classic pattern for a negative message:

LO 1 Identify how to structure a negative message

1. Buffer
2. Statement of disappointing news, plus reason
3. An alternative or compromise to soften the disappointment
4. A positive, goodwill-building closing

In more complicated situations, you should expand each paragraph to elaborate your points and to manage your reader's response effectively. For example, later in this module you will meet Penelope Stefanopoulos, who is writing to a customer of Pergola Products with whom she is not acquainted but whom she would like to preserve as a customer, if possible. She

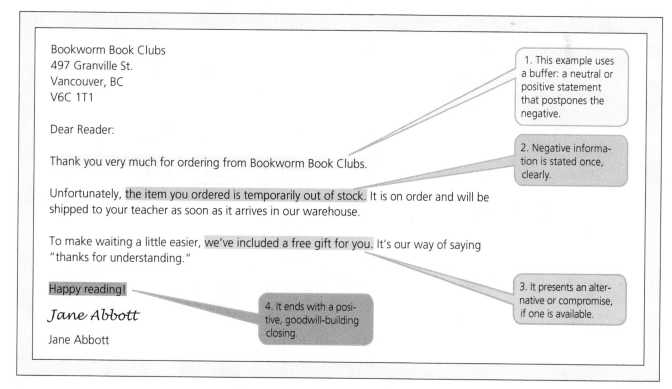

Figure 1 This sample negative message uses a standard organizational pattern.

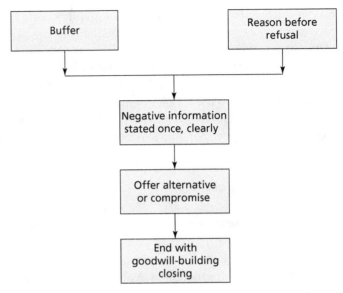

Figure 2 A flowchart shows the standard organizational pattern for a negative message.

will use a version of the first organizational pattern outlined in Figure 1. She has two options for the beginning of her letter (see Figure 2):

1. She can use a buffer, as Jane Abbott did in her letter in Figure 1.

2. She can give a reason before her refusal.

In the case where you do not already know the person you are writing to, try to build as much **goodwill** as you can. After breaking the bad news, consider offering an alternative or compromise (if possible). End with a goodwill closing.

Goodwill: A positive disposition that the reader has toward you or your organization

LO 3 Develop the ability to write a good buffer to soften negative news

BUFFERS

Buffer: A neutral statement often used to begin a negative message

Good buffers can be hard to write. Figure 3 lists a few tips to help you write a good buffer.

When to Use a Buffer	What Makes a Good Buffer?	What Makes a Buffer Good?
• When you know your reader values cultural indirectness (many non-North American cultures prefer indirect rather than direct statements) • When you need to thank your reader for something • When openly stating the negative sounds too abrupt or rude	• Start with the positive • Thank the reader for something he or she has done (see Figure 6) • Describe what happened or list facts relating to the situation • Refer to an enclosure in the message	It should accomplish these things: • Put the reader in a positive frame of mind • Not give the bad news, but not suggest a positive response either • Provide an effective transition to the negative news

Figure 3 What you need to know about buffers.

Exercise 1: What Is a Good Buffer?

Evaluate the following sample buffers for how good they are. Use the information in Figure 3 as your criteria to evaluate the degree to which each buffer is effective. Revise where necessary.

1. Dear Mr. Todd,

Thank you for your letter of May 7 in which you requested a replacement blade to your straight razor after extensive usage caused it to break.

2. Dear Mr. Sauron,

It is with great regret that I am sending you this replacement ring. We were unable to recover the original, as you requested, because it was recently destroyed after its bearer fell into an active volcano.

3. Dear Ms. Looser,

Congratulations! You have been selected as fourth runner up in this season's North American Idol contest.

4. Dear Mr. Vassani,

The members of the selection committee were very impressed with your credentials, your work, and especially your expertise in the area of groundwater contamination solutions, but they decided to offer the position to the other short-listed candidate. We felt the other candidate better suited our needs at this time.

5. Dear Colleague,

The process of organizing the program for the 2011 Business Communication Association Conference has been completed. With much regret, I am writing to report that your proposal(s) could not be included in the final schedule.

Case 1★★ We Regret to Inform You . . .

LO 2 Read critically to identify important information and make inferences

Abdul Akbar reread the letter that Penelope Stefanopoulos had just handed him (Figure 4). He didn't know where to begin in his explanation about the errors the customer had made with the product. As a chemist in the research and development division of Pergola Products, Abdul was a first line of defense for administrative assistants like Penelope in customer service, who dealt extensively with inquiries and complaints from consumers about Pergola's vast array of household products.

Penelope agreed that they couldn't refund the replacement cost of the shirt, but she also knew that she would have to explain to the customer why the Bleach'Em Out pen couldn't work when he used it in the way he described. She was wondering if Abdul could tell her anything about the chemistry of mixing together these different products.

Abdul nodded. He said he might have to do some research to find out what was in the GooBGone formula, but the most immediate problem that he could see was that the dryer heat would set an ink stain (which was usually permanent unless it was an erasable formula), so Jared, the letter writer, had been starting at a serious disadvantage. Abdul explained that the products that Jared had used first were all pretreaters—meant to be done before the shirt went into the washer the first time. The Bleach'Em Out pen is an on-the-go stain remover. It interacts on a molecular basis with the pretreaters so combining the two treatments risks potential discoloration or further setting of the stain.

photosindia/Getty Images

Figure 4 Letter of complaint for Bleach'Em Out stain removal pen.

The packaging instructions were clear: they warned customers against using this pen on ink stains. The material safety data sheet of the citrus cleaner, GooBGone, stated that its citrus and petroleum base was incompatible with oxidizing materials such as chlorine and strong acids. Abdul noted that the Bleach'Em Out pen contained chlorine bleach, so the interaction of the two substances likely caused the greenish colour.

Penelope replied that what Abdul had told her should work well as the basis for the letter. She didn't think the customer would need the actual chemical formulae—that would be too much detail. She decided to work up a draft of her reply, and then see if she needed any more concrete data.

Abdul offered to email the website address for the GooBGone product in case she wanted to quote from it. He also suggested that the customer might package up the shirt and send it to him at the lab. He noted that he had a few things to try to remove the stain that Jared would not have access to, as a regular consumer. Abdul offered to try to remove the stain, if Penelope's customer was interested.

Penelope agreed enthusiastically because his offer would allow her to offer the customer an alternative. She began reviewing her options for writing the reply. She remembered that she also had some brochures about cleaning and some samples in her office of new cleaning products that were just coming onto the market. Another option would be to send him some of those.

> Professional Communication Assignments

1. We Cannot Refund the Cost of Your Shirt

In the role of Penelope Stefanopoulos, write a reply to Jared LeBlanc in which you refuse to refund the cost of his ruined shirt. Use the information in this module to help you organize and draft the negative message. Use the details from the case itself and from Figure 5 to help you develop the content for the letter. Your main goals are to give Jared the bad news, to have him read, understand, and accept the bad news, and to maintain as much goodwill with him as possible.

Audience: Jared LeBlanc, the customer who ruined his shirt

Purpose: To convey the bad news that you will not be able to grant his request for reimbursement

Genre: Business letter

2. Documenting How to Handle Reimbursement Requests

Writing as Abdul Akbar, draft a memo to Penelope Stefanopoulos that outlines the problem. Although you have already spoken to Penelope about the problem, this memo will serve as documentation of how the situation was handled internally. Use the discussion in this module to help you organize and draft your response to the request for reimbursement. Your main goals in writing this memo are to document the facts of the case and the reasons for not being able to agree to reimburse the customer.

Audience: Penelope Stefanopoulos, customer service representative at Pergola Products

Purpose: To describe the facts of the case and explain the reasons for not reimbursing the customer

Genre: Memo

Bonny Brite Bleach'Em Out Stain Removal Pen is not a pretreater; it is an on-the-go stain remover.

Directions for Use:
1. Remove excess food from stain.
2. Press the tip of pen onto the stain several times to release stain remover solution.
3. Rub pen tip carefully across the stain to remove it. If necessary, release more liquid onto the stain and continue to massage it in gently.
4. **Please Note:** If treated area will come in direct contact with sunlight, wipe with a damp cloth to remove excess solution from fabric.

Works Well On: Tea, wine, grape juice, chocolate, barbecue sauce, ketchup, coffee
Do Not Use On: Ink, grease, blood, lemon juice

Figure 5 English instructions on the packaging of Bonny Brite Bleach'Em Out Stain Removal Pen.

ANALYSIS: ORGANIZATIONAL STATUS AND REFUSING JARED'S REQUEST

Organize your negative message according to your relationship with the recipient. In Penelope Stefanopoulos's situation in Case 1, she is writing to a customer who is not part of the Pergola Products organization, so she will use the standard negative letter format (see Figure 1). In this

LO 4 Demonstrate how to structure a negative message to recipients who have more or less status within the organization than you do instance, Penelope has no pre-existing relationship with Mr. LeBlanc, but she does want to build as much goodwill with him as she can to retain him as a customer. Consequently, she is likely to offer him an alternative or a compromise following the refusal and then end with a strong, goodwill-building closing. If she were writing to a coworker with similar status to her own or a subordinate, Penelope would structure her message differently. She would structure it yet another way if she were writing to her boss.

For example, Figure 6 uses a direct approach to communicate bad news, the writer's resignation from a job. It also outlines one pattern to use when drafting a negative message to a superior. The annotations highlight the main attributes of the letter structure:

1. Identify and describe the problem

2. Give background, if necessary

3. Describe options for fixing the problem

4. Recommend a solution and offer assistance to solve problem

In cases such as Figure 6, it is unlikely that the letter will announce the news; it is more likely that Armand will have spoken or at least emailed with Catherine about this transition. The letter is required for formal reasons, such as unit reviews within the company that look for patterns in people leaving a large organization, for example. The letter also has the effect of smoothing over the transition. The offer to help with the search for a successor, while unlikely to be accepted, shows a concern for the organization and reflects well on the writer.

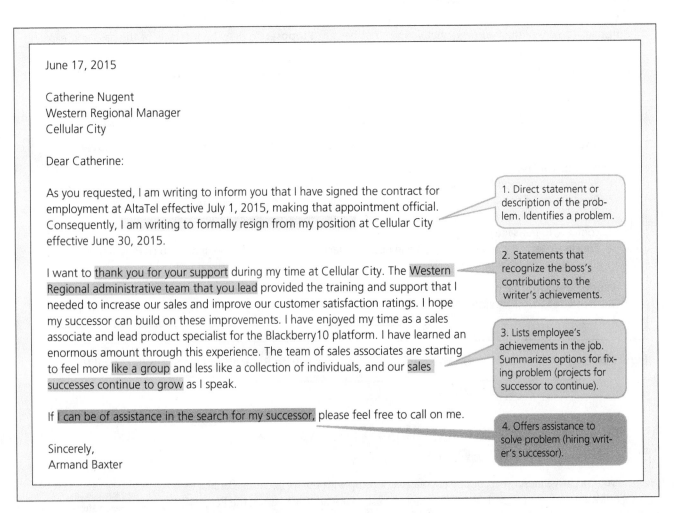

Figure 6 Sample letter conveys bad news from a subordinate to a boss.

Andreas Saldavs/Shutterstock

Figure 7 is an example of the same bad news (the writer is resigning) conveyed to subordinates. The annotations highlight the organizational structure of the message:

1. Describe the problem clearly and briefly
2. Supply an alternative or compromise, if possible
3. Ask for input or advice, if appropriate

As in the letter to the superior, Armand states the bad news directly. Although this situation offers no possibility of compromise, Armand does introduce an alternative. He notes that he will not be leaving before he arranges the client accounts—a direct concern for his readers who face an uncertain future with his departure from the job. He then invites his employees to take an active role in the search that will appoint his successor.

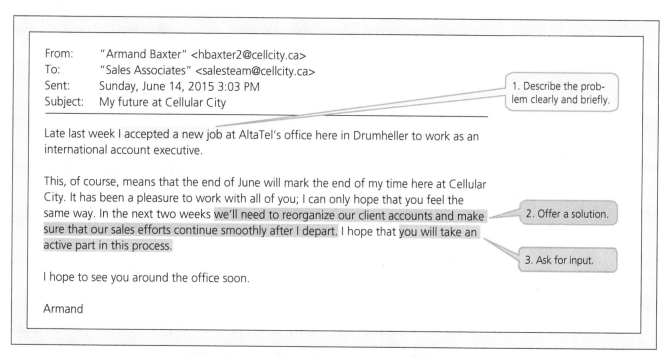

Figure 7 Sample letter conveys bad news to subordinates and peers.

Rich Melnyk, publisher of the Edmonton Moon, had a problem. To reduce costs, in 2007 the paper had stopped delivering print subscriptions to the outlying areas in Northern and Central Alberta. They also had cut the size of the paper from 75 pages to 50 pages. Given this string of events, Melnyk had little choice other than to raise the price for subscriptions.

Figure 8 shows a sample letter that aims to inform subscribers of an increase in the cost of the *Edmonton Moon* newspaper while maintaining them as customers.

October 1, 2015
0763241

Fred Keynes
8443 90th Ave.
Edmonton, Alberta

Dear Subscriber,

In our booming province, prices are rising for all products, and the Edmonton Moon is no exception.

The huge increase in the price of oil, which has benefits for all of us in Alberta, has affected the cost of delivering your newspaper to your home. The price of newsprint has also jumped. We've absorbed these extra expenses as much as we can, but have now reached a point where we must pass some of these increased costs to our customers. Effective November 1, 2015 your subscription to the Edmonton Moon will be $21.50 per month plus applicable taxes. This still represents a saving to you of 10% off our regular price.

While no one likes to hear about increased prices, we hope you will understand this is necessary in order to continue providing you with the exclusive coverage of sports, city news, and popular culture only found in the Edmonton Moon.

Our hard-hitting local news commentary and award-winning sports reporting combine to deliver the best value of any newspaper in Edmonton.

As an Edmonton Moon subscriber, you will still have free access to our digital edition, a full online version of the newspaper that's yours to read anytime, anywhere.

If you have any questions or comments, please do not hesitate to contact our customer service centre at 1-800-492-MOON (2121).

Thank you for reading the Edmonton Moon.

Rich Melnyk

Publisher, Edmonton Moon

---

1 Strathcona Road, Edmonton, AB T6G 5X7 Canada ● 1-800-668-MOON

Figure 8 Sample negative message to subscribers.

Professional Communication Assignments

3. The Price of Your Paper Is Going Up

Read the letter in Figure 8 informing subscribers that rates for the newspaper will increase starting November 1. As you read, analyze the structure and strategies used to deliver the bad news and then evaluate the quality of this letter based on the discussion in this module.

1. How effective is this letter at informing readers of the cost increase while maintaining them as subscribers?
2. What strategies does Melnyk use to manage readers' responses and emotions to the information?
3. What structure has Melnyk used to organize his negative message?
4. What makes this structure effective/ineffective for you, as a reader/subscriber?
5. What revisions would you make to the formatting, strategies, or sentence structure to improve the effectiveness of this negative message?

Audience: Course instructor

Purpose: Analyze the negative message and explain how it works

Genre: Memo from you to the course instructor

4. Discontinue Your Paper

Imagine that you are a subscriber to the Edmonton Moon and that you received a copy of this letter. After much consideration, you decide to discontinue your subscription. Write a letter to Rich Melnyk breaking the bad news to him. Use one of the structures for a negative message outlined in this module to organize your letter.

Audience: Rich Melnyk, Publisher of the Edmonton Moon

Purpose: To express your dissatisfaction with the price increase and to try to motivate him to consider alternatives so that you could re-subscribe

Genre: Business letter

Exercise 2: Evaluate and Revise This Negative Message

The letter in Figure 9 delivers bad news to parents of a class of grade 7 students who will have to change teachers only a few weeks into the new school year. Read this letter and, using the information outlined in this module on writing effective negative

---

St. Xavier Senior School

October 3, 2015

Dear Parents/Guardians,

As your child may have told you, his/her grade seven math teacher has been absent for a week now. Unfortunately, this week, due to personal reasons, Mr. Jahvinder had to resign. To our students' credit they have expressed great concern for Mr. Jahvinder. Though I must respect Mr. Jahvinder's privacy, I want to assure the students that he felt a great responsibility to each of them, so his decision was truly based on what will be best for the children.

With that said, the focus needs to be on our next steps. Presently, Mrs. Maciaq is the substitute teacher and has been devoting many hours to catch up on the paper grading and planning of lessons. She has been available before and after school, as well as during lunch hour. In the meantime, we have begun the interview process to find the best person for this position. While we want to expedite the process, we will only hire the best qualified to teach grade seven mathematics to our children.

We appreciate your patience and understanding during this process. Please let Mrs. Maciaq or me know of any concerns you might have.

Sincerely,

Hazel Broadview

Hazel Broadview
Principal

1459 Carlton St., Halifax, NS B3H 3B8 ● 123-456-7890

Figure 9 Sample negative message to parents.

messages, analyze and evaluate it. Decide which organizational pattern has been used as the basis for this message. Examine such details as whether the writer has used a buffer, and so on. Finally, when you complete your analysis, revise the letter to correct or improve any flaws that you noticed in your evaluation.

MODULE SUMMARY

- The classic pattern for negative messages begins with a buffer, moves to a statement of the bad news, offers an alternative or compromise, and ends with a positive, goodwill-building closing.
- An alternative opening for negative messages begins by giving a reason before the refusal.
- Use buffer statements to soften the bad news; use them when you have an opportunity to thank the reader or to summarize the facts of the case in a neutral manner.
- Structure bad news messages depending on the recipient's status within the organization: use a direct structure and omit the buffer when dealing with people you work with regularly.

Module 9
Writing Persuasive Messages

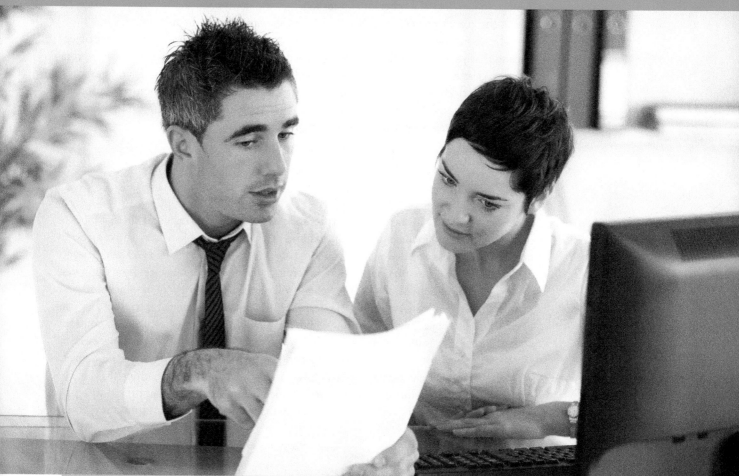

Wavebreakmedia/Shutterstock

LEARNING OUTCOMES

LO 1 Identify and distinguish direct request and diagnostic or problem-solving messages

LO 2 Organize direct request and diagnostic or problem-solving messages

LO 3 Anticipate reader objections

LO 4 Demonstrate that the solution will benefit both the reader and the organization

GETTING STARTED

Sometimes the right thing to do is so obvious that it takes very little to persuade the rest of your team members to agree on a plan of action. Enjoy these moments—they are rare. More often than not, you will have to persuade your coworkers, your supervisor, and others that the plan of action you have in mind is the one everyone should follow. If you are new to an organization or are a junior member of the team, the burden of proof will be on you to persuade the rest of the team that yours in the right solution. In this module you will learn how to recognize and respond to communication situations where your readers may resist or oppose the message that you must deliver. This type of communication is called a **persuasive message** and it includes **direct requests** and diagnostic or **problem-solving messages**.

In the first case, you will meet Sheri Safir, who is writing to the Ontario Assessment Review Board to ask them to reconsider their ruling of the Moonstone Valley Centre for the Arts as a private club. In this message, she makes a direct request that members of the review board reconsider their earlier designation of the community service group as a private members club. In the second case, Adam Zeleski solves a problem for his supervisor, Gerry Michaels—creating more storage space near the entrance to their office. Adam needs to write a persuasive message to convince the other employees to adopt the new policy and use the new space; he then has to consider an employee's request for an exemption from the new policy.

The discussion in this module shows you how to analyze and anticipate reader objections so that you can counter them convincingly. You will then learn how to organize your direct request message. Next you will learn about diagnostic or problem-solving messages, in which you identify a problem shared by you and your reader and propose a solution. In this type of message, the main challenge is to show your readers how your solution benefits them and to counter any objections they might have to your solution.

Problem-solving message: A message that identifies a problem and proposes a solution for the reader to approve or carry out

TYPES OF PERSUASIVE MESSAGES AND HOW TO WRITE THEM

LO 1 Identify and distinguish direct request and diagnostic or problem-solving messages

A persuasive message is one that you expect your reader to resist or oppose. Different types of persuasive messages include direct requests and diagnostic or problem-solving messages. In both of these types of messages, writers aim to persuade readers to act based on their message. Direct request messages ask readers to do something. Generally, the request is something that readers may not want to do or that they believe will not benefit them. Writers of direct request messages must anticipate where readers' resistance or opposition originates so that they can overcome those objections. Similarly, diagnostic or problem-solving messages also confront potential reader resistance or opposition. In a diagnostic or problem-solving message, writers identify a problem shared by writer and reader and propose a solution that readers must enact.

Direct requests: Messages in which you ask your reader to do something for you

Direct requests are messages in which you ask your reader to do something for you. For example, you might want to 1) change your readers' minds, and 2) prompt them to act by writing back to you. Persuasion involves getting readers to do more than think: it requires them to act.

Overcoming Objections

LO 3 Anticipate reader objections

Motivating readers to act takes more effort than persuading them to consider a different point of view (the goal of argument in most essay-writing situations). Inciting readers to action requires knowing how or what they think as well as understanding what motivates them. For example, barriers to action include objections that readers may have to the proposal or request. Successfully responding to and answering objections can make readers much more likely to grant your request. To discover what objections readers may have, ask them, if possible. If you are unsure that you understand, ask follow-up questions to clarify. If it is impossible to ask, then you need to analyze both your reader and the situation to anticipate possible objections.

To anticipate objections they might have, you need to know that most people's objections are rooted in three areas:

- *Practical reasons.* Readers may object for practical reasons, meaning they do not see how your proposal or request meets their needs or is advantageous to them. If you show how your idea benefits them, they are more likely to change their minds.

- *Misunderstanding or misinformation.* If readers are misinformed or misunderstand something about your proposal or request, they may object to it. By clarifying the misunderstanding, you can remove their reasons for resisting your message.

- *Emotional reasons.* Sometimes people object to your proposal or request because they are invested in keeping things as they are. By constructing a thorough argument, you can overcome objections based on emotional reasons.

Exercise 1: Overcoming Reader Objections

For the proposals or requests described in the following examples, generate a list of possible objections that the following groups of people might have to them:

- Your boss
- Your coworkers
- Your employees
- Your customers

1. A new policy that the organization will no longer cover postage costs for employees' personal mail

2. A proposed increase in the wellness spending account for employees who have more than five years' service from $500 a year to $750 a year; wellness spending accounts for employees with less than five years' service will remain at $500 a year

3. To qualify for full reimbursement of travel expenses, all employees must supply airline boarding passes for both departure and arrival segments of all travel taken on behalf of the organization

4. Any proposed expenses beyond the corporate credit card's $1000 limit must be approved in advance by division managers

5. All customers who pay the full amount of their bill in advance of installation are entitled to a 4 percent discount on the total cost of their purchase

How to Organize a Direct Request Message

Figure 1 is a direct request letter that asks readers to fill out and return a survey to evaluate their recent customer service experience. This message requires two actions of readers: to fill out the survey and to mail it back to the writer.

The letter uses the following organizational pattern for making a direct request:

1. Introduction:

   Gives background to request

   Delays request to avoid being abrupt

2. Asks for the requested actions

3. Gives complete information to allow the reader to act

4. Provides incentive to act

5. Counters possible objection to request

Adapt the pattern to best suit your message and context. For example, if you know your reader well and he or she is acquainted with the context for your message, you can skip the

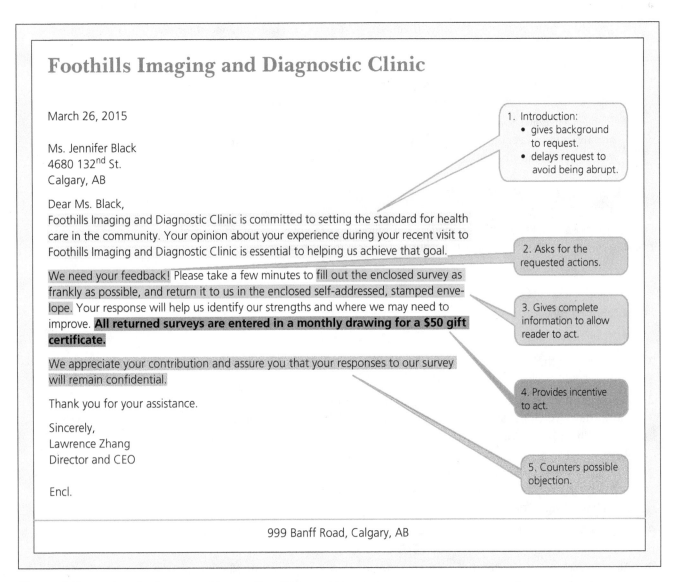

Figure 1 Example of a letter making a direct request.

introduction by making your request immediately. Similarly, if you don't anticipate any objections to your request, don't include item 5 in your message.

Exercise 2: Analyze and Revise a Direct Request Letter

Figure 2 is a sample persuasive letter aimed at convincing a book club member to make his selection for the trimester. Read and analyze the letter to answer the following questions:

1. What is the structure or organizational pattern of this letter?
2. How effective do you think the persuasive appeal is in this letter?
3. How could you reorganize the content of the letter to make it more persuasive?
4. What sentences in the letter could be revised for better cohesion, conciseness, and emphasis?

When you have identified the aspects of the letter that could be improved, revise it to make the appeal more compelling.

Book Lovers' Book Club

3/829711006
Mr. Hayden Mitchell
123 Wistler Cresc.
Fernie, BC

November 4, 2015

Dear Mr. Mitchell,
A few weeks ago we sent you a letter mentioning that you had missed your deadline of October 19 for making your book purchase for the fall trimester. Attributing your lateness to forgetfulness, we then gave you a few extra days to make your reading choice at your leisure.

All the same, we have determined that, despite the extension, you have not made your purchase of the trimester, and we are concerned at your silence.

In our view, you are an important member of the book club and your satisfaction is our priority, which is why we decided to offer you additional time to make your purchase: your new deadline of purchase is November 16. If we haven't heard from you by this new date, we will assume that you wish to receive our selection of the trimester, chosen by our reading committee and we will then expedite it to you.

We continue to keep our promise of offering the best economical choices at 40% off the public price. I invite you to review our catalogue.

As soon as possible, please telephone our toll-free customer service number at 1-800-123-4567, or consult our website at www.bookloversunite.ca. If you live near one of our stores, I invite you to pay us a visit where you will be impressed by the welcome and the exclusive products offered to members of Book Lovers' Book Club.

Be assured, Mr. Mitchell, of my best wishes,
Monica Pritchard
Director of sales and service

2244 Kings Street, Charlottetown, PEI
www.bookloversunite.ca

Figure 2 Sample persuasive letter.

Case 1★★ Define "Nonprofit Community Service Organization"

When the phone rang Sheri Safir knew the voice on the other end of the line: her accountant, Fred Johnson. Fred had helped her set up her business, including getting incorporated, and had given her valuable advice at many points along the way as her business developed.

Stuart Jenner/Shutterstock

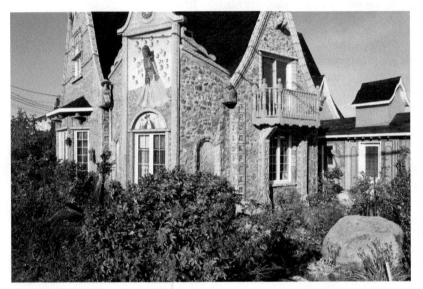

Barrett & MacKay/All Canada Photos/
Getty Images

She felt he had done good work for her and that he was a valuable member of her professional network. Because she did not have any pressing concerns with her accounts, she asked Fred if there was something she could do for him.

Fred replied that there was, in fact, a favour he would like to ask. He was on the Board of Directors of the Moonstone Valley Centre for the Arts, and the board was having a problem with the Ontario Assessment Review Board. They would not allow the Art Centre to designate itself as a nonprofit service organization. As a result, they taxed the Centre as if it were a private club. So the organization was paying significantly higher taxes than it would if it were a community service organization. Fred was hoping that as language expert at Tech Writing Solutions, Sheri might write a letter to the review board explaining that the Arts Centre *does* qualify as a nonprofit service organization.

Sheri replied enthusiastically—this was something she was good at. She had a few questions, though. For one, why did the review board say the Arts Centre was a private members' club? Didn't it run art classes and other programs for the general public? Could anyone sign up for the classes?

Fred replied that, yes, it actually ran a large number of classes for all ages, from painting to sculpture to pottery. The classes drew people from across the community, and some teachers were not even members of the Arts Centre, although many were. It was expensive to pay the higher taxes, and Fred noted that the Centre was finding it increasingly difficult to operate with that designation, so it had become a priority to change it this year.

At this point Sheri was certain she wanted to help. She asked Fred about the timeline for the project: how fast did he need the letter? His answer was October 23; the board of directors would meet the Assessment Review Board in Toronto on the 24th. He asked whether that date would work given Sheri's busy schedule. He also noted that the board would like to review a draft a day or two earlier so they could ensure it contained all the relevant information needed to make the argument.

Sheri saw that this timeline gave her three weeks to write the letter. She offered to send a draft by October 20, and Fred replied that date was perfect. He also noted that the Arts Centre wanted to reimburse her for her time and asked her for her rates for this project.

Sheri replied that she would not charge for this project because it gave her a chance to give back to the community. She explained that she enjoyed helping community organizations, especially when they contributed to the welfare of people in the community the way Moonstone Valley Centre for the Arts certainly did. In one of her previous lives as a teacher, she noted, she had taught service-learning courses, so she knew how

THE LEGISLATION
ASSESSMENT ACT
ONTARIO REGULATION 282/98
NON PROFIT SERVICE ORGANIZATION

3(1)   The residential class consists of the following:
        2. Land not used for residential purposes that is:
           iv Land owned and occupied by *a non profit service organization,*
           a non profit private club, a non profit cultural organization or a non
           profit recreational sports club, other than land used as a golf course
           or ski resort.

        2.1 "Service Organization" means an organization whose
        primary function is to provide services to
        promote the welfare of the community
        and not only to benefit its members

> Green highlighted text indicates the term being defined.

> Yellow highlighted text indicates the definitions of the term, "non profit service."

Our Belief
The Moonstone Valley Centre for the Arts meets this qualification fully.

Figure 3 Text from the Ontario Assessment Act, Regulation 282/98, defining what constitutes a nonprofit service organization.
Source: Quoted from Ontario Assessment Act

such organizations contribute to the general well-being of the community. She explained that drafting the letter would be fun.

Fred was thrilled with Sheri's offer. He said that his administrative assistant Delia would email the regulations from the Assessment Review Board. That would give Sheri the exact wording to use in her letter.

Sheri hung up the phone and turned back to her computer. A few hours later she received Delia's email (see Figure 3).

ANALYSIS: ARGUE MOONSTONE'S TAX STATUS

The letter that Sheri Safir will write is a persuasive message that includes a direct request. She needs the Assessment Review Board to reconsider its ruling. The board members have ruled that the Moonstone Valley Centre for the Arts is a private club rather than a nonprofit service organization. Sheri's goal is to change the board's mind by showing how the centre serves the needs of nonmember citizens of the Moonstone Valley area.

Sheri Safir wants the Board to do two things for her: 1) change their minds about the Arts Centre, and 2) act by revising the centre's designation. Next, Sheri Safir must persuade the Arts Centre Board of Directors to rename the organization. As mentioned earlier in this module, persuasion involves getting readers to do more than think: it requires them to act.

Although the standard advice is to ask readers to explain any objections that they might have to your proposed course of action, sometimes it is not possible to do so. Certainly, Sheri Safir cannot because she is not acquainted with members of the Assessment Review Board. In this case, she needs to analyze her readers and anticipate their possible objections. Sheri assumes these attitudes by her readers on the review board:

LO 2 Organize direct request and diagnostic or problem-solving messages

- Not acting means more tax revenue for the board members' employer, the Ontario government

- They will consider an opposing viewpoint
- They want to do their jobs as members of the review board properly and well
- They will find Sheri a credible speaker from her position as president of Tech Writing Solutions, a consulting firm that does communications contract work for the Ontario government

To anticipate objections they might have, Sheri analyzes the three main areas where most people's objections are rooted:

- *Practical reasons.* Sheri quickly realizes that the primary practical objection her readers might have to her argument is also the crux of it: that nonprofit groups that provide benefits primarily for their members are not service organizations. She needs to show readers how the Arts Centre serves a much broader community base than just centre members.

- *Misunderstanding or misinformation.* Sheri knows that her readers do not understand the ways in which arts organizations provide community outreach to young people and how outlets for artistic expression can make a lasting impact on young people's lives. By explaining the less tangible aspects of experiences with fine arts, Sheri can show her readers that the Centre for the Arts provides valuable service to the community.

- *Emotional reasons.* The Assessment Review Board has recently received a Ministry directive to apply the definition of "service" more selectively to private members clubs. As a consequence, some board members may resist Sheri's persuasive appeal because they want to use her case to fulfill the Ministry directive. To ensure that her organization is granted the "service" designation, Sheri must provide detailed evidence to show how Moonstone Valley Centre for the Arts completely fits the definition of "nonprofit service organization." By constructing a thorough argument, she can overcome this particular type of objection.

Professional Communication Assignments

1. Write the Letter for the Moonstone Valley Centre for the Arts

Assume the role of Sheri Safir and draft a letter for Fred Johnson explaining how the Moonstone Valley Centre for the Arts fits the Ontario government's definition of a non-profit service organization. In your letter, include appropriate evidence to support your claims about the work that the Centre for the Arts does, and make as strong a case as you can for the centre fulfilling the Assessment Review Board's own definition of the term. Use the information in this module to help you develop a convincing case for the centre.

Purpose: To convince members of the Ontario Assessment Review Board to designate Moonstone Valley Centre for the Arts as a nonprofit service organization

Audience: Members of the Ontario Assessment Review Board, who rule on, among other things, whether a nonprofit organization fulfils a service function in its community

Genre: Letter

2. Write a Persuasive Memo

Write an email to the board of the Moonstone Valley Centre for the Arts in which you argue that they should change their name to better reflect their community mission as a nonprofit service organization. In your letter, suggest a new name for the organization and provide arguments to support your position that the new name would be an improvement. Anticipate opposition from the board: they have used the current name for over 20 years, and it has a lot of brand awareness in the region. Using the information in this module, develop an argument that should persuade them to agree to your request.

Purpose: To show the board how they will benefit from having a new name and identity for the organization

Audience: The board is the primary audience, but members of the organization are an important secondary audience

Genre: Letter

DIAGNOSTIC OR PROBLEM-SOLVING PERSUASIVE MESSAGES

A second type of persuasive message is a diagnostic or problem-solving message, which identifies a problem that you and your reader share to which you are proposing a solution. You have two primary aims: 1) to convince readers that the solution is good and 2) to get them to behave differently to solve the problem. The main challenge to writing this type of message is showing your readers how your proposed solution will benefit them. You must demonstrate that you and the reader are mutually benefited by solving the problem. This approach draws readers into the message to improve the chances they will consider your solution. As when you are writing a direct request message, you should also consider whether readers might have objections to the solution that you propose. Review the previous discussion on overcoming objections for strategies you can use to analyze the rhetorical situation and anticipate possible reader objections.

LO 4 Demonstrate that the solution will benefit both the reader and the organization

Diagnostic Persuasive Message

The email in Figure 4 is a diagnostic persuasive message. Read the message, noting the annotations that highlight the organizational pattern used to develop and present the argument. You must understand your reader's perspective to anticipate possible objections to

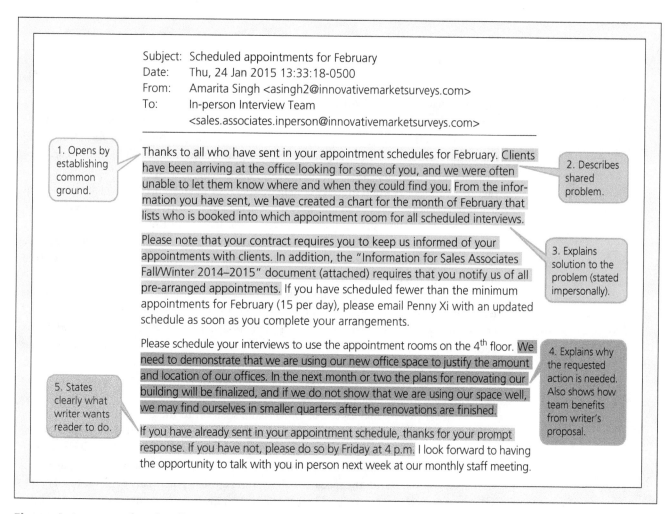

Figure 4 An example of a diagnostic persuasive email message asking employees to use new office space to conduct market survey research.

your proposal or idea as well as to demonstrate how both of you benefit from your solution. For example, in Figure 4, Ms. Singh notes in the third paragraph that the amount of space that their division receives is directly related to how often they all use the space. For the survey research team to continue to enjoy their spacious office area, they need to schedule their work in it. If the space appears to upper management to be underused, it will be reallocated to another division. Ms. Singh reminds them that they all benefit if they all use the office space, the underlying goal of her message.

The message in Figure 4 uses a standard pattern of organization for diagnostic or problem-solving messages. Address these topics in this order:

1. Open by establishing or building common ground between writer and readers

2. Describe the problem shared by you and readers

3. Explain the solution to the problem (use neutral language to keep the discussion impersonal)

4. Explain why the proposed action is necessary and how readers benefit from this solution

5. Explain clearly what you want readers to do

For complex persuasive situations, you may need to devote a paragraph to each of these steps; in more straightforward situations, a sentence or two may accomplish your goal. Adapt the pattern to fit your purpose and audience as you write.

Case 2★★ Please Hang Your Winter Gear in the New Company Cloakroom

Gerry Michaels had asked Adam Zeleski to solve the winter coat problem before Gerry got back from his sales trip. Gerry wanted him to figure out the best solution and write a memo to everyone telling them to fall in line. Gerry was heading to the airport for a week-long trip around the southern United States to line up new customers for Elite Swimwear. Elite Swimwear had surprised everyone by becoming a successful designer and manufacturer of high-end swimwear, when industry commentators swore that Canadian-designed and manufactured fashion couldn't compete globally. Located in the thriving city of Barrie, Ontario, its success wasn't obviously assured, although it was located just north of Toronto and just south of the two largest lake and cottage districts in the province. However, through the hard work, shrewd business sense, and design flair of the co-owners, Elite Swimwear was a flourishing (if improbable) success.

One of the problems Barrie had was snow—lots of it. Given the amount of snow that fell on Barrie most winters, many of Elite Swimwear's employees left their cars at home and cross-country skied, snowshoed, or drove their snowmobiles to work. Snowmobiles in the parking lot instead of cars weren't a problem, but storage of all the employees' winter gear associated with these modes of transportation was a problem. The coat racks were groaning under the weight of snowsuits, scarves, ski pants and coats; and boots and shoes everywhere made walking through the office difficult.

As he left, Gerry had asked Adam to find a solution to the outerwear problem before someone injured themselves falling over someone else's ski boots. Adam had considered several solutions, including installing an army of coat hooks and boot racks along the hallway leading to the company offices. A major objection to this solution, he conceded, was that, although workable, it would clutter the spacious hallways and create a potentially negative first impression for visitors to the company. Then Adam had an inspiration: an old storage closet at the end of the hallway could be cleared out and made into a cloakroom. Coat hooks could hold the snowsuits, ski pants, and winter coats; a shelf above the coat hooks could store helmets, hats, and gloves; and a series of low racks could support boots and shoes, organizing them and raising them off the floor so that they could dry quickly. A bonus was that one sweep of the cleaner's mop could clean up the dirt and snow as it dried off the footwear. Employees, who entered mainly through the front door, could strip off their traveling gear and change into their street shoes in the cloakroom before making their way to their desks or the plant. They could even build a rack for skis and a series of hooks for snowshoes in one corner.

Adam proposed the solution to Rachel Fielder, company CEO, who enthusiastically endorsed the idea. A quick phone call to Gerry secured his approval. Gerry also directed Adam to a carpentry company that had completed several earlier jobs for the company. MacDuff Framing and Carpentry started on the project right away. Before Adam knew it, the cloakroom was nearly ready for use. All that remained was to announce the new facility to company employees. Adam thought it was the kind of message that should be spread orally, but Gerry wanted every employee to receive an email directing them to the cloakroom and explaining any rules associated with it, and he asked Adam to draft the email.

Exercise 3: Overcoming Reader Objections: Using the Company Cloakroom

As noted earlier, reader objections generally originate from three areas:

- Practical reasons
- Misunderstanding or misinformation
- Emotional reasons

1. Using these three general areas, brainstorm a list of objections that employees at Elite Swimwear might have for using the new company cloakroom. To do this, you will need to determine and evaluate the perspectives of the different groups of employees. First, determine whether office staff, sewing machine operators, cutters, and so on may have differing perspectives. Also consider whether their mode of transportation (car, snowmobile, snowshoe, cross-country skis) might affect their perspectives on using the cloakroom.

2. Next, generate a list of benefits that employees and the company will share if everyone uses the cloakroom. You can develop these benefits based on the counters to the objections that you listed in item 1.

3. Using both your list of objections and your list of benefits, generate a corresponding list of arguments or reasons that you could use to overcome the employees' various objections.

4. As your instructor directs, write a one- to two-page memo to the instructor that summarizes the best ideas from your three lists. Expand the ideas into mini-arguments, as appropriate, to help you see how these ideas can help you better reach different segments of your audience of employees at Elite Swimwear (for example, will sewing machine operators have different objections from the office staff?)

ANALYSIS: PLEASE USE THE CLOAKROOM

Adam knew that several of the company's employees would probably object to using the new cloakroom, so before he began drafting the memo to inform them of the new policy, he spent a few minutes generating a list of possible objections based on the three areas that generally gave rise to objections: practical reasons, misunderstanding or emotional reasons. He suspected that most of the objections that his coworkers might have to using the cloakroom would be practical or emotional reasons such as fear of personal items being stolen or resistance to changing habits. He would have to counter such objections in his explanation so he jotted down some potential solutions he could offer to relieve his readers' concerns.

Once he was ready to begin writing, he identified one or two possible points he could make to establish common ground with his coworkers/readers. It was going to be easy to describe the problem, Adam decided, because nearly everyone had complained about tripping over boots or skis. They would all understand the necessity of maintaining a safe working environment. He decided he would probably not need much detail to describe the solution because most of his readers were already familiar with the renovation and its purpose.

Adam knew that he also needed to highlight for his readers several ways in which they were all going to benefit from having the new cloakroom available, so everyone would finish by feeling good about the cloakroom and happy to make use of it.

> Professional Communication Assignments

3. Write the Email Announcing the Opening of the New Winter Wear Cloak Room

Writing as Adam Zeleski, draft the email message to all employees regarding the use of the new employee cloakroom. Because employees are used to the current system where three or four of them share a coat tree near their desks, some have voiced concerns about not being able to keep an eye on their belongings and equipment while they work. Other employees who drive to work have a minimum of items to hang up, and they want to continue the current system, since they did not cause the problem the cloakroom is designed to fix. Rachel and Gerry have drafted a list of rules to communicate to all employees about cloakroom use (see Figure 5). Include those rules, as appropriate, in your draft.

Purpose: To convince all employees at Elite Swimwear to hang their winter outerwear in the new company cloakroom

Audience: All employees at Elite Swimwear, including designers, cutters, sewing machine operators, and office staff, who may or may not snowmobile, snowshoe, or cross-country ski to work regularly

Genre: Email

4. Request an Exception

You are an Elite Swimwear employee who works in the company plant. Your spouse drops you off at work every day, so you do not have the winter gear that has contributed to the clutter around the premises. You want to be able to leave your coat on the hook near your workstation so that you can quickly put it on when you have to supervise incoming or outgoing shipments, which occur at least three times a week (and sometimes more often). You have found that when you have to walk to the front of the plant to get your coat each time, it slows down this step of production. You spoke to Adam Zeleski about an exemption from using the cloakroom, but he said you would have to make your case in writing to Gerry Michaels and Rachel Fielder yourself because they had said "no exemptions." Make your case.

Purpose: To explain how using the cloakroom will inhibit you from doing your job and to offer an alternative solution that solves the problem

Audience: Gerry Michaels, president of Elite Swimwear, and Rachel Fielder, CEO of Elite Swimwear, both of whom now hang their winter wear in the new cloakroom

Genre: Email

Rule for Cloakroom Use

All employees will use the cloakroom to store their outerwear while they are working at Elite Swimwear.

All footwear should go on the lower racks and not on the floor.

All helmets, etc. should be stored on the shelves above the coat hooks.

All equipment must be stored using the racks and hooks provided for that equipment.

Employees may store shoes on the boot racks for use when they arrive each day.

Figure 5 Rules of cloakroom use.

MODULE SUMMARY

- Direct request messages overcome objections by giving practical reasons, clarifying misunderstandings or misinformation, and responding to readers' emotions.

- Organize a direct request message by giving the background to the problem, asking for the solution, giving the reader the information they need to act, creating incentives for the reader, and countering objections.

- Diagnostic or problem-solving persuasive messages aim to convince readers that the proposed solution is good and to get readers to behave differently to solve the problem.

- Organize a diagnostic message by establishing common ground, describing the shared problem, explaining the solution to the problem and why the requested action is needed, and showing how readers benefit from writer's proposal.

Module 10

Proposals

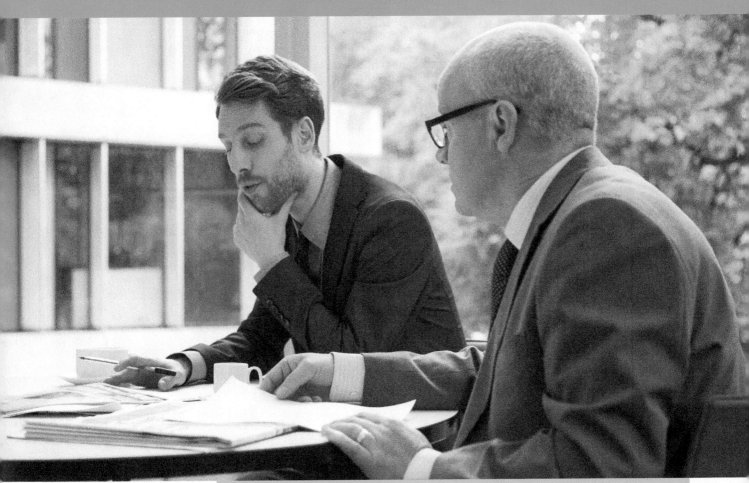

LEARNING OUTCOMES

LO 1 Think of proposals primarily as persuasive documents

LO 2 Use logic, credibility, and emotion to convince your audience to accept your proposal

LO 3 Structure unsolicited proposals using a problem–solution model

LO 4 Organize and format a proposal document

GETTING STARTED

Proposals share a common purpose: they attempt to persuade people that your idea is a good one. Proposals range from high stakes ("Will you marry me?") to much lower (a text suggesting you get together with some friends at a bar). Even résumés are a kind of proposal: you are proposing that a company hire you. All of these share the essence of written proposals in business contexts: a good idea that you try to get others to join in on.

To write a successful proposal at work, you need to establish that you are worth listening to (credibility), create logical reasons, and generate enthusiasm for your idea. Solicited proposals generally state the problem that needs to be solved; these kinds of proposals argue in favour of your solution to the problem. Unsolicited proposals, however, must first establish that there is a problem before identifying how to solve it. As you prepare to write a proposal document, make sure you know which of these two kinds of arguments you are writing.

WRITING PERSUASIVE PROPOSALS

Writing a good proposal is writing a persuasive proposal. Proposals are all about convincing your reader to say yes. Proposals present an idea or plan to do something, often to solve a problem or provide a service or product. In a competitive situation, you have to show how your idea, solution, and abilities are superior to those being offered by the writers of competing proposals. **Solicited proposals** (where someone has requested proposals be submitted—that is, has circulated a Request for Proposals, or RFP) generally result in a competitive situation, where only one or two successful ones will be chosen, but not always. For example, in Case 1 the president has distributed an RFP for internal proposals. In this case, if the ideas proposed are all appropriate, they will all be accepted. In other noncompetitive situations, you may be submitting a proposal that you were motivated to write by observing a problem that needs a solution. This is an **unsolicited proposal**. In this case, your reader is not expecting the proposal, so you will have to convince her or him that the problem you have identified really does exist and is significant enough to need a solution. In situations where every proposal is likely to be accepted, you are writing a persuasive document because you still need to show readers that your idea is worthwhile and you have the expertise to complete the project.

When someone has requested a proposal, you won't have to convince the requester to accept it. Nevertheless, RFP set criteria for acceptable projects, so you will need to show how your team's proposed projects are suitable and fit those criteria. If you are suggesting an activity that doesn't fit the criteria well you will need to make a well-supported argument to show why the requester should consider your idea. By presenting a clear, well-developed argument, you could persuade readers that your idea is still valid and worth pursuing.

PROPOSAL WRITING AND PERSUASION

Proposals achieve persuasion when they convince readers to act: to select your proposal from among competing solutions to their problem, approve your proposed project, and get started. To persuade readers in a proposal, use a logical argument supported by evidence, a demonstration of your credibility, and an emotional appeal to help readers feel the importance of your argument. This section shows you how and when to use these appeals in a proposal to make it as effective as possible.

Logic

Logic refers to the series of claims and supporting evidence that you develop and organize to discuss your solution to the problem. In the case of a competitive solicited proposal, the point of the argument is to show readers how the writer can develop and deliver the solution described. The logic should also explain the benefits of the writer's particular solution and emphasize how this solution is superior to other possible solutions.

LO 1 Think of proposals primarily as persuasive documents

Solicited proposals: Proposals that have been requested by an organization via Request for Proposal (RFP)

Unsolicited proposal: A proposal that you prepare without being asked to by a potential client

LO 2 Use logic, credibility, and emotion to convince your audience to accept your proposal

Credibility

Credibility is essential in a proposal because it can only persuade readers if they trust the writer and respect what he or she has to say. You can create trust and respect on the part of readers in four ways:

1. Show readers that you are knowledgeable about your subject matter
2. Include a thorough and detailed discussion of the issues relevant to the topic
3. Provide details about your qualifications and the resources available to you on this project
4. Submit a work schedule that is realistic and detailed

Show Your Knowledge of the Topic   Part of your credibility in a proposal grows out of the logic of your argument: if your ideas are reasonable and your evidence provides solid support, then your readers will grow to trust that you are competent and trustworthy. When you use some of the vocabulary appropriate to your topic, you also demonstrate your knowledge and "membership" in the group of experts on that topic. It is important, however, to strike a balance between using technical terms appropriate to the subject and the knowledge of your readers, who may not be experts in that area. Define technical terms and use only the vocabulary you need.

Include a Thorough Discussion of Issues Relevant to the Topic   You also demonstrate your expertise and trustworthiness on your topic by accurately presenting the right amount of information about your topic. Be concise while including details that your reader both needs and wants to know. State and develop ideas appropriately and then stop. When readers find what they need to know in your discussion, they will feel that you are a credible speaker on your topic.

Provide Details About Your Qualifications and Resources   Another aspect of your credibility is the experience, expertise, and track record that you bring to the project. Describing your background and your record of success on previous projects instils confidence in your reader about the proposed project. Include details that build your credibility by showing that you have the skills and the resources to successfully complete this project as well. For example, if you need expertise in an area that you don't currently have, you could name contacts you already possess who will provide that expertise for you. When you show that you can anticipate potential problems as well as access the connections that allow you to supply missing elements, you build a strong ethical appeal that improves the persuasive power of your proposal.

Submit a Realistic and Detailed Work Schedule   The fourth area that helps build credibility is in the work schedule you provide with the proposal. Take the time you need to accurately and thoroughly project the various stages of the project. When readers assess your planning, they see that you have thought through the project and accurately evaluated the time it will take to complete. If you show that you have a reasonable plan for hitting your deadlines, you are more likely to convince readers that you *will*, in fact, hit those deadlines.

Emotional Appeal

The emotional appeal in a proposal refers to the legitimate use of readers' emotions or feelings to engage their minds and build assent. Persuasion is not complete until readers do more than say, "Yes, you have a point." Detached interest is not persuasion. You want readers to move beyond uncommitted interest to actually doing something, even changing their behaviour. In the case of proposal writing, you want readers to select your proposal, approve your ideas, and allow you to start the project.

Emotion is the main tool that helps readers become invested in your project and that moves them from interest to assent or action. It's not unethical to show readers why your ideas are important and set up opportunities for them to become invested in your proposal, but it is unethical to use emotional appeals that are unconnected to your subject matter to evoke a response in your reader. For example, advertisements that propose purchasing a product as a solution to consumers' insecurities (in other words, "drink this beer to become more attractive to others") aim to manipulate viewers into choosing their product. In a proposal, you should focus on showing readers how the solution you propose will benefit them and be superior to other possible solutions. If you make readers feel the truth of your statements, you are likely to persuade them to choose or approve your proposal.

Here are two ways to create an effective emotional appeal in a proposal:

- Use concrete examples and vivid details
- Incorporate figurative language, including comparisons, where appropriate

Case 1★★ Why Our Organization Should Sponsor a Dragon-Boat Racing Team

Paul Steinberg looked down at his notes and announced that the last item on the meeting agenda was that corporate head office wanted each store to put together a proposal outlining ideas for community service projects for next year. Eyebrows raised around the table. Every year the employees at Douglas Mountain Recreational Equipment (DMRE) devoted several weekends to raising money for a local charity. In the past, the employees at each store decided what group they wanted to support independently of the head office, so the request for proposals was a new initiative.

Graves

Paul explained that Doug Black, the president of DMRE, felt that the company was straying too far from the corporate image in what employees were choosing to support. For example, last year one store in Southwestern Ontario did a series of fundraising projects for the local cancer centre. No one actually objected to them supporting such a good cause, but Black had decided this directive would encourage everyone to pursue more sports or fitness-related activities that better fit with the company's vision and mission. Paul explained that this change made sense because that is what DMRE did—sell recreational equipment. Black felt it was important to show company employees living active and healthy as well as helping lifestyles. Paul caught glimpses of a few eyes rolling, but he wasn't surprised. His team was a group of particularly independent-minded young people. He knew they enjoyed giving back to the community, but he also knew some of them would resent this interference from the company president.

Julia Ke was an enthusiastic and energetic member of his team who was particularly adept at identifying groups in the community who most needed support. Paul knew that some of the projects they had taken on in the last year or two were the result of her instigation, like putting a new roof on the Denise Carr Women's Shelter. However, these projects had also been tenuously related to DMRE's mission. After much discussion, the team had decided the shelter's need outweighed corporate's preference. He was bracing himself for her reaction, but she surprised him.

"I don't think that's out of line," she said, "since Doug gives us time off for these projects. If he's going to compensate us the way he does, I guess it makes sense that he should have some say in what we do. But I *do* think reroofing the women's shelter last year was worthwhile, even if the public didn't associate our work with DMRE." Julia then asked the group what they wanted to do this year that was more recreational-equipment related.

Paul suggested that the group brainstorm some ideas and see what most people were in favour of doing. He pointed out that once the group had picked out a project they would have to submit a written proposal to the president. A few groans met these words. Paul explained that the president wanted a written proposal so that he could give feedback to ensure that it fit with the company's goals.

"I know what we can do," exclaimed Frances. Everyone turned to her. "Let's sponsor a dragon-boat racing meet! That would be so much fun! We could form our own team, but also invite some of the businesses around town to start teams and compete with us. We can also invite racing teams from other cities in the area as well. We can use the meet to raise money to support something like the Boys and Girls Club. They organize sports activities for underprivileged kids in the city. That should fit Mr. Black's criteria. We could hold the meet right here on Clear Lake."

Tran thought that was a cool idea. He explained that his cousin was on a dragon-boat racing team that practiced on Lake Winnipegosis. He had also seen one that trained out of Nanaimo Harbour, and he said that it looked like a lot of fun.

Kelly suggested that they could run or sponsor a marathon or a rock-climbing event for adolescents. Several other ideas were quickly tossed out, and the meeting quickly transformed into an uproar as staff members threw out suggestions and spoke over one another. Paul called the meeting back to order and asked for a volunteer to write the proposal. Julia raised her hand meekly. He thanked Julia before instructing everyone else to email their suggestions to her. Julia would compile a list, send it around for everyone to vote on, and then take the top four favourites, research them, and outline how they might work as service projects for next year.

Professional Communication Assignments

1. Proposing Three Service Projects for the DMRE Sales Team

Take on the persona of one member of the Douglas Mountain Recreational Equipment sales team and write a proposal describing three possible service projects that the sales team could undertake for the following year. This case is not obviously set in any particular region of the country, so locate it in your area and develop three of the ideas proposed by members of the sales team for service projects that are appropriate to your location (see Figure 1). Be sure to select ideas that are related to sports and recreational activities, as requested by the company president.

Direct your proposal to Doug Black, the president of DMRE. Of course, Paul Steinberg is your initial and secondary audience.

Use all available resources (internet, library, yellow pages, etc.) to research your three activities so that you can write a clear and complete description of them in your proposal. Use the discussion in this module on writing proposals to help you develop your ideas, organize your arguments, and present them clearly, concisely, and convincingly.

Audience: Doug Black, the president of DMRE

Purpose: To persuade Black to approve your proposal

Genre: Proposal

Dragon-boat racing meet to raise money for a local group (need suggestions)

Hold a marathon

Organize a rock climbing event for adolescents and young adults

Participate in local walking/running/biking event sponsored by someone else

Organize spring cleanup drive for Clear Lake (or Thunder River)

Hold mountain bike ride to raise money for low-income families in city

Hold a golf tournament to raise money for local group (need suggestions)

Habitat for Humanity—help build some houses?

Set up a program to collect used sports equipment at the store to donate to local children's groups or underprivileged young people

Organize and run Environmental Awareness weekend at the mall

Figure 1 Sales team suggestions for possible service projects.

2. Write a Proposal That Suggests Service Projects That Do Not Fit the Corporate Image

Writing as one of the employees in Case 1, draft a proposal in which you suggest three service projects that aren't clearly related to fitness and recreation. In this case you are going to have to make well-developed and supported arguments as to why your ideas are appropriate and should be approved even though they aren't directly related to the president's recent mandate.

Use all available research sources to collect information about the three projects you propose and situate them in your local area so that your evidence and arguments are concrete, specific, and compelling. In your proposal, focus on showing Mr. Black how these projects will benefit both DMRE and the local community. If you want to show how the projects are indirectly related to fitness and recreation, go ahead.

Audience: Doug Black, the president of DMRE

Purpose: To persuade Black to approve your proposal

Genre: Proposal

ANALYSIS: DMRE SUPPORTS AN ACTIVE LOCAL COMMUNITY

Use Concrete Examples and Vivid Details Use descriptive verbs and adjectives to create a compelling experience for readers. Include information that helps to make your subject matter come alive. For example, if Julia Ke is arguing that the proposal to organize a spring cleanup of local waterways is most appropriate because it fits the company environmental stewardship program, she can make her argument more or less compelling by adding or omitting vivid details. Of these two versions, which one do you find most interesting?

Version 1: We propose to organize a weekend spring cleanup scheduled for April to invite community members to join the staff in collecting garbage from the waterways around our city. This cleanup project will fit well with DMRE's environmental stewardship program.

Version 2: This year we will invite community members to don their rubber gloves and boots to join us in our 1st Annual Waterways Spring Cleanup in April. Armed with decomposable garbage bags, rakes, and shovels, we will gather on the shores of Clear Lake, Thunder River, and Burrow Creek and work together to restore the pristine beauty of our local waterways. This project represents a new and innovative direction for our team, which has not, in the past, participated in DMRE's environmental stewardship program.

Although version 2 is longer, it includes more information about the proposed project and some specific details that help readers better imagine the shape the activity will take. Black will also know which waterways the team plans to work on and the type of work they intend to do during the cleanup (pick up garbage, etc.).

Incorporate Figurative Language, Including Comparisons, Where Appropriate
Although many people associate figurative language with literary texts and poetry, it is equally useful in business and professional communication. You can use apt comparisons as well as rhetorical figures to help readers feel the significance of your ideas. For example, of these two statements which create the most impact on you, as a reader?

> *Version 1*: We will all enjoy the garbage-free banks of the local lakes and rivers later in the summer.

> *Version 2*: On those hot, sultry afternoons in July, our novice canoe classes will paddle quietly *like early settlers first come to this area, unspoiled by human intrusion.*

The simile, *like early settlers first come to this area, unspoiled by human intrusion*, expands on the verb *enjoy* from version 1, painting for readers the picture of local waterways as they were before widescale human development, which has made necessary the proposed environmental cleanup. The simile links Julia's argument for this being a worthwhile project to the company's image as environmentally conscious. It also invokes the company's adherence to the "Leave No Trace" principles of environmental ethics in a way that should be an effective emotional appeal to the company president.

HOW TO WRITE UNSOLICITED PROPOSALS

LO 3 Structure unsolicited proposals using a problem–solution model

Unsolicited proposals present different rhetorical challenges to one that your boss or instructor has asked you to write. One important part of such a proposal is showing readers that the problem exists and is significant enough to need solving. You can define *significance* in financial terms—for example, the cost or lost income that the problem represents for the organization. You can also define significance in terms relating to corporate image—for example, the problem generates bad publicity or public criticism for the company. The point is that you want to show readers that the problem is an issue and it needs a solution. Choose whatever terms you think will have the best impact to persuade your reader.

The second part of the challenge in writing this type of proposal is describing your solution to the problem and showing readers why it is the best option. What may be obvious to you is not necessarily obvious to readers, so explain what makes it the best solution. Show readers how your solution will benefit them and/or the organization. When readers share your view of the problem, they are more likely to agree with your analysis and conclusion.

Use this pattern to organize the argument in this type of proposal:

1. What is the problem? (Define and explain it)
2. Why should we solve this problem? (Why is it significant?)
3. What should we do to solve this problem? (Describe your solution)
4. Why should we choose the solution you propose? (Emphasize its benefits)

By the end of the proposal, you should have convincingly answered all of these questions.

Alyssa Klein-Moore looked at the two forms that she had pulled out of the drawer. Both of them had "Client Information" printed at the top, but a quick glance told her the questions on each were slightly different. She searched the form for a publication date to determine whether one was a more up-to-date version of the other. No such luck. The instructions didn't indicate when to use each form either. She would have to ask someone, again. She snuck a peek at Mrs. Chato, who was waiting patiently for her to hand over the form. Alyssa looked around the office but everyone was busy. Surinder was on the phone, Jorge was meeting with a client, and she remembered that Munir was on a coffee run. Alyssa's training would have been much smoother if she had a training manual so that she didn't have to ask someone about everything.

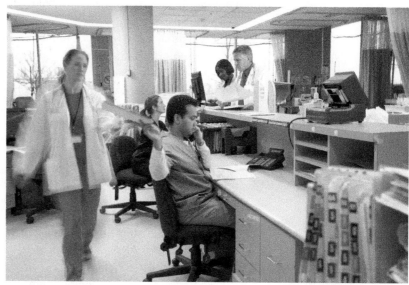

UpperCut Images/Getty Images

Alyssa liked working as an administrative assistant in Hamilton Dental Clinic, but without any training procedure or manual, it was hard and delicate work finding out what she needed to know to do her job. Everyone was so busy that she constantly had to interrupt them to ask simple questions. She was jotting everything down that she learned in her notebook, but the list of new jobs seemed endless.

A suggestion came back to her that her dad had made on the phone the previous evening when she was describing her first two days to him. "Why don't you offer to make a training manual for the office?" he had said. "That way you can learn how to do everything, you will have a reference if you forget something, and it will be useful for the next person they hire who won't have to rely on everyone else in the office to teach them the way you have to do."

She wondered if the dentists in the office would agree to her spending some time putting the manual together. Would they object to paying her to do it? It would be more productive if she could look things up rather than waiting until someone was free to ask. The manual could actually save the practice money in the long run because other new employees could use it too. They could even take it home and study it at night so that they could figure out in advance where to find the information quickly and efficiently.

Surinder hung up the phone and turned to Alyssa, indicating which form should go to Mrs. Chato. Surinder noted that the office really should get rid of the old files, but everyone was too busy to clear them out. There was no way Alyssa could do this during normal working hours—maybe coming in on a Sunday would be necessary.

"What we need is an employee training manual," said Alyssa. "Do you think Dr. Watson would be willing to let me put one together, Surinder?"

Surinder thought that this was a good idea. She paused for a moment and then suggested that rather than talking to him, Alyssa should write up a proposal. That way Alyssa could explain the financial advantages thoroughly—calculate how many hours the established staff lose helping new employees, how many weeks it takes for new people to become completely productive, and how a manual could shorten that time. Then Dr. Watson could circulate the proposal among the other doctors. Surinder pointed out that Alyssa was likely to get approval fairly quickly if she could show how the manual would save the practice time and money.

Just before lunch, Alyssa managed to seize a few moments to talk to Dr. Watson about her idea. He agreed that the office could definitely use a more systematic method of training new staff.

"We also need to see some numbers," he noted. "If you can show us why a manual is the best solution and also quantify the savings for us, I should think the other dentists would be receptive to making the training manual a part of your duties during down periods in the office until the project is finished. Yes, I do think the written rationale is the way to go here."

Exercise 1: Identify the Problem

Part A: Use Case 2 as the basis for the discussion in this exercise. With one or two of your classmates, draft some ideas that could be useful in writing an unsolicited proposal for Dr. Watson. Generate a list of statements or phrases that help you 1) define the problem that Alyssa identifies at Hamilton Dental Clinic, and 2) demonstrate the significance of the problem.

Remember to define the problem in terms that will make sense to the dentists at the clinic, rather than to Alyssa herself or some of the other staff members. When you are discussing the significance of the problem, generate as many different terms of significance as you can to help you view the problem from many different angles (for example, financial, customer service, corporate image, etc.). The more angles you take, the better you can consider which terms of significance will be most compelling for Dr. Watson and his colleagues.

Part B: When you feel that your discussion has exhausted the possibilities for analyzing the problem and its significance, use some of the statements or phrases generated during your discussion to write one-paragraph drafts of your argument for the proposal. Add evidence where appropriate to support your claims. As you draft, pay attention to your credibility as a writer for this project and the emotional appeal that is a companion to your logical argument.

Exercise 2: Describe a Solution

With one or two of your classmates, discuss Case 2, paying particular attention to the range of solutions that are possible to solve the problem that Alyssa Klein-Moore (or your group from Exercise 1) identified at Hamilton Dental Clinic.

Cover these topics in your discussions and make notes of useful ideas that are suggested:

1. What solutions are possible to train new employees at Hamilton Dental Clinic?
2. Which solution(s) is/are most appropriate for Hamilton Dental Clinic?
3. In your group's estimation, which are the top two solutions to the problem as you or Alyssa Klein-Moore defines it and why?

In your discussion, you should aim to generate as many possible solutions to the problem as you can. When you have created a list that gives you a range of interesting possible solutions (expand on those suggested in Figure 2), evaluate each suggestion with an emphasis on how well it fits the context of Hamilton Dental Clinic.

Possible formats for training information:

Manual (print: easily updated, may become outdated quickly; electronic: easily updated, easily accessed, easily lost if employees can't find file; new employees can print off .pdf to take home or access on home computer . . . what else?)

Video (problem: production values; is this best way to present information? Need a script, video camera; how easy is this for new employees to use? View on computer screen? No way to make print copies . . . what else?)

Wiki (electronic entries, easily updated, downside is employee knowledge needed to use it. . . what else?)

What other new technology could I use? (must take into account demographic of employees, technical abilities, etc.)

Figure 2 What is the best format or genre for training materials?

For example, what sense did you get of the demographics of the staff working at the clinic? How appropriate does your group think a wiki might be for new and existing employees at the clinic? Decide on the top two solutions and explain what makes you rate them as the best.

Exercise 3: Describe the Benefits of the Solution

Using one of the top two solutions that your group chose in Exercise 2 and through discussion with one or two classmates:

1. Generate a list of benefits that you can see in the solution that your group chose. (Make sure to consider ways that the solution benefits readers and the organization as a whole. Designate someone in the group to record the useful ideas that come out of the discussion.)

2. Evaluate how effective you think the benefits that your group has generated will be on the various potential readers of your proposal.

3. Develop the argument for each benefit by drafting (collaboratively or individually) a paragraph for each one. As you draft, think about which benefit is most persuasive for your potential readers. Also think about which ones might be most useful when you draft the proposal to create the training material.

Professional Communication Assignments

3. Write the Proposal to Create Training Material for New Employees at Hamilton Dental Clinic

Writing as Alyssa Klein-Moore, write an unsolicited proposal to Dr. Watson and the other dental partners and associates making a case for the necessity of creating training materials for new employees at Hamilton Dental Clinic. Explain the problem that you see and why it is necessary to solve this problem. Use the information supplied in Figures 2, 3, and 4 as evidence to support your arguments quantifying the amount of time and money that the training information would save the practice. Include an explanation as to why the manual (or some other approach, if you think there is a better one) is the best solution to the problem. You can argue for using either a print or electronic (or both) version

Financial savings

Hours spent learning

Day 1: 7 hours × $10.00/hr. = $70.00

Day 2: 7 hours × $10.00/hr. = $70.00

Day 3: 6 hours × $10.00/hr. = $60.00

Total for 3 days: $200.00

Projection: 3 weeks of learning @ 4 or 5 hours a day: 5 × 15 × $10.00/hr. = $750

Total after 3.5 weeks: $950.00

Hours spent teaching

After 3.5 weeks, staff will have spent approximately 62 hours teaching procedures (**N.B.** Staff use fewer hours because new employee spends time alone practising new procedure): 62 hrs × $15.00/hr. = $930.00

Total training costs for one new employee: $1880.00

Figure 3 Financial cost of training one new employee.

Hours spent learning procedures: estimate for proposal budget

Hours spent creating materials: estimate for proposal budget

Hours spent designing materials: estimate for proposal budget

Hours spent testing materials

Hours spent revising materials

Figure 4 Estimate costs of creating training materials (hours × $10.00/hr. wage).

of the manual based on which format you think would be most useful in the office.

Audience: Dr. Watson and the other medical partners

Purpose: To persuade Watson to approve your proposal

Genre: Proposal

4. Write an Unsolicited Proposal Offering to Solve a Problem that You Observe at Work or at School

Identify a problem at work or on your school campus that you have some ideas about how to solve. Find out who would approve a proposal for solving such a problem, and address your unsolicited proposal to that individual. Use the information in this module, especially the information in the following sections to help you organize and present your ideas so as to convince your reader(s) that the problem is significant enough to require a solution and that you have a well-thought-out plan for how to do it.

Audience: You must specify this

Purpose: To persuade your audience to approve your proposal

Genre: Proposal

FORMATTING A PROPOSAL

LO 4 Organize and format a proposal document

The preceding section described what kinds of arguments you should make in an unsolicited proposal as you write it. Figure 5 outlines a format for structuring unsolicited proposals. Use the headings given in the figure—they are standard and readers will look for them as a

1. Problem Statement
   - Describe problem
   - Demonstrate why it needs a solution

2. Solution Description
   - Describe solution
   - Show why it is the best solution
   - Demonstrate how it benefits the reader/organization

3. Methods
   - Explain how you will solve the problem

4. Qualifications and Resources
   - Show why you are the person to solve the problem

5. Work Schedule
   - Timeline for completing the project

6. Budget
   - Estimate costs for solving problem/completing the project

7. Call to Action
   - Request approval to move forward with project

Figure 5 Outline for structuring an unsolicited proposal.

way to conceptually organize your information. Note that in the first two sections, you both describe and explain the problem and then you describe and explain your proposed solution. In these first sections you grab and hold your reader's attention through the persuasiveness of your descriptions of the problem and the solution. If you do not successfully convince readers of the validity of the problem, the information that you present in the rest of the proposal will be less compelling.

Sections 3 to 7 provide details about your actual plan for solving the problem, as well as a timeline and budget. Readers who are persuaded that the problem and solution you describe are valid will find this additional information useful to decide whether to give you permission to proceed.

Exercise 4: Draft the Problem Statement for Proposal

Part A: Individually or in groups of two or three people, draft the problem statement for your proposal for Hamilton Dental Clinic, using the ideas that you and your group generated in Exercise 1. Develop your description of the problem as fully as you can, including relevant evidence drawn from Case 2, so that you present a persuasive argument that the problem exists and needs solution. Also pay attention to the credibility that you are building for yourself and your reader's engagement with the subject matter. Use the techniques described earlier to ensure that all three of your rhetorical appeals are strong.

Part B: Individually or in groups of two or three people, draft the solution section for your proposal. In this section, pay close attention to the logical appeal that you are creating to make sure that your claims are convincing and supported by logical and relevant evidence. Use the ideas from your earlier discussions to help you develop your ideas and arguments fully. Be sure to develop the other rhetorical appeals effectively as well.

HOW TO WRITE A PROPOSAL IN RESPONSE TO A REQUEST FOR PROPOSALS (RFP)

When responding to an RFP, consider the needs expressed by the issuer in the proposal. These needs will form the backbone of the criteria for evaluating submissions. Unlike most class situations, only one proposal will be chosen—there is only one passing grade to be handed out! Information on the Contracts Canada website notes that bidders may not contact the organizations requesting the bids without compromising the bid process. This warning means that you must interpret the RFP without feedback from the issuer, making a careful and accurate analysis essential. A careful analysis of the RFP also helps you understand what information should be included in the proposal.

Here are three steps to use in analyzing an RFP:

1. Determine what kind of proposal is requested
2. Identify the evaluation criteria outlined in the RFP
3. Determine what information to include in the proposal

Determine What Kind of Proposal Is Requested

Under the heading "Requirements" (see Figure 6), the RFP specifies that one contractor will be selected ("a Contractor"). It also states the deliverable requested—"an innovative creative advertising and social marketing campaign"—and the length of the contract—"one year with potential for extension for two additional years." Our analysis of this section of the RFP reveals that this is a competitive bid with a creative marketing campaign being produced. In contrast, when an instructor in one of your classes requests a proposal, the situation is noncompetitive, because every student's proposal will be accepted, if he or she proposes a reasonable and well-thought-out idea for a paper or project.

Identify the Evaluation Criteria Outlined in the RFP

In the RFP partially reproduced in Figure 7, the criteria are described in the section titled "Evaluation Process." The mandatory criteria (in other words, the information that must be supplied in the proposal) are the following:

The products

1. One sample national integrated campaign that includes print and one other media

---

Requirements

Municipal Services is seeking a Contractor to update existing marketing materials or develop new materials, for an innovative advertising and social marketing campaign. The campaign will last one year with potential for extension for two additional years provided the initial campaign meets our objectives and budget. The successful bidder will provide a campaign strategy including an innovative approach, media partners, social media strategy, and an overall plan that includes a detailed critical path that covers the implementation time frame for each media product and the proposed budget breakdown.

Figure 6 What kind of proposal is requested?

Source: © Pearson Education, Inc.

Figure 7 Identify the criteria outlined in the RFP.

Source: © Pearson Education, Inc.

2. Example of one national multi media campaign that includes TV and social media

The personnel

3. List the personnel who would lead work in the major project categories and their prior accomplishments

4. Hourly rates of these key people

The organization

5. Evidence from the organization that it is financially capable of developing these campaigns and delivering these products

Other

6. Once bidders make the initial cut (the proposal includes 1 to 5), quality of the proposals will be evaluated by a point system

It is fair to assume that those items listed first are the most important criteria to the evaluators. In this case, the sample products appear first, not surprisingly. Proposal readers are immediately interested in the type and quality of campaign ideas submitted by the bidders. After they have reviewed the sample work proposed, evaluators are secondly most interested in assessing the members of the team assembled to produce the creative work. They want to know that the team members are qualified and capable of completing this project. Thirdly, evaluators are interested in a breakdown of costs for developing the proposed products, and fourthly, they want a commitment from the bidding organization that it can and will meet its financial obligations in developing these products.

Determine What Information to Include in the Proposal

The third step in analyzing the RFP is to determine what information needs to be covered in the proposal. This step is similar but not identical to identifying the evaluation criteria. For example, often the team that you assemble offers strong support for your ability to complete the project you propose. In this case, you want to describe your (or your team's) qualifications and certifications to do the work. Discussing qualifications includes both formal education and some description of previous creative projects you may have completed.

This analysis gives us useful information about the criteria and priorities of the evaluators of the RFP. The next stage of proposal development is to pull together the team and actually generate the deliverables stipulated in the RFP criteria. Once you've outlined your ideas for the potential solution, you should select a format for the proposal. Often, a partial format may present in the criteria stated in the RFP (see the next section for more information on formatting a proposal). Once you have drafted the proposal, review your analysis of the RFP to ensure that you have not gone off track anywhere and that you have included all relevant information and criteria.

Case 3★★★ "Varscona County Community Get Fit! Campaign": Proposal for Varscona County Municipal Services

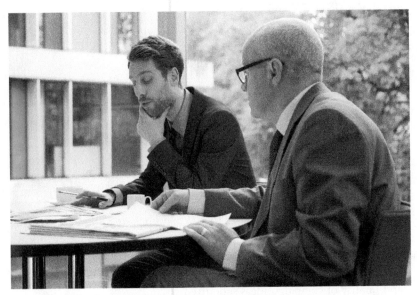

Compassionate Eye Foundation/Dan Kenyon/Digital Vision/Getty Images

Jacob Horne stopped by his mailbox on his way to his cubicle. There was a stack of papers and envelopes, but one in particular caught his attention because it had a bright yellow sticky note on it with his supervisor, Ron Tennant's, scrawl across it: "I think we have a shot at this one. Look through it and drop by my office to talk before you start the draft." Jacob removed the note so he could see the two pages underneath. He skimmed the title: "Varscona County Community Get Fit!"—it was a Request for Proposals from Varscona County Municipal Services (see Figure 8). He briefly rifled through the other papers in his mail to see whether there was anything else he needed to attend to right away, but it all appeared to be routine. There were no other yellow sticky notes from Ron. As he passed Ron's office, he asked him if he had time to talk about the RFP from Varscona County Municipal Services. Ron asked Jacob to read the request and come by in 20 minutes or so.

Ron began by suggesting that Jacob could be the lead person on this proposal because he had had great success with the last government contract. Jacob replied that while this was true, Monique contributed important work to that project, too. He asked if she could be assigned to this proposal as well. Ron pointed out that Monique was pretty much mired on a City of Ottawa contract right then, so she might only be able to contribute ideas and not much text, at least until the end of the month. Jacob and Ron talked for 10 or 15 minutes about the requirements discussed in the RFP. Together they identified the key personnel from Tennant and Marshall Marketing who would have the expertise to create this advertising campaign. Jacob took notes as they talked (see Figure 9). Ron suggested that Jacob check the Contracts Canada website for details or any changes about the bidding process and suggested a deadline of a week's time for the draft.

Trade Agreement: NONE
Tendering Procedures: The bidder must supply Canadian goods and/or services
Attachment: None
Competitive Procurement Strategy: Best Overall Proposal
Comprehensive Land Claim Agreement: No
Nature of Requirements:
ADVERTISING SERVICES
Prentice, James
Telephone No. - 780-901-4567
Facsimile No. - 780-204-2001

THERE IS NO SECURITY REQUIREMENT ASSOCIATED WITH THIS SOLICITATION.

VARSCONA COUNTY COMMUNITY GET FIT!

REQUIREMENT

Varscona County is seeking a Contractor to update existing marketing materials or develop new materials, for an innovative advertising and social marketing campaign. The campaign will last one year with potential for extension for two additional years provided the initial campaign meets our objectives and budget. The successful bidder will provide a campaign strategy including an innovative approach, media partners, social media strategy, and an overall plan that includes a detailed critical path that covers the implementation time frame for each media product and the proposed budget breakdown.

OBJECTIVES AND PURPOSE

This campaign (part of Municipal Services larger social marketing campaign) supports Varscona campaign to increase the use of the county recreational facilities in an effort to improve overall health outcomes for the county. Over the long term (3–5 years+), the campaign, together with other initiatives, seeks to create an active citizenry and build favourable health outcomes. For the 2015–16 fiscal year, the goal remains the same; that is, to encourage citizens of Varscona county to engage in physical activity. For Option Year 1 (FY 2016–17) and Option Year 2 (FY 2007–18), objectives and requirements will be similar to those of FY 2015–16.

EVALUATION PROCESS

The successful bidder must satisfy all of the criteria in the Request for Proposal including: providing an example of one national integrated campaign that includes print and one other media; providing an example of one national multi media campaign that includes TV and social media; and listing the personnel who would lead work in the major project categories; complying with the certification requirements described in the RFP; and providing hourly rates; and evidence that the bidder has provided verified proof of financial resources to perform the work.

PERIOD OF THE CONTRACT

The period of the Contract will be from date of award to March 31st, 2015 with the first Option period running from April 1st, 2015 to March 31st, 2016 and the second Option period running from April 1st, 2016 to March 31st, 2017.

BASIS OF SELECTION

The responsive bid with the lowest cost-per-point will be recommended for award of a contract. Delivery Date:

Above-mentioned

The Crown retains the right to negotiate with suppliers on any procurement.

Documents may be submitted in either official language of Canada.

Figure 8 Example of a Request for Proposal.

Source: © Pearson Education, Inc.

Creative team members: Me, Monique, and Rita

Media choices: Ron suggests billboard (+print) and internet (+television)

-Must discuss with Monique and Rita to decide if these are the right ones

Ask Fred Marshall for financial workup to show T&M Marketing can finance development of campaign

Pull résumés for Rita and Monique for qualifications section (see Figure 10)

Draft due week Monday (April 17)

Figure 9 Jacob Horne's notes from his discussion with Ron Tennant about the Varscona County Municipal Services RFP.

Professional Communication Assignments

5. Write a Solicited Proposal for Varscona County Municipal Services RFP

Use the information in the next section to help you, writing as Jacob Horne, to draft a proposal that responds to the Request For Proposals (RFP) in Figure 8. If you have a background in marketing or advertising, you may already have enough knowledge and experience to develop a publicity campaign. If not, conduct some internet or library research to gather enough background (aim for some plausible ideas at this point) to develop ideas for a social marketing campaign.

Also check out the Contracts Canada website (www.tpsgc-pwgsc.gc.ca/app-acq/amac-cpsa/amac-cpsa-02-eng.html) for information about writing proposals for government business. Use information from Figure 10 to write your proposal.

Audience: James Prentice

Purpose: To persuade Prentice to award the contract to Tennant and Marshall Marketing

Genre: Proposal

Points to Emphasize About Creative Personnel

Monique Ducharme
- Concordia University, BFA 2008
- Centre des arts visuals, 6 courses (graphic design, figure drawing, animation, etc.)

$40.00/hr.

Experience:
- Dove Real Women Canada, 2007
- Public Works Canada, Clean Water Campaign, 2009

Rita Sharma
- Ontario College of Art and Design, EMDes 2007
- OCAD, BFA 2004

$65.00/hr.

Experience:
- Featured artist, McClure Gallery, Montréal, QC, 2008
- Public Works Canada, Clean Water Campaign, 2009
- Ride the TTC, 2005

Me
- UBC, BComm (Marketing), 2008

$35.00/hr.

Experience:
- Public Works Canada, Clean Water Campaign, 2009
- Outstanding Marketing Project for 2009 (awarded by Tennant & Marshall)
- Pulse Marketing Board of Canada, Saskatoon, SK 2009

Figure 10 Jacob Horne's notes summarizing qualification and credentials of his creative team.

6. Write a Solicited Proposal for Hamilton Dental Clinic

Reread Case 2. Dr. Grant Watson (the practice owner) has requested that you develop training materials for the office. He has asked two employees to come up with ideas, but he only intends to accept one of the two proposals. Writing as Alyssa Klein-Moore or Munir Abbasi, develop a proposal to create training materials for the office that Dr. Watson will want to use. Draw on the information in Case 2 and the proposal criteria in Figure 11 for your draft. Use the standard generic proposal format in Figure 12 to structure your proposal.

Audience: Dr. Watson and the other medical partners

Purpose: To persuade Watson to approve your proposal

Genre: Proposal

The training materials must be

- Easy to update
- Compact and usable
- Accessible in all parts of the practice
- Clear, concise, and complete
- Inexpensive to produce and update

Figure 11 Proposal criteria for Hamilton Dental Clinic.

- Problem Statement/Background
- Methods/Procedures
- Qualifications/Resources
- Work Schedule
- Budget

Figure 12 Standard generic format for a proposal.

ANALYSIS: FORMATTING A SOLICITED PROPOSAL

When Jacob sits down at his desk to work on the RFP from Varscona County Municipal Services, the first thing he will do is analyze the RFP carefully to determine what information James Prentice, the issuer of the RFP, wants in the proposal. The RFP contains the criteria that Prentice and the selection committee will use to evaluate and choose from among the proposals. In a competitive situation such as this, only one proposal will be chosen. Information on the Contracts Canada website notes that bidders may not contact the organizations requesting the bids without compromising the bid process. This warning means that Jacob has to interpret the RFP without feedback, making a careful and accurate analysis essential. If he is successful, he will bring at least $25,000 and a year (or longer) of new business to Tennant and Marshall Advertising.

Our analysis of the RFP reveals a partial outline for the organizational structure of the proposal: two sample campaign ideas; personnel, qualifications, and certification; and budget. This structure is a variation on the standard generic format for a proposal (see Figure 12). Jacob will likely adapt this generic format to the implied format from the RFP. In other words, he will add the sections not specified in the RFP, as appropriate, to ensure readers have the complete information they need to evaluate the proposal. Instead of the "Problem Statement/ Background," he uses two headings adapted to the subject matter of the project: "Sample Print and Billboard Campaign" and "Sample Television and Internet Campaign" (or whichever of the second media his team chooses in each case). He will evaluate whether a discussion of methods or procedures for developing the campaigns is appropriate to his readers' needs, as identified in his analysis. He can adapt the "Qualifications/Resources" headings to his situation and call it "Personnel: Qualifications, Certification, and Commitment." In this section he describes the qualifications and credentials of the creative people working on the campaigns. This information he compiles from the resumes that everyone at Tennant and Marshall Marketing keeps on file for proposal writers to use (see Figure 10). Because the RFP highlights budget information (the hourly wages of personnel and a legal commitment from Tennant and Marshall that it can finance this project), Jacob may consider moving the budget discussion before the work schedule in the proposal. Prentice has requested atypical information as part of the financials, so Jacob thinks about whether this part of the discussion should be highlighted rather than relegated to the end of the proposal, as is standard.

If your analysis of the RFP does not suggest a format for the proposal, use the standard format presented in Figure 12.

QUESTIONS A PROPOSAL MUST ANSWER

A proposal is an informative document, and readers come to it expecting to gather complete information about the project that you are proposing to create. They have specific questions that they want you to answer. The following list summarizes the questions that readers expect to have answered when they finish reading your proposal:

- *What problem will you solve?* Answer this question in the problem statement section.
- *How will you solve the problem?* Answer this question through your discussion in the problem statement and methods sections.
- *What will you produce for the reader?* Answer this question in the problem statement.
- *Can you accomplish what you propose?* Answer this question through your discussion in the methods, qualifications and resources, and work schedule sections.
- *What benefits do you present?* Talk about how the reader benefits from selecting your proposal in the problem statement and the qualifications and resources discussion.
- *When will you complete the project?* Your work schedule answers this question.
- *What will it cost?* The budget discussion answers this question.

Of course, you are not just answering these questions; you are also constructing a persuasive argument to convince readers to choose your proposal. For example, to answer the question, "Can you accomplish what you propose," Jacob plans to sketch out a clear and detailed work plan so that readers can imagine his team working through the project stages of the four marketing campaigns specified in the RFP. He is also going to emphasize his team's history of meeting or exceeding deadlines in earlier projects. This provides evidence to support his claim that they will complete the campaign designs as promised. Without evidence, the claim is an assertion (a statement without proof); add evidence to make it into an argument. The following assignment helps you turn the answer to one of these questions into a persuasive argument.

Exercise 5: Writing an Argument with Evidence

In groups of two or three, place yourself in Jacob Horne's position (or one of the other two members of his creative team, Monique Ducharme and Rita Sharma) and discuss possible benefits that the creative team at Tennant and Marshall can offer to James Prentice and Varscona County Municipal Services. At least one person in your group should record the group's ideas. In your discussions, come up with ideas that answer the question, "What benefits do you present?" When you have brainstormed a number of good benefits, decide where they would fit best in the proposal: in the problem statement, in the qualifications and resources section, or somewhere else in the proposal.

When you feel you have exhausted the possibilities for discussion, either individually or collaboratively draft two paragraphs that include both claims and evidence that you could use in a draft of the proposal. In one paragraph, develop benefits that will fit in the problem statement/background section. In the other paragraph, discuss benefits that will fit in the qualifications and resources section. If you identified benefits that fit other parts of the proposal, develop them into suitable paragraphs as well. Ensure that you include evidence to make your case convincing.

As your instructor requests, hand in drafts of the paragraphs with the names of everyone in the group who participated.

MODULE SUMMARY

- There are two main types of proposals: solicited proposals (Requests for Proposals) and unsolicited proposals.

- Good proposals use a combination of logical arguments, credibility, and emotional appeals to persuade readers that their proposals should be accepted.

- Writing unsolicited proposals requires that writers show the problem exists and is significant in addition to offering the best solution to the problem.

- Analyzing an RFP requires that writers determine what kind of proposal is requested, identify the evaluation criteria outlined in the RFP, and then determine what information readers want to see in the proposal.

- A proposal must answer the following questions:

  - What problem will you solve?
  - How will you solve the problem?
  - What will you produce for the reader/client?
  - Can you accomplish what you propose?
  - What benefits do you present?
  - When will you complete the project?
  - What will it cost?

Module 11

Informal and Interim Reports

LEARNING OUTCOMES

LO 1 Define an activity report and organize one appropriately

LO 2 Describe the purpose and audience for an activity report

LO 3 Identify the information that should be present in a trip report and organize that information appropriately

LO 4 Describe the purpose and audience for a trip report

LO 5 Define a meeting report and demonstrate how to structure one appropriately

LO 6 Describe the purpose and audience for a meeting report

GETTING STARTED

The majority of your writing at work will involve writing informal or short reports: activity reports, trip reports, and meeting reports. When we think of reports, we often imagine the thick, heavy, massive texts that are every worker's nightmare—if they have to write them.

Success as a writer at work, though, may very well depend on your ability to master the short report: write clearly, concisely, and quickly about work-related topics. Developing your skills in these genres depends on learning about how they are structured and what kinds of information readers expect in them.

The first section of this module begins with activity reports, which detail your accomplishments for the month. This section presents the information you need to know to write an informative and persuasive activity report. The middle section of this module introduces you to trip reports. Trip reports are filed following employee travel at the organization's expense. This section discusses your purpose in writing the report, the content it presents, and your audience. The third section of this module looks at meeting reports or minutes. Meeting reports are usually kept by the administrative assistant of an organization, and they serve as a permanent record of what happened at the meeting. They showcase the decision-making and analytical skills of those who attended the meeting and act as a legal and official report of the meeting. This section also includes a generic structure for a meeting report that you can adapt to your specific situation.

WHAT IS AN ACTIVITY OR STATUS REPORT?

Activity or status reports—also known as progress reports—are required at many organizations from all employees as a way to track company and employee productivity, either generally or on specific projects. These reports also allow employee input and enable them to comment on their past and future activities.

LO 1 Define an activity report and organize one appropriately

Content

The following information is normally included in an activity report:

- Details of completed work
- Description of problems encountered
- Summary of solutions to problems
- Outline of work remaining to be completed

The terms *status, activity,* and *progress reports* are sometimes viewed as interchangeable, but there are subtle differences between them. As the name suggests, a status report often focuses on one large project, with the discussion reporting where the writer is in the process of completion (in other words, what is the status of this project?). A progress report is very similar to a status report in that the writer emphasizes what has been accomplished so far and what remains to be done before the project is complete. The progress report may not focus on just one project, however; it may report on a series of projects in mid-process. Informal reports (in fact, *all* reports) have goals from the organization's perspective and from the employee's perspective. While demonstrating their competence on past work, employees can also shape their future work by making suggestions or offering solutions to problems raised in the report.

The activity report is generally used by organizations to keep track of what employees are doing day to day or week to week. They include reporting on all of an employee's activities rather than the effort toward completion of a single project. At the same time, these distinctions are not cut in stone; different organizations evolve different traditions of naming, so if you are asked to write one of these reports at a new organization, ask a few questions about the content and emphasis so that you can decide which area to emphasize in your report.

Figure 1 outlines an activity or status report structure. Use it if your organization does not have an established format.

Introduction or project description

- Summarize the project you are working on
- Summarize your progress
- Briefly identify obstacles you overcame
- Assess whether your project is on time and on budget

Work completed

- Detail task by task what you have done
- Evaluate your progress against the plan
- Describe any problems encountered and how you solved them
- Note what you've learned that may benefit others

Work remaining

- Assess remaining work against the plan
- Detail tasks remaining before completion
- Anticipate possible problems and offer potential solutions

Cost (if budget is involved)

- Report on what budget you have spent, what remains, and why any discrepancies exist (for example, unforeseen costs associated with solving problems)

Assessment of progress so far: Conclusion and recommendations

- Assess whether you will complete the project as planned
- Propose any necessary revisions to the schedule or plan

Figure 1 Typical structure for a progress or status report.

Readers expect to gain specific information from a progress or activity report. They want these points:

- A descriptive title announcing report content
- An executive summary to skim for project context or background
- A discussion of how this work contributes to the organization's larger goals (its relevance)
- A report on positive and negative project developments so they can learn from your solutions

Note that your readers want to learn from the discussion in your report.

Case 1★★★ Accounting for Your Productivity at Afoyalan Pharmaceuticals

It was the 29th, and Martin Dasher realized that his first project of the day should be a status report to summarize his accomplishments for the month. It was due tomorrow. Martin didn't have to review his notes to know that he had spent all of April working on a nonprogramming project: user testing the newly developed online employee training materials. Developing and running the usability tests had been a huge stretch for him, and although he felt he had done a great job, he was tired of document production and wanted to get back to his real job before he got too far behind on his own projects.

He had taken over for Nirmala Eko, Afoyalan's technical writer, when she left on maternity leave just as the beta version of the training materials was finished; she wouldn't be back until July 1. Megan Korrigan, the human resources department head, and Sefu Afolayan, company president, had insisted that the training materials for the new system come online as soon as possible. Mr. Afolayan had decided that Martin knew the most about the new program, so he should take over the user testing phase.

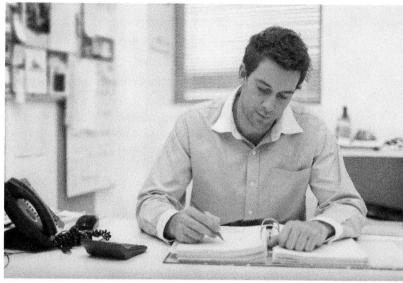

Hybrid Images/Cultura/Getty Images

One of things that had excited Martin when he started at Afoyalan Pharmaceuticals 18 months ago was the relatively small size of the company. With only two programmers in the IT department, he could work on more aspects of information technology beyond programming. Although the user testing project wasn't exactly what he had in mind, it had been interesting. At the same time, he wanted to get back to programming. He decided to write his status report to accomplish two goals (in this order): 1) convince Sefu Afolayan that it was time Martin returned to programming, and 2) to demonstrate the great job he had been doing in Nirmala's place.

A quick look at his notes showed Martin that he had lots of details to cite in recording his progress over the month (see Figures 2 and 3). Opening a new file next to his notes, he

---

Summary of problems found in modules 1 through 4

- Three problem areas in module 1

    1. Wrong visual in Figure 1.8 (original didn't show the crucial detail on screen)
    2. Ambiguous phrasing in step 1.3
    3. Added glossary to define delimited terms of program

- One problem area in module 2

    1. Deleted steps 2.1 to 2.3 from first draft because no one used them

- Four problems in module 3

    1. Added definition of "repeated selection" to glossary because users didn't see its specialized use
    2. Added three more figures to steps 3.3–3.5
    3. Added callout detail to Figure 3.7 to highlight relevant information
    4. Corrected two broken links in step 3.8

- One problem in module 4

    1. Ambiguous phrasing in step 4.3; changed "add three spaces between elements" to "hit 'enter' three times"

- Additional problem in module 2

    1. Deleted Figure 2.3 to end user confusion generated in step 2.4

- Additional problem addressed: redesigned the "repeat selection" icon

Figure 2 Martin Dasher's notes on progress over the past month.

April Status Report

Martin Dasher

Persuasive Goals for this Report:

1. Convince Sefu that I should get back to programming right away (calculate $$ saved by eliminating several steps from inventory control process)
2. Show that I worked hard on this user testing and did a good job, even though this is not related to my training or usual job responsibilities (I'm a good team player!)
3. Show why Valerie can finish user testing and meet May 18 for full operations

Main points to make:

1. **What we got done:**
   - First and second phase testing completed
   - Identified and corrected 11 problems in modules 1 through 4

2. **What we still have to do:**
   - Final phase testing for modules 3 and 4.

3. **Budget:** See Megan for exact figures, we are not over projection (we weren't two weeks ago). Then we had spend $8,000 of our $15,000 budgeted for this process. We should be close to $10,000, but I have to check this.

4. **Projection for hitting deadline:**
   - Not much left to do: Final test of modules 3 and 4
   - Users are lined up (Becky, Todd, Mira, Amir)

We should hit May 18 launch date.

Figure 3 Martin Dasher's financial notes for writing his April status report for Afolayan Pharmaceuticals.

	Re:	Budget for Employee Training Materials on New World Order program
Send	**From:**	megan.korrigan@afolayanind.ca
	To:	martin.dasher@afoyalanind.ca

Hi, Martin,

Here are the budget figures: the project has spent $9,741.32, as of April 27. You have $5,258.68 left to complete the project. Note that any funds spent between April 27 and today (Apr. 29) have not reached me yet, so you should subtract them from these figures if you want exact amounts.

Cheers,
Meg

Figure 4 Email from Megan Korrigan about the usability testing budget for the employee training online learning modules.

listed his main persuasive goals for the report. The big question was how to convince his boss that he was more valuable as a programmer than as a user test coordinator.

Moving him out of Nirmala's position would create a problem, so he would also need to suggest who could complete the testing in his place. He also needed an important neglected project to add urgency to his reassignment. He *had* been working on an important project before he was reassigned. He'd just have to reacquaint himself with the details of that project. As for his own replacement, Valerie McCorkindale from human resources had been helping him; she could easily coordinate the final tests. Martin had them set up so they did not need technical expertise, and she was better than he was with people. Martin opened the status report template (see Figure 1 for the template structure) and filled in the basic financial details (Figure 4).

ANALYSIS: MARTIN AIMS TO RETURN TO PROGRAMMING

Martin Dasher writes an activity report every month. In part, his report assesses the status report of user testing new training materials for the company. Martin's boss wants to know whether this project is on schedule to launch as planned. In addition to showing the project is on schedule, Martin also wants his boss to remember that Martin's assigned work has been neglected over the past month. He wants Sefu Afoyalan to send him back to his programming work.

Purpose

Martin hopes to accomplish several goals with his activity report:

LO 2 Describe the purpose and audience for an activity report

1. To ensure he returns to programming
2. To showcase his activities in user testing, although not his area of expertise
3. To update his coworkers and company president, Mr. Afoyalan, on the status of the employee training materials
4. To reassure the reader that all the training materials will come online May 18

Audience

The audience for a status or activity report is broader than you might think. The **initial audience** for Martin's report is Sefu Afoyalan, the company president, who supervises all employees at the small company. In addition, Martin will send a copy of the report to Nirmala Eko so that she can follow the training materials' progress while on maternity leave. Megan Korrigan is another reader who wants the training materials online quickly to train employees who will work with the new program. Martin may also CC his coworkers who help test it so everyone knows where they are in the process. The report will be archived so other employees may refer to it later.

Initial audience: The person to whom you send your completed work; often, there are many other audiences who will also read it

Persuasive Goals

Another interesting aspect to this status report is the persuasive element by which Martin aims to get his programmer job back as soon as possible. Martin notes the need for a convincing case if he is to move back to his former job. He suggests that he will include an estimate of the money to be saved when he finishes his proposed "fix" for the company database. Providing good reasons will encourage Mr. Afoyalan to decide in Martin's favour.

Exercise 1: What Is the Difference Between an Activity Report, a Status Report, and a Progress Report?

As a discussion among groups of two or three people or individually as a writing exercise, discuss or draft answers to the following questions:

- If the terms "activity report," "status report," and "progress report" refer to the same kind of document presenting the same kind of material, why do you think these three different terms have developed?

- What differences in content or purpose can you infer from the three different terms?

- Would you organize your discussion in, say, an activity report differently from a progress report? Why or why not?

Professional Communication Assignments

1. Write a Draft of Martin Dasher's Activity Report

Using the information from the case; the information in Figures 2, 3, and 4; and the discussion on activity, status, and progress reports, write a draft of Martin Dasher's activity report for the president of Afoyalan Pharmaceuticals. In your draft, try to accomplish the persuasive goals that Martin identifies in his notes in Figure 3, as well as including all relevant information drawn from the case to demonstrate that Martin is a conscientious and hard-working employee who earned his paycheque last month. Remember that your primary goal in writing this report is to ensure that Martin is returned to his original position as a company programmer.

Audience: Sefu Afoyalan, fellow employees at Afoyalan Pharmaceuticals

Purpose: To show your competence as a worker and to have someone else take over user testing the training materials so you can return to your original work

Genre: Activity report

2. Write an Activity Report for Your Business Communication Instructor

Write an activity report for your business and professional communication instructor to report on what you accomplished this week (or over the last two weeks) toward the reading and assignments in your business and professional communication class. Your goal in writing this assignment is to show your instructor how hard you have been working on the course and to convince him or her that you will complete the rest of the assignments in this course in a timely fashion.

Audience: Your business and professional communication instructor

Purpose: To demonstrate your hard work and learning so far in this course

Genre: Activity report

TRIP REPORTS

Many organizations require employees to write trip reports when they return from travel on company business. Sometimes the trip report is a form with blanks to fill in, but some organizations request a written document to establish that the trip was taken. A trip report is usually a short (250 to 500 words) memo report and records the trip's date, destination, and purpose. It includes details to prove the writer took a productive trip where he or she represented the organization effectively and accomplished the goals set out for the trip. It also itemizes trip-related expenses. From the primary reader's perspective, the trip report should prove the employee took the trip and completed the work that motivated the trip. Secondary readers want the report to summarize the main functions of the trip. Consider who else besides your immediate boss might read your trip report.

Content

The content of a trip report varies depending on the business trip's length. The headings allow you to describe the trip's general intent and its outcome or success. Attachments include original receipts for travel (boarding passes or taxi receipts), food (restaurant or credit card receipts), and accommodation (your hotel bill), if your organization reimburses travel expenses after the trip. Attachments may also include documents (for example, brochures, reports, other types of information) relevant to the purpose for the trip.

Case 2★★   How I Spent My Training Seminar

"So how was the course you took in Toronto?" asked Midori Fujioka as she passed by the door, her arms loaded with file folders. Casey MacLean replied that it had been great, if a bit overwhelming. She gestured to a pile of brochures, papers, and handwritten notes about the inventory control program, *OrderNow*. She described how the instructors went over the basics the first half of each day, but then after lunch, got into how to use the functions that Casey and her colleagues would need for tracking and updating inventory at Parsons Electronic Superstore. Casey had spent part of the previous week at a two-day workshop learning how to use *OrderNow*, recently purchased by Parsons Electronics. Casey had gone to the workshop as the only full-time employee in charge of store inventory. Midori had decided the best way to learn the new program was to send Casey for training and have her teach her part-time counterparts, Lim Kuang and Frank Delacroix, who shared inventory management responsibilities for the store on the late, weekend, and holiday shifts.

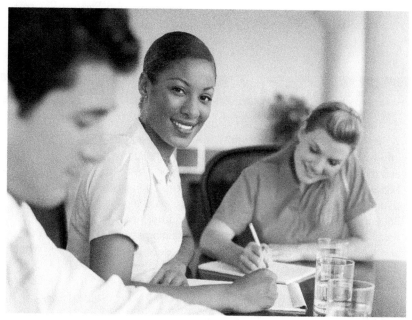

George Doyle/Stockbyte/Getty Images

Midori was happy that the course had worked out, and she asked Casey to arrange a meeting with Lim and Frank to teach them what she had learned. Midori noted that she would also need a trip report as soon as Casey could write it, but by Friday at the latest.

Casey agreed and asked if she should include copies of her notes and the instructional materials. Midori said no, not this time, and asked Casey to file the handouts they gave her in the educational materials filing cabinet. Midori asked Casey to just summarize the highlights in her report so the office had a record of what she had learned.

Casey turned to her filing drawer and decided that it was best to get the trip report started immediately. Flipping through her files, she found what she needed: a copy of a report from an earlier trip. It would be a good model. It had the correct headings, and best of all, as Casey remembered, Midori had said it was a good report. She located the earlier report file in her documents folder and saved the file with a new name. Then she deleted most of the information, leaving only the headings. She fanned the papers from her trip across the desk and paused for a moment, debating. She had actually missed the morning session of the second day because of a bout of food poisoning. "How should I handle that in the trip report?" she wondered.

ANALYSIS: CASEY REPORTS ON HER TRAINING TRIP

From the writer's perspective, the trip report shows that he or she took the trip as planned and accomplished work on the trip. In Casey MacLean's case, she wants to show that she attended the training seminar and learned the main functions that Parsons Electronics needs to properly manage its inventory. If problems arose or the trip was less successful than hoped, the writer has a more challenging task in writing the trip report. For example, because Casey got food poisoning at dinner on the first day, she had to miss the first half of the second day. She has to report this absence and explain what course material she missed. She also needs to explain how she plans to or has compensated for her absence. For example, she may outline a plan to learn what she missed by self-study or attending a second seminar later in the month. Midori Fujioka is primarily interested in two points: 1) Casey learned the functions that Parsons Electronics most needs to manage its inventory, and 2) Casey can train the other employees using what she learned at the seminar.

Professional Communication Assignment

3. Write a Trip Report for Casey McLean

Writing as Casey McLean, draft a trip report using the information provided in the case, the format in Figure 5, and the previous discussion on writing trip reports. Write to Midori Fujioka as your primary audience, keeping in mind that other employees and even the owner of the company, Bill Parsons, may read your report in the future. Include detail to show that Casey did attend the training seminar and learned the information she needs to use the newly purchased inventory control program, *OrderNow*.

Audience: Midori Fujioka

Purpose: To persuade your readers that the trip was worthwhile

Genre: Trip report

Trip date and destination

Purpose of the trip

Background of the trip

Details of the trip

- Who went
- What happened
- Outcome/results
- Implications

Conclusions/recommendations

Any follow up

Attachments

Figure 5 Generic format for a trip report.

MEETING REPORTS

LO 5 Define a meeting report and demonstrate how to structure one appropriately

LO 6 Describe the purpose and audience for a meeting report

Meeting reports are informal reports that record details about a meeting to provide a permanent record of what happened, who attended and said what, what decisions were made, and what work remains for subsequent meetings. Sometimes called *meeting minutes*, meeting reports are often kept by the secretary of an organization or the administrative assistant of the division and circulated before the next meeting for participant review. A first order of business at the next meeting is often to discuss the previous meeting report, revise it if necessary, and vote to accept the report as an accurate record of that meeting.

Purpose

A meeting report accurately and concisely records what happened at an organizational meeting. It acts as an official and legal record of the meeting discussion. Readers of meeting

Figure 6 Generic structure for a meeting report.

reports can vary. Some readers read to discover what happened at the meeting because they could not attend. Others review the report because they were present and must approve it for accuracy. From the organization's perspective, meeting reports provide a historical record of its work and important decisions.

Content

As noted, meeting reports briefly summarize the items on the meeting agenda and the discussion about each item. Generally, these reports record the committee or group name, the date of the meeting, and its location. They often summarize the follow-up action that was chosen, the person selected to take action, and the deadline for completing it. Meeting reports also record who attended the meeting, as well as those who should have but did not attend. Next the report records any discussion about agenda items and the outcome or decision reached about each. It ends by identifying the date and time of the next meeting and any agenda items that were identified for it. Figure 6 outlines a generic structure to use or adapt for a meeting report at your organization.

Audience

Meeting reports are archival documents (they record the events of a meeting for later reference or review) rather than transactional documents (documents generated to accomplish a specific action with a group of readers). Readers for a meeting report can vary widely, and they are often far distant from the meeting itself. They can include 1) members of the committee, those who attended and those who did not (the initial audience for the report); 2) administrative staff evaluating the work of the committee or group (the **gatekeeper audience**); 3) others who want to verify action taken at the meeting; 4) the new head of a committee interested in those issues the committee or group has handled in the past (**secondary audience** for the report); and very occasionally 5) legal teams who investigate ethical problems to determine whether specific issues were discussed and when (a version of the **watchdog audience**, but with more power than watchdog audiences usually have).

As a writer of a meeting report, you likely want to accomplish several goals: 1) to show that your group makes well-thought-out and significant decisions, 2) to demonstrate the group works hard and accomplishes things, and 3) to illustrate the proficiency and accuracy of your own communication skills.

Gatekeeper audience: Readers who decide who else will read your document

Secondary audience: People who will read your document for different reasons than the primary audience

Watchdog audience: Readers who may obtain your document and read it for political, legal, or social reasons

Mike Harrington/Iconica/Getty Images

"Hello, everyone," said Helen Bean, smiling at her assembled staff. There were six people altogether who comprised the executive of the Daily Bread Food Bank. Today they had one newcomer to their monthly meeting, Paul Marceaux. He was a student at the local college and as part of his program he hoped to write a grant to raise money for the Food Bank. Helen introduced Paul to the rest of the team. On Paul's right was Marci Aziz, the chief fundraiser. Helen noted that Paul would be working closely with her. Beside Marci sat Jin Han, the head driver and ace mechanic. He supervised other volunteers on food pickup and did minor service on the fleet. Helen continued by introducing Eamon O'Malley, who did the accounting books, and Arthur Banda, who managed the food bank. She pointed out that Arthur also acted as the scribe at the food bank's meetings because he had the most legible handwriting. Helen then noted that one more member of the executive, Ivan Alexandrov, could not attend the meeting.

Paul was then asked to introduce himself. He described how he had volunteered a lot with literacy programs and raising funds at the canvassing level but had never had the chance to write grants to raise money. He explained that he was a second-year business student also doing a minor in service learning.

Marci welcomed Paul and described how she was focusing on connecting with local businesses such as restaurants and grocery stores to gather donations for the food bank. That kept her pretty busy, she said, and as a result she was not finding time to locate sponsors for their transportation end, which was almost as important as having food on the shelves. Jin agreed, noting that without trucks the food didn't get onto shelves, but they also wouldn't need trucks if there was no food to transport.

Helen noted that they did have one more thing on the agenda. In February, Eamon had offered to meet with local car dealership owners to see what kind of deal they might give the food bank if the executive were to purchase a new van. He was happy to report on that meeting. He explained that he had visited all the local dealerships and gathered both official and unofficial prices for a van. He noted that Robson Motors had offered to give the food bank a van from their leased fleet and charge it a fraction of the original price, but in exchange Mr. Robson also wanted his dealership logo splashed all over the van. Eamon told Robson that the Daily Bread executive would need to discuss this generous offer. He then distributed a half-sheet of paper with dealer names, van information, and prices on it. Everyone sat quietly for a few minutes studying the figures.

Eamon, after a minute, asked Jin how he would feel about advertising Robson Motors as the volunteers made their rounds. Jin shrugged and said that he thought it didn't matter so long as the Food Bank logo and name also figured prominently on the van. He then asked about the mileage on the used van, pointing out that this, as well as its maintenance and repair records, were more important than the paint job. He noted that a beat-up van could cost the organization money in towing and repair charges way above the low price, not to mention the inconvenience of breaking down by the roadside. The others around the table nodded at Jin's comments.

Arthur noted that Robson was offering them a good price. He suggested that maybe they could get some more information about the specific van and if it was in good shape, accept the offer. Paul suggested that Robson might also be willing to include some warranty for maintenance and repairs as part of the deal.

Helen thought that was a great idea. She also suggested that maybe they could apply for a grant to cover infrastructure costs. She asked Paul if he had found any funding possibilities that could cover these types of expenses in his preliminary research. Paul responded that those grants were rare. Marci suggested that they could make a convincing argument to one of the agencies that having roadworthy vehicles was central to Daily Bread's mission.

Helen agreed. She then ended the meeting by asking Marci and Paul to research potential funding sources more fully, Eamon to gather more information about the use history of the van offered by Robson Motors, and Arthur to circulate the minutes of the meeting so that Ivan could read them.

Professional Communication Assignments

4. Write the meeting report for the Daily Bread Food Bank Executive Committee

Writing as Arthur, the food bank manager, or Shelley, his assistant and a food bank volunteer, draft a copy of the minutes for this meeting of the executive committee of the Daily Bread Food Bank. The minutes or meeting report will bring a sixth member of the committee, Ivan, up to date on the group's discussions at the meeting, and it will also serve as a record of the group's activities. The meeting report will record the start of Paul's activities with the food bank as well as the organization's efforts to update its van fleet for collecting food donations around the city. Use the information in the preceding section of this module to help you write an informative meeting report for the Daily Bread Food Bank.

Audience: Ivan Alexandrov, the members of the Executive Committee, and the members of the board of directors of the Daily Bread Food Bank

Purpose: To accurately and concisely record what happened at the meeting and what action was taken or decided on

Genre: Meeting report

5. Write a Meeting Report for a Group to Which You Belong

If you are a member of a school or work committee, record notes at the next meeting so that you can write a report of that meeting. Use the discussion in this section to help you format and draft an accurate and appropriately detailed account of the meeting. Your report should be a document that other members of the committee could approve as an accurate record of the meeting and that will inform individuals who could not attend the meeting about the main items discussed and the actions or decisions that were made or approved.

Audience: The other members of the committee meeting, your instructor, and classmates who may be interested in the activities of this committee

Purpose: To accurately and concisely record what happened at the meeting and what action was decided on or taken

Genre: Meeting report

MODULE SUMMARY

- Activity or status reports document two types of activities: employees' general productivity, and progress on a specific project.

- Activity reports include descriptions of what work has been completed, problems encountered (and overcome), solutions to problems, and what work remains.

- Trip reports are short and document trip dates, destination(s), purpose for the trip, who went, what happened, results, reflections on trip's outcome or success, and receipts for trip expenses.

- Meeting reports or minutes are a permanent record of what happened at a meeting and include who attended, what they said, what decisions they made, and what work remains for later meetings.

Module 12

Research Reports: Recommendation, Analytical, and Informational

Sergey Nivens/Shutterstock

LEARNING OUTCOMES

LO 1 Describe what a research report is and explain how to gather information to write one

LO 2 Identify how to find and evaluate print and online published sources

LO 3 Prepare for, conduct, and complete an interview

LO 4 Create and administer survey research and evaluate and analyze survey data

LO 5 Format and draft a research report

LO 6 Understand and manage the political elements of writing a business report

GETTING STARTED

Reports are the engine that drives the modern organization, providing the power required to make good decisions about the future of an organization or business. For example, the municipal government might notice a rise in vandalism cases involving 12- to 15-year-olds in your town in the later afternoon, after school ends and before many parents finish work. The members of city council might discuss the role the city should play in developing activities or programs targeted to this age group to prevent bored teenagers from getting into trouble—in a similar case in Stettler, AB, the council voted to fund a skate park. Generally the solution is proposed in the form of a written report that outlines the problem, examines the potential solutions, and often recommends the best solution to the decision makers.

In this module, you learn about writing formal reports that require some type of research to find the best solution. The different types of reports (informational, analytical, and recommendation) refer to what the writer does with the research they gather. An informational report examines a subject in depth but generally does not recommend solutions to the problem it examines. Analytical reports go a step beyond informational reports by providing discussion and analysis; they might even include several recommendations for readers to choose from, but they stop short of identifying one best solution. Readers of analytical reports have to choose the best solution for themselves. Recommendation reports, then, go beyond analytical reports by seeking to solve the problem and recommend the best solution. If you are unsure of which report your readers are expecting, ask questions until you are clear about the purpose for your report.

Most research reports grow out of a question or problem that needs a solution. Many problems can have several solutions, but careful research can help you decide which one is the best solution. This module introduces you to the basic methods of report writing research: using published sources, interviewing experts, and creating surveys. Interviewing and survey research are primary sources; published documents and website materials are secondary sources. Primary research in report writing focuses on people as a source of information (interviews or surveys). Secondary research includes published sources of information, including books, journal or magazine articles, reliable internet websites, and .pdf documents. Next, the module shows you how to transform your research findings into a draft report. You learn the basic components of a formal report and the rhetorical considerations for each section. The second to last section explores useful information about repetition of text in research reports and the shifts in the discourse used from section to section. The module ends by considering the political implications of report production and addressing the ways in which even a singly-authored report should be a collaborative project if it is to achieve its goals.

RESEARCH METHODS FOR RESEARCH REPORTS

Research reports come in three main genres or types:

LO 1 Describe what a research report is and explain how to gather information to write one

- Information reports (collect and present information on a subject)
- Analytical reports (collect, analyze, and present information on a subject; offer a range of solutions)
- Recommendation reports (collect, analyze, and present information on a subject; recommend the best solution)

Research reports address real questions to which people need good quality answers. If answers are immediately obvious, no report is needed. When a report is assigned, it is because a lot of research must be done to identify a range of possible answers or solutions. In the context of business and professional communication, primary research refers to the report writer working with people to find answers. Generally report writers use interviews or surveys to collect information (opinions and ideas) from people. Secondary research refers to published texts. Vast amounts of published information are available in libraries and online.

RESEARCH METHODS: SECONDARY SOURCES
Online Key Word Search

LO 2 Identify how to find and evaluate print and online published sources

The simplest way to begin a search online is to type key words linked to the topic into one of the many internet search engines: google.com or google.ca (select "Search pages from

Canada" if you want exclusively Canadian webpages), yahoo.com or yahoo.ca, cuil.pt, ask.com, or lycos.com, among others. A key word search using *business plan* brought up over 500,000,000 hits, far too many, suggesting that the search terms are too broad and need to be refined. However, at the beginning of a research project, the first few screens of links will likely provide ample starting points. You can also use metasearch engines to locate information that may be useful to your project. **Metasearch engines** allow you to search for more focused content. For example, globalspec.com searches websites for engineering materials and specifications.

As they appear onscreen, evaluate the sites themselves and the information they contain to determine the reliability and trustworthiness of each. Sites that exist mainly to sell products or services are less reliable than government- or educational-sponsored websites. Figure 1 summarizes some tips for evaluating the credibility or trustworthiness of the information that you find online and in print.

Remember to keep records of the citation information for all of the sources that look useful. Save the URLs for reliable sites and record the date that you visited the site; you will need that information later for citation purposes.

Figure 2 identifies the information that you should record for each website. To save headaches later, record this information for sites that seem less useful, but that you might use in the future.

Metasearch engines: Web search engines that compile results derived from several other search engines

Considerations	Print Sources	Online Sources
General trustworthiness	If library sources, they have already been evaluated for credibility and purchased. Library sources have a high rate of dependability.	Anyone can post anything. Most websites have no screening mechanism for content. Material can range from highly credible to highly suspect.
Author	What information can you find about the author? What else has the author published? What have other writers said about this text or author (book reviews, review essays, texts published in response)?	Is there an author identified? What additional information can you find about this person? What are their credentials on this topic and generally? What organization(s) is he or she affiliated with? Can you find reviews or evaluations of this writer's work?
Publisher	Who published the document? Is it a reputable and recognizable publishing house? What kinds of other publications does this publisher issue?	Check the site URL. Websites associated with the government or postsecondary educational institutions (.gov, .gc.ca, .edu, .uschoolname, etc.) are more trustworthy than commercial sites (.com, .net, etc.). Nonprofit-sponsored websites (.net, .org, etc.) can vary in their reliability.
Date or timeliness	How recent is the text? Is timeliness important to your topic? Historical documents don't lose credibility with age; in contrast, research on the genome project, for example, should be as current as possible.	When was the website last updated? Does the website acknowledge recent developments on a topic? If sources are included, how recent are their publication dates?

Figure 1 Tips for evaluating the trustworthiness of print and online sources.

(continued)

Considerations	Print Sources	Online Sources
Bias of content discussion	What perspective does the text or writer take on the topic? To what extent does the writer maintain a neutral stance towards the topic? Can you detect a political or philosophical slant to the ideas? How does this slant affect the information in the text? How will your use of this information affect the text that you are writing?	What perspective does the writer take on the topic? Does the writer try to sell you a product or service or specific point of view? Does the writer maintain a neutral attitude towards the topic (reporting rather than commenting or evaluating)? What political or philosophical slant can you detect towards the discussion of the ideas? How might this slant affect the information on the site? How will your use of this information affect the text that you are writing?
Evidence and quality of sources	What evidence does the writer use to support his or her argument or position? Did the writer conduct primary or secondary research to support their views? Does the text have a bibliography and citations? How credible and recent are the sources cited by this writer? Lack of or out-of-date sources can seriously undermine credibility for some topics.	What evidence does the site use to support the position it advances? Is the information based on credible research or published sources? Does the site provide sources for statistical or proprietary information? How credible and recent are the sources cited on the website? Lack of or out-of-date sources can seriously undermine credibility for some topics.

Figure 1 (*continued*)

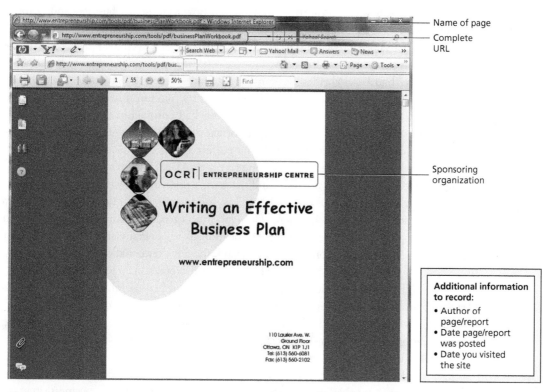

Figure 2 To document your sources accurately, record as much of this information as you can for each source you use.

Source: www.entrepreneurship.com> publication (OCR Entrepreneurship Centre).

Case 1★★ Should Secret Garden Treasures and Gifts Open a New Location in Vancouver?

Chris Cheadle/All Canada Photos/
Getty Images

Kay McKenzie bustled through the front door, her arms filled with boxes and bags. She had just returned to her store, Secret Garden Treasures and Gifts, the night before and was anxious to show her sales team the new products she had found. She had returned with items from six artisans who worked along the west coast of Vancouver Island. She unwrapped a Haida carving of the sun with inlaid mother of pearl and delicate patterns of ash and cherry wood. The artist who had created the mask was going to send more pieces. They were expensive, but amazing. She then lifted a life-size yellow and green glass banana slug out of the box. "Aren't these great?" she exclaimed.

Kay pulled out several more unique pieces that Josh Irvine thought were well-chosen for the store. It catered to a discerning clientele in Toronto's hottest urban redevelopment area, the Docks. At first there had been mostly nightclubs and bars around Secret Garden, but elegant residential towers and unique shops were drawing increasingly larger crowds and more wealthy visitors and residents to the area. Business had certainly picked up in the last three years, and Kay was constantly thinking about how to grow her business and bring in more unique products and appreciative customers. She had suggested that Josh return to school for some business credentials to help with her plans. She even paid for part of his tuition, an incentive that he couldn't refuse, although he hadn't planned to return to school.

In fact, he had been thrilled to join Secret Garden after he graduated because he needed a break from books and teachers. Kay had to talk him into hitting the books again, but he had to admit it had been a terrific idea. Josh had enrolled in the School of Retail Management, and he was pleased to see the information was relevant and useful to the business. Kay thought that Vancouver might be perfect to set up a second Secret Garden. Although Josh agreed that a second location was a good idea, he wasn't sure Vancouver was the right location—it was too far away, and neither he nor Kay knew that market well.

Kay thought that Josh could take over in Toronto temporarily while she could get away to do some research and scout locations. Her plan wasn't to do anything right away, but to explore the opportunity of opening a second location. With so many artists and artisans on the Gulf Islands, not to mention Vancouver Island, she felt they could collect some amazing stock. Some of the stock could be shipped to the Toronto store, adding to its unique offerings.

Kay felt that Josh's business studies background would be useful to determine if this idea was feasible. She asked him to research Vancouver as a location, digest what he could find, and report what she should do to expand Secret Garden. She asked him to identify the hottest location in Vancouver—maybe Granville Island would be a place to start. It has a similar feel to the Docks.

Josh asked if she wanted him to scout possible sources of merchandise. Kay felt that she had enough ideas about that already. She wanted him to look at the small business situation there: What help does the B.C. government offer new start-ups? What government-sponsored programs could they apply for? How did renting compare to buying based on per-square-foot costs? What sales would they need to generate to make a profit and keep the location open?

How many employees would they need? She stressed that she didn't want him to just describe; she needed his advice to evaluate the information he found.

Josh had scribbled some notes while he and Kay were talking. He realized he needed an outline of what topics to cover in the report. He would do that right away and get Kay's approval before she left the store.

ANALYSIS: CONSIDERING A VANCOUVER LOCATION

In Josh Irvine's case, Kay McKenzie has requested a recommendation report (she asked him to study a problem and recommend a solution). To study the problem, he conducts some research to identify what topics to cover in the report. He knows he has several options for gathering information:

LO 3 Prepare for, conduct, and complete an interview

- Print and online sources (secondary sources)
- Interviews (primary source)
- Surveys (primary source)

Josh decides to start with trade books, textbooks, business magazines, journals, and websites to learn what topics to cover. Then he will choose one or two professors at the university with expertise in these areas to interview. He will also consider other contacts (family members, friends, and acquaintances) who could offer insight and advice. After brief consideration, he decides that surveys of the general population to collect opinions, preferences, and shopping habits will be much less useful to his report. He decides not to do survey research on this project: "I can see developing a survey as we get closer to analyzing the clientele for this new store, but for this report I need basic information on starting a new business." He then decides to start with the internet. Figure 3 shows the results from this initial search. After that he will research textbooks at the school bookstore, and then end up at the library. He thinks that a librarian at the information desk can help him identify good sources as well as help him find some of the sources he has seen but can't track down.

After Josh reads the information on business plans from several URLs that turned up in his search, he has a better idea of the topics he should research for his report. He also

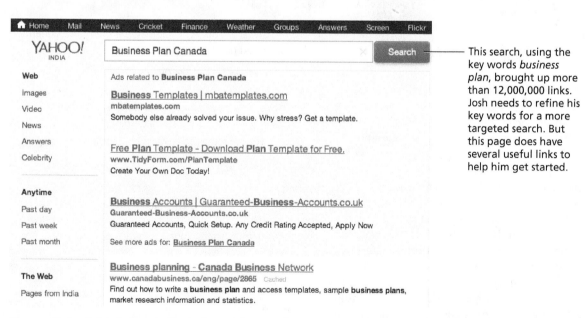

Figure 3 An initial search for information on business plans using yahoo.ca brings up some useful links that help Josh get started.

Source: Screen capture of results from a Yahoo search engine.

eliminates several topics because he is not creating a business plan for Kay McKenzie, but a document more closely tailored to her question about whether to expand into Vancouver. This report will, in fact, precede a business plan. He decides to also collect data to use later for a convincing business plan that Kay could take to her bankers.

Once he knows what topics he should research for the report, Josh realizes that his job has barely begun. He also needs to research the local and provincial business scene in Vancouver. He can use the internet to search for government- and business-related websites, as well as real estate and financial websites, to gather the raw data he needs about Vancouver as a site for Kay's business. He also hopes that he can figure out what areas of the city may be the best choices of location for a new unique gift shop.

Online Database Search

Josh's review of the information on various business websites has given him a great starting point. However, he isn't going to stop with a review of websites; he will also search the databases at his school library to locate trade publications and academic journals for articles relevant to his project. He will search for business-related publications in one or two of these databases:

- ArticleFirst (FirstSearch)
- Canadian Newsstand—Major Dailies (EZProxy)
- Factiva (Dow Jones)
- LexisNexis Academic (LexisNexis)

Access these databases by visiting your school library's webpages. You may need your school user ID and password to do the search. Some of these databases have full-text articles online; others contain abstracts of the articles. You will have to visit the library to find these journals or books from your online search.

⟩ Professional Communication Assignments

1. Write a Report Recommending Whether Kay McKenzie Should Open a New Store in Vancouver

Adopting the persona of Josh, write a research report for Kay McKenzie that evaluates whether she should open a second branch of Secret Garden Treasures and Gifts in Vancouver. As your instructor directs, write your report as either an analytical report (you make several recommendations based on your conclusion but do not specifically recommend one course of action) or a recommendation report (analyze the data and recommend to Kay McKenzie what you think she should do). Use the information in the case as well as the discussion in the module to help you write the report. Collect information from reputable websites to research the prospects for new businesses in Vancouver, B.C., and use this information to help you decide what to recommend to Kay. Include relevant data about start-up costs, projected time period to profitability, and details about potential local, regional, or provincial programs that may help Kay develop her business. Also include graphs and

charts, where appropriate, to display the costs and benefits of her proposed plan.

Audience: Kay McKenzie, owner of Secret Garden Treasures and Gifts

Purpose: To show Kay McKenzie why Vancouver is/is not a favourable location for her new store

Genre: Formal report (analytical or recommendation)

2. Write a Status Report for Case 1

Writing as Josh Irvine, write a status report for your boss, Kay McKenzie, reporting on the progress you've made so far on your research report. A status report is a persuasive document that demonstrates your competence, hard work, and ability to solve problems as an employee of the organization.

Audience: Kay McKenzie

Purpose: To demonstrate to your boss, Kay McKenzie, that you are doing a good job of looking into the feasibility of opening a second store location in Vancouver

Genre: Status report

Exercise 1: Annotated Bibliography of Sources for Your Research Report

Conduct two online searches, one using internet search engines such as google.ca, yahoo.ca, cuil.pt, or ask.com and one using three databases from your school library. Locate at least three useful website sources and three useful articles or books drawn from your database search. Use these sources to create an annotated bibliography. An annotated bibliography consists of two parts:

- Citation information for each source
- Summary and analysis of the useful content in each source

To create an annotated bibliography, carefully record the citation information for each source.

- *For print sources:* Author, title of publication, publication information, publication date, page numbers
- *For online sources:* Title of page, author (if listed), sponsoring organization, date page was posted, date you accessed the page, page numbers (if listed), complete URL

For the annotations, write at least two paragraphs:

- Summarize the main content or argument of the webpage or article.
- Analyze the ways in which you expect this source will be useful or is relevant to your project.

The sources that you select for your annotated bibliography should cover a variety of topics related to your report, including both the topics to cover and the specific content that you will need to write your report.

RESEARCH METHODS: PRIMARY SOURCES

Interviews

After he has collected as many relevant and useful print and online secondary sources as he can use, Josh Irvine decides to talk to some experts. People with expertise in the areas he has chosen will help him tailor the general information from the secondary sources to his specific situation—in this case, Kay's proposed business venture. He considers whom among his contacts he might talk to.

Who to Interview People with expertise are another potential source of information for any project. Josh generates a list of everyone he knows who is a good source of expertise, including acquaintances. He has taken several business courses in his program, so he identifies those instructors as individuals who can help him review the content to discuss in his report. However, they are busy people, so he must prepare carefully before the interview to ensure that it runs efficiently and on target. He also recalls that some websites from his earlier search had email or chat connections to ask an expert questions about business law and regulations in B.C., entrepreneurship, and other topics. These contacts can also help him answer specific questions that arise as he assembles and interprets his data about business in Vancouver.

Figure 4 Prepare for interviews.

The Interview Process   Josh had taken a journalism class in high school, so he knows the basics about interviewing (see Figure 4). He knows the three stages to a successful interview:

- Preparing for the interview
- Conducting the interview
- Using the interview information

Educate Yourself   To prepare for the interviews, Josh considers what he wants to learn from each person during the interview and prepares a list of questions for each interview subject. He realizes that he must also do more research before the interview. If he goes into the interview already knowing the basics of, for example, business plans, he won't need to waste valuable time having his interview subject teach him. That way he can focus on asking more advanced questions that will improve his report quality. With background knowledge, he can generate more effective follow-up questions. As he thinks about gaps in his knowledge and whom to ask about which topic, Josh realizes that he doesn't know much about each person's areas of expertise. He decides to do a quick internet search on each person to learn more about their interests and specialties so that he can make the best use of the interview time.

Prepare a List of Questions   When Josh feels knowledgeable about his subject matter and his interview subjects, he is ready to draft questions to help direct each interview (see Figure 5). He starts with the basic journalists' questions: Who? What? Where? When? Why? How? These questions help generate more specific questions about the topics. Then he reviews his notes, assessing what he has omitted.

When he has exhausted his ideas about possible questions, Josh reviews the list and reorganizes the questions until they progress logically and smoothly through his research areas. A computer file allows him to compose, arrange, and print the list to make a legible handout for the interview.

• Ask questions that cannot be answered with a simple "yes" or "no."

• Ask questions that you cannot find answers to somewhere else.

• Ask questions to help you understand difficult ideas or concepts.

• Include background, where necessary, to provide context to your questions.

Figure 5 Strategies for asking good questions.

After filling in the blanks he saw after reviewing the project as a whole, Josh decides his list is ready:

1. He can cross out the questions as he works through them

2. He will use this list to control and direct the conversation to collect the information he needs

3. He has extra questions in case his interview subject answers efficiently and there is ample time at the end

When Josh feels prepared, he decides to schedule the interview. First he calls Dr. Spengler, the professor who taught his Issues and Innovations in Retailing class. When he connects to Dr. Spengler's voicemail, Josh leaves a clear, concise message requesting the hour-long interview, summarizing the subject of the interview, and leaving his cell number to return the call. After disconnecting, Josh decides to email Dr. Spengler in case he doesn't check his messages regularly. Email will also give Josh the opportunity to more fully describe his goals for the interview.

Exercise 2: Write an Email to Dr. Spengler Requesting an Interview

As Josh Irvine, draft an email to Dr. Spengler requesting an interview and explaining why you want to talk to him. Remember that Dr. Spengler is a busy person and may not feel he has an hour to talk to you, so consider and include some type of motivation to convince Dr. Spengler to agree to the interview.

Audience: Dr. Spengler, a business professor from a class you took last term

Purpose: To persuade Dr. Spengler to grant you an hour-long interview

Genre: Persuasive email message

Length of the Interview   Josh asks Dr. Spengler for an hour-long interview because he has several complex topics to learn about. Josh feels he can persuade Dr. Spengler to talk to him for an hour, but any longer will be too great a time commitment. In addition, an hour of directed conversation, careful listening, and note taking is mentally draining. After an hour, neither he nor Dr. Spengler will be at their sharpest, and it is important not to waste his interviewee's time. If they have topics left to discuss at the end of the hour, Josh decides, he can schedule a follow-up interview.

Note Taking During the Interview   "Should I take notes or record these interviews?" Josh asks to himself. Digitally recording an interview is much easier, especially if you have a voice recorder. Josh knows he can borrow a voice recorder from his cousin, but he also knows that it always takes 10 or 15 minutes to train the device to recognize the speaker's voice, and he isn't sure that his interview subjects will want to spend this time to get organized. "Do I want to take that time from my interview to set this up?" reflects Josh. However, the digital recorder will also eliminate transcribing time by converting the audio file into a text file, and it is easier to skim a printed page than handwritten notes to extract the important points from the interview. Then Josh remembers from an earlier class that the instructor had urged them to always take notes, whether they are recording an interview or not, in case the equipment fails. Josh finally decides that if he can borrow a digital recorder for the interviews, he will. Otherwise, he will take detailed notes during the interview.

Conducting the Interview Josh made sure he arrived at his interview with Dr. Spengler five minutes early. "Thanks for agreeing to talk to me, Dr. Spengler," he said as he shook his former professor's hand. "I really appreciate you giving me a few minutes of your time to help me with this project for work. I have registered for your class on starting a small business in the fall term, but unfortunately I need to know more about it now."

"Well, I always enjoy seeing former students continue on with the work after they leave my class," said Dr. Spengler. "Why don't you check out the books that I've ordered for that class as possible sources for your report? A couple of them are really good and one even uses some examples from business in B.C."

"Great, I definitely will. I will also have a jump on the fall reading," noted Josh. "Let's start by me describing where I'm going with this report. Then I have some questions, but if something occurs to you while I'm talking, please interrupt me." He briefly described Kay McKenzie's request; then he posed his first question: "Dr. Spengler, what would you say are the top three things someone starting up a new business should beware of?"

As the other man talked, Josh listened carefully, noting in a word or two the important points being made. Josh had decided to take notes and go back and fill in details as he remembered them immediately after the interview. He was careful to look up frequently, making eye contact with Dr. Spengler and nodding and smiling to convey that he was listening, he understood, and he was finding the information important. This kind of response is called *active listening*, and it lets the speaker know that you are engaged with their words (see Figure 6).

Josh was busy during the interview, listening carefully, thinking about what was said, formulating follow-up questions, and ensuring they covered the areas that he had identified in his preparation. Several times, when Dr. Spengler seemed to drift off topic with a particularly complex point about economic theory, Josh tactfully brought him back to the main point, "Wow, Dr. Spengler, listening to your explanation of risk theory shows me how much I still have to learn. It is a fascinating area, isn't it? But what your explanation makes me wonder is whether and how we can use this predictive theory to minimize risk for the small business owner?"

Josh was startled to see that his hour was up. He still had a few more questions, but a brief glance showed that he had answers already embedded in earlier questions. "This has been fantastic, Dr. Spengler. You have helped me so much, not only with what I need to know for this report, but what I want to know as I continue in this program. Thanks again for your time and your valuable expertise."

"You're very welcome, Josh," replied Dr. Spengler. "I have enjoyed thinking about some of these subjects in the context of an actual business in a real location."

"I think I understood everything you said pretty well," added Josh. "But if I have questions as I look over my notes and try to apply your ideas to my research, would it be okay if I contact you for one or two things?"

"Yes, certainly," answered Dr. Spengler. He went on to explain that he would be out of town the following week, however, so Josh should email him for a faster response.

"Again, thank you." Josh gathered his notes and papers as he left.

- Make eye contact
- Smile and nod
- Where appropriate, rephrase what the speaker has said to show you understand his or her point

Figure 6 **Strategies for listening well.**

Using the Interview Information   Josh left Dr. Spengler's office and headed to the library. While details of the interview were still fresh, he reviewed his notes and filled in points. After half an hour, he had recorded everything important that he could recall from the interview. He numbered all the pages and then wrote Dr. Spengler's full name, official title and position, and the interview date on each page so that he could cite this information on his references page. He still needed to interview a second professor, as well as check out the books that Dr. Spengler had mentioned. Then he would explore the online information he had gathered about small business regulations and incentives in B.C. in the context of ideas from the interview.

When Josh began drafting his report, he used the interview data collected in several ways:

- As evidence to support decisions he made about how to proceed
- As a credible source, cited to support his recommendations about opening the new store location
- As an expert defining technical terms related to the report topic
- As summary of the method he chose to assemble his research

He reported some of his interview subject's comments directly through citations. He also summarized the responses as background to clarify technical concepts or explain his process in answering Kay McKenzie's question.

Josh Irvine decided that survey research wouldn't help him answer the question posed by Kay McKenzie. We turn now to a different scenario in which survey research is the only way to answer a supervisor's question. In the following case we meet An Kim, who is charged with determining the best choices for literacy events for young adults at a local community centre.

Surveys

Surveys are useful for gathering opinions and ideas from a wide variety of people so that the survey results can be quantified (or counted) and compared to other surveys. This is why, in Case 2, Mr. Joshi suggests to An Kim that she survey the young adults in the Ritchie community. The advantages to using a survey are that you can reach a large number of different people, ask them the same questions, and count and compare their responses. Disadvantages to survey research are respondents' unwillingness to fill out the survey, their concerns about the confidentiality of their responses, and loaded survey questions that distort respondents' answers. Unless you have a budget for conducting survey research that allows you to pay respondents, you have to consider how to motivate people to fill out your questionnaire. Think about the ways in which your gathering of information may benefit them so that they will donate their time and opinions.

One way to create an online survey is to use one of the internet sites listed in Figure 7 or one that you may already be familiar with. These websites allow you to generate a survey quickly and easily. With some providers (for example, SurveyMonkey), a basic survey of 10 questions is free; more advanced features may be purchased. The site's services include collecting and analyzing responses. You can create a mailing list inviting participants to complete your survey, and when you have finished gathering the data, you can download it in a spreadsheet or results report. Although they make parts of survey creation relatively simple, they do not create good survey questions for you, so you should know how to write good questions to gather the information needed for your report.

Writing Good Questions   The heart of good survey research is writing good questions that get answers to help with your research. There are two types of questions to ask: **closed-ended questions** and **open-ended questions**. Closed-ended questions offer respondents a

LO 4 Create and administer survey research and evaluate and analyze survey data

Closed-ended questions: Questions that require respondents to choose one of several answers provided by the survey

Open-ended questions: Questions that leave a space for the respondent to fill in an answer in their own words

The following online survey sites allow you to create free trial versions or free short surveys of up to 10 questions:

SurveyMonkey: www.surveymonkey.com

Checkbox Technologies: www.checkbox.com

Surveyspro: www.esurveyspro.com

Surveyspros also offers a free trial version of their more expensive service.

Figure 7 Online websites that offer free trial versions or free short survey options.

list of possible answers from which they can choose. You control the answers and respondents choose the one that best fits their situation. Open-ended questions ask respondents to use their own words and to explain why they hold the views they do. Open-ended questions allow respondents to give surprising or unanticipated answers. Figure 8 gives examples of open-ended and closed-ended survey questions.

Open-Ended Survey Questions	Closed-Ended Survey Questions
1. What is the best gift that you've ever received?	1. How often do you visit a gift store to buy a present for someone? ☐ More than once a week ☐ Once a week ☐ Once a month ☐ Several times a year ☐ Never
2. Why was that gift the best one you've ever received?	2. What types of stores do you usually shop at to buy gifts for other people? ☐ Department stores ☐ Electronic stores ☐ Clothing stores ☐ Home furnishing stores ☐ Gift stores ☐ Other—Please list:_____

Figure 8 Examples of open-ended and closed-ended survey questions.

Figure 9 Undefined technical terms can produce inaccurate responses.

You can see from the examples in Figure 8 that closed-ended questions are the easiest to tabulate; you just count up the responses for each choice. The open-ended questions are more challenging because you have to decide how best to categorize and count many, perhaps quite different, responses. At the same time, open-ended questions give you more accurate information because respondents can choose the answer that best suits them; closed-ended questions force respondents to choose one predetermined answer that may not match their experience well.

Remember as you create survey questions that the more questions you ask, the more likely it is that respondents will not complete or return the questionnaire. Similarly, open-ended questions take more time and effort for respondents because they have to formulate an answer and write it down. Checking boxes is much faster and easier. To increase the chance that more people complete your survey, limit your use of open-ended questions. Use them to identify the most important information that you need to know.

Dos and Don'ts for Question Writing

Do Use Plain Language to Ask Questions   Avoid complex sentence structure and use **plain language** to make questions easy and fast to understand. In Figure 9, the first question uses undefined technical terms, yet asks responders to make a choice. Some people would have to guess at their answer. The revised question explains without technical language the choices open to the respondent.

Plain language: An approach to writing that emphasizes the needs of readers to make sense of documents through direct, simple, and unadorned prose and well-organized documents

Do Ask Specific Questions   Ask questions that respondents know how to answer. Vague or ambiguous questions force them to make up answers or abandon your survey because they do not understand what you want. Figure 10 forces readers to stop and consider the question.

Figure 10 Ask questions clearly.

Loaded question: Have you ever received a single gift that you liked?

Neutral question: Generally, how happy have you been with most of the gifts that you have received?

Figure 11 Use neutral language to gather unbiased responses.

Don't Ask Loaded Questions   Loaded questions are ones that signal to your respondents how you want them to answer (see Figure 11). The first question steers respondents to respond critically. The revised second question uses neutral language. Neutral language gathers unbiased responses.

Don't Ask Several Questions in One Sentence   Do not phrase questions so they ask more than one thing in the same sentence. Such questions often offer one area of response so respondents cannot tell to which part of the question the answer corresponds (see Figure 12).

Creating Good Responses   The second half of writing good survey questions is creating suitable responses. Of course, you only need to provide responses with closed-ended questions. Choose from several options for responses:

- Yes/no answers
- Rating scales
- Comparative rating scales
- Category scales

Yes/no answers require respondents to check "yes" or "no" in response to the question. Figure 13 presents a list of options that respondents can answer "yes" to by checking the box or "no" by leaving it blank. As you can see in this example, you can obtain a lot of information from one question if you use some ingenuity and format it as a list.

Rating scales enable respondents to represent their responses using numbers. The number represents the strength of their response. Scales allow these options:

- Choose one of the listed numerical responses
- Give a number to the responses listed
- Select among a range of numbers
- Select a number that corresponds to a word or phrase that describes the response

Multiple questions in one: Should Secret Garden stock more gift ideas or more artwork?

Multiple questions subdivided:

Which should Secret Garden stock more of?

☐ Gifts

☐ Artwork

☐ Books

Figure 12 Subdivide multiple questions.

1. Which types of stores have you shopped at in the last year to buy a gift for someone?

   Check all that apply.

   ☐ Department store

   ☐ Electronic store

   ☐ Clothing store

   ☐ Home furnishing store

   ☐ Gift store

   ☐ Bookstore

   ☐ Other—Please list:_____

Figure 13 Yes/no questions generate a lot of information.

Likert scales traditionally use a five-point range, although other ranges, such as seven and nine, are also possible. Represent the intervals as a list or on a line graph with numbers. Figure 14 shows two Likert scales, one that uses a numbered line and the other a numbered list.

Comparative rating scales allow respondents to rank their responses. Figure 15 is an example of a comparative rating scale.

Categories provide general ranges of answers for people to select. For example, you may not be able to calculate exactly how many gifts you give in a particular month, but you likely have a general sense and could fit yourself into a scale that identifies categories such as "frequently," "occasionally," or "almost never."

Choose Your Survey Medium   You have several choices for distributing your survey. You can post it online using a site such as SurveyMonkey.com, you can distribute print copies, or you can use telephone conversations. Whichever method you choose, prepare your questions so they are clear and easy to understand. Use the tips in Figure 16 to prepare your questionnaire.

2. **This neighbourhood needs more specialty stores.**

   1. Strongly agree

   2. Agree

   3. Neither agree nor disagree

   4. Disagree

   5. Strongly disagree

1	2	3	4	5
Strongly agree	Agree	Neither agree nor disagree	Disagree	Strongly disagree

Figure 14 Two layouts for a Likert scale response. The first one is a numbered list; the second one is a numbered line.

---

3. Please rate your three favourite types of gifts to give:

___ Books

___ Music

___ Clothing

___ Travel

___ Kitchen items

___ Tools

___ Furniture

___ Cash

___ Artwork

Figure 15 A comparative scale asks respondents to identify the types of gifts they prefer to give.

Reporting Survey Data   After creating your survey, you need to locate those people who will respond to it. If you use a print survey, you can leave copies of it in a public place for respondents to pick up and fill in. Be sure to include information on how to return the form to you. If you want to survey a particular population, you must decide how to contact those people and how many you can afford to contact. Keep track of who returns the survey so you know what your response rate is. The higher your response rate, the better quality your data will be.

Open-ended survey questions produce **qualitative data**—data that is not easily counted but adds important details. To tabulate qualitative data, read through the words looking for patterns and group similar responses together. Qualitative data gives a context to the numeric patterns arising from quantitative data. If many respondents give you the same answers to a question, this data is considered quantitative because you can count it. Answers to closed-ended questions are **quantitative data** as well. For closed-ended questions, count the totals to each answer and write the totals directly onto a blank survey sheet. Look for patterns in your data that help you generalize your results. When you use quantitative data in your report, present the data in a table or graph so readers can see the patterns that you think are important.

Qualitative data: Data that answers research questions through words, stories, and observations

Quantitative data: Data that can be represented in numbers, tables, and charts

---

- Give the survey a title.
- Write a short introduction to encourage respondents to finish the survey.
- Order your questions from easy or factual to more complex to create the feeling that the survey will be fast to answer.
- Leave space for respondents to write answers to open-ended questions.
- Edit the survey form to include only questions you really need answers to.
- Leave lots of white space so the form looks inviting.

Figure 16 Tips for preparing survey forms.

Look for ways to present data from surveys that illustrate the points you want to argue in your report. Graphs and charts compare survey answers so your readers can see the significance of your findings.

Exercise 3: Create a Survey to Identify the Gift-Giving Practices of People in Your Age Group

In groups of two or three people, create a one-page survey that helps you gather information about the gift-giving practices of students at your institution. Use the information in the previous section to help you design a persuasive, easy-to-fill-out questionnaire that respondents want to answer.

Audience: Your classmates as potential respondents

Purpose: To create a well-designed survey

Genre: Survey

Case 2★★ Collecting Survey Data to Write a Report for a Nonprofit Organization

An Kim, who worked part time at the Ritchie Community Centre and was a full-time Humanities major at Ritchie College, said hello to the centre manager, Mahavira Joshi. Mahavira asked how her day was going and thanked her for going out of her way to find him. He said he had just heard from the provincial government that the Ritchie Community Centre had been awarded a $3000 grant to hold a series of events for young adults at the drop-in program at the centre.

An was tempted to offer Mahavira a high five in celebration but thought better of it. Instead, she offered an exuberant "Congratulations!"

Mahavira appreciated An's enthusiasm. He then explained the terms of the award: that any events paid for by the grant had to be related to literacy in some way and they had to bring young people ages 15 to 20 (more or less) to the centre. He said that he had no idea of the interests of this age group, so that's where he hoped An could help with research. His idea was that a survey of this group might help to find out what they would think was cool, what might bring them to the centre.

An agreed, noting that there were several online survey sites they could use, such as SurveyMonkey. Mahavira said he liked the idea of an online survey, thinking that it might fit that age group—that it was free was a big benefit too. Mahavira asked if An could prepare a report for the board of directors. He didn't want a big report, just an informal but informative one to circulate in advance and be discussed at the board meeting next month. He wanted to present the members with a range of options so they could make the final decision.

.shock/Fotolia

An said that she could email the survey to some of the students at her school, maybe also put it out to some of her social media contacts. If it was a short survey, An said that she thought most of her group would be likely to fill it out right away.

This sounded good to Mahavira. He suggested that perhaps she could work with Ben Dunwoody on this. Mahavira thought that between An and Ben they could brainstorm some initial suggestions for activities for the survey. He added that perhaps their friends on social media could also add input on what would be exciting to generate even better ideas. An thanked him for the suggestion and said she would go look for Ben.

Mahavira told An that he was looking forward to reading the report, noting that it was great to have the grant money to promote the centre's mission. He added that if An had any problems or questions to let him know and he would do what he could to help.

Exercise 4: Create a Survey for Ritchie Community Centre

Writing as An Kim or Ben Dunwoody, create a one-page survey that you can use to gather information about literacy-related social activities that 15- to 20-year-olds would find appealing. If you wish, you can use one of the web survey sites to create an online survey for this exercise (see Figure 7). Use the information on creating good survey questions to help you develop a survey that this demographic would want to fill out and that will provide you with insights as to the activities this group would want to support. Make sure your questionnaire will provide you with information that would help you write the report described by Mahavira in Case 2.

Audience: 15- to 20-year-olds who are interested in cool literacy-related activities

Purpose: To persuade this demographic to give you useful and interesting ideas for activities they would spend time attending

Genre: Survey (up to 10 questions)

GENRES OF THE RESEARCH REPORT

Research reports can take several forms, depending upon the writer's goals in preparing them:

- *Information report.* A writer who has been asked to *explore* a problem chooses an information report format. Information reports introduce the topic, explain relevant background, assemble research on the topic, and end by interpreting and summarizing the problem. Information reports do not recommend solutions.

- *Analytical report.* A writer who has been asked to *study* a problem and devise a series of possible solutions chooses an analytical report. Analytical reports explore the topic or problem, collect data and research to explore potential solutions to the problem, and identify several solutions for readers to consider and choose from among.

- *Recommendation report.* A writer who has been asked to *solve* a problem chooses a recommendation report. Recommendation reports allow the writer to examine the problem in depth, analyze the data and research related to the problem, discuss possible solutions to the problem, and empower the writer to judge and recommend the best solution of those considered.

Formal and Informal Research Reports

Reports can be formal or informal, depending upon the nature of the problem and the level of formality of the organization. Formal reports are usually many pages long, bound into a permanent cover, and include traditional sections and front matter such as a cover letter, an executive summary, and appendices. Informal reports are usually shorter, do not contain front matter or appendices (although they may include a references page), and may be formatted as a memo directed to the writer's supervisor.

WRITING THE REPORT

LO 5 Format and draft a research report

Analyze the Research Results

When you have gathered the information you need, the next step is to analyze it to find a solution. You may have already developed a sense of the solution to the problem as you did your research. In Case 1, Josh Irvine has two questions to answer: 1) should Kay McKenzie open a second location in Vancouver, and 2) what would be the best location for the new store? Josh likely already has a sense of the first answer based on his research, but the answer to the question about location may or may not be obvious. Without actually visiting the areas, he can only guess, but telephone conversations with two or three commercial real estate agents about possible hot locations in Vancouver gives him some expertise to draw on.

You may already have a strong sense of what you want to say in the report, but you should still study your research carefully to ensure that you recommend the best solution. Set up criteria as you analyze your information to ensure you remember the top priorities for the solution.

Identify Appropriate Evidence

A report is an argument to persuade readers of your recommendations' validity, so identify persuasive evidence in your results that supports your discussion. Even information reports use financial and other types of data to develop graphs or charts that illustrate and support your conclusions. If appropriate, include photographs or drawings to illustrate details that build your case. Reports should offer multiple ways for readers to understand the information that you've gathered. For example, Josh Irvine could include maps of the neighbourhoods he recommends as well as graphical representations of financial data to support his recommendations.

Draft the Report

The report does not have to be drafted in order. Start with whatever topic seems easiest to write about. Once you have written a complete draft, you can work on making the sections fit together coherently.

Format for a Research Report: Direct Organizational Pattern A research report is a multi-page document that presents the information that readers need to understand the problem and solution that you propose. It consists of conventional sections that accomplish different goals. These sections should be ordered according to your readers' attitudes toward your report and its findings. For example, if readers have a positive attitude toward your subject matter (say, your boss has followed your project, approved early suggested results, and now eagerly awaits your final recommendations), choose a direct pattern of organization that places conclusions and recommendations up front in the report, immediately following the executive summary.

Figure 17 shows a direct organizational pattern. Use this pattern if you believe readers will respond positively to your report. For example, if Josh Irvine decides that Kay McKenzie should definitely open a new location for Secret Garden in Vancouver, he would likely use a direct pattern of organization because he can expect, from her initial enthusiasm, that she supports this recommendation. If, however, he decides to

- Executive Summary
- Conclusions/Recommendations
- Introduction/Purpose/Problem
- Background
- Research Methods
- Findings or Results
- Implications (what does this mean?)
- Appendices (sources; raw data; supplementary charts, graphs, or tables; etc.)

Figure 17 A direct organizational pattern for an analytical or recommendation report.

recommend against a Vancouver location, he might use a different organizational pattern to show her why the expansion is a potentially bad idea. In this case, he would use an indirect pattern.

Format for a Research Report: Indirect Organizational Pattern An indirect pattern of organization defers the conclusions and recommendations of the report until the logical end. This indirect pattern allows you to work through the problem, analyze your data and research, and demonstrate in a clear, logical manner that your conclusion is solid and not easily refuted by opposing viewpoints. This pattern shows and persuades readers at the same time that the outcome they resist supporting is, in fact, the best one. See Figure 18 for an example of an indirect pattern of organization for a report.

Report Section Content Whether you use a direct or indirect pattern of organization for your report, include the following types of information in sections of the report as listed. This overview follows an indirect pattern of organization, presenting the writer's conclusions and recommendations at the end, after he or she has made the case for the analysis presented.

- The *executive summary* or *abstract* briefly summarizes the report subject. It presents the recommendations made in the report and the reasons for these recommendations.

- Executive Summary
- Introduction/Purpose/Problem
- Background
- Research Methods
- Findings or Results
- Implications (what does this mean?)
- Conclusions/Recommendations
- Appendices (sources; raw data; supplementary charts, graphs, or tables; etc.)

Figure 18 An indirect pattern of organization for an analytical or recommendation report.

It briefly describes the topics discussed in the report and the depth with which you discuss them. As you organize the information in your abstract, choose a method that fits the information you want to convey in this section. Do not use the same organizational pattern you used in the report.

- The *introduction/purpose/problem* is part of the main body of the report that summarizes the project. It explains the report's purpose and describes the problem that the report solves.

- The *background* updates readers on the history of the problem and relevant information that helps them understand your discussion and your solution(s) to the problem.

- The *research methods* section describes the methods used to collect the information presented in the report. If you used interviews or surveys to gather information, this section of the report provides the details that readers need to evaluate the validity of your results. This section should convince readers that you've used sound research principles so that they can feel confident about the reliability of the solution(s) you recommend.

- The *findings* or *results* section summarizes the information relevant to the report discussion. Often this section includes graphical representations of data to display trends and insights based on your research. Use graphs to show patterns to readers and to turn the raw numbers into information that readers can easily process and understand. If you conducted a survey or interview, present the data or information relevant to your solution. Usually this section does not interpret or explain your data. The explanation and interpretation comes in the next section of the report, the implications. This pattern borrows from that used in scientific research reports, where results are discussed separately from the arguments about their significance. This separation allows readers to assess the results without having the writer overtly shape those results. Include relevant results, not every result. Be aware that readers look for mention of negative results as well as positive ones. They want to learn from what you have done so they can avoid making similar mistakes.

- The *implications* section interprets your results and explains what they mean. If necessary, repeat or refine charts and graphs to highlight the significance of your results. When you explain why they are significant, you transform your information into knowledge that readers can use to shape their actions. Also describe any limitations on your results.

- The *conclusions* and *recommendations* may be discussed together or separately. The conclusion does not usually introduce new ideas or insights; instead it summarizes the main points of the report. Use paragraphs or a numbered list to remind readers of the important conclusions reached in the report. When discussing your recommendations, list the action items you recommend to solve the problem. Your action items are new information, so explain why you chose this course of action and why it will be effective. Readers also expect you to use your experience on this topic to recommend actions on related decisions and to comment on future research or activities related to this project, so don't cut your discussion of recommendations too short.

- *Appendices* include information supplementary to the report, such as completed survey forms, analyses of data, lists of works cited, references, or notes. If your material for the appendix is extensive, consider subdividing it into several appendices for quick reference. One appendix is sufficient if you have a reference list.

Formatting Conclusions and Recommendations   As you draft your conclusions and recommendations, consider the best way to format these on the page to draw your reader's attention to them. Consider pulling out one or more bullet points that concisely summarize the main points. Readers can skim the bullet points to decide whether to read further.

Format your recommendations as bullet points or a numbered list. If the conclusions are self-explanatory, the list may be all you need. However, if readers need additional information or you want to persuade them to accept your recommendation, include some concise elaboration to accompany the bullet point. Figure 19 shows examples of both formatted and unformatted conclusion and recommendation sections. Consider which a busy reader would prefer to receive.

The underlying persuasive message of your report should demonstrate your knowledge of correct research methods, your ability to follow those methods to collect accurate and useful data, and your ability to organize and interpret this information. Aim to communicate the reliability of your research so that readers trust it as a foundation for good decisions.

Example 1

Conclusions and Recommendations

This report demonstrates that we can solve the problem of budget overruns on department photocopying if we monitor more closely who is making copies and how many copies each person makes. Though it is impractical to have individuals self-report their photocopying usage (we have tried this approach but found large discrepancies between the hand-recorded numbers and the electronic tally on the machines) or to assign an employee to oversee photocopying, we can install a device that requires user ID and password before individuals can access the machine. The device will track who makes copies and how many copies they make. Barb can oversee this usage, query those who make excessive copies, and monitor the copy budget. We recommend the purchase of either a tracking device that is compatible with our current photocopier (see appendix A for two choices available) or the purchase of a new photocopier that has this software already installed (see appendix A for machines available).

Example 2

Conclusions

- We must monitor photocopier usage more closely.
- Self-reporting and employee surveillance have been unsuccessful in the past.
- Purchase of new technology will enable electronic monitoring and recording of copier use.
- Our choices:
  a. Buy a device to restrict copier use that fits on our current copier.
  b. Purchase a new copier with limited access software installed.

Recommendations

1. Purchase limited access software that is compatible with our current copier.
2. Issue user IDs and passwords to all employees.

Figure 19 Example 1 buries conclusions in a paragraph, whereas Example 2 highlights the main ideas in bullet points.

THE LANGUAGES OF THE REPORT GENRE

Reports are a genre (type of document) that employs different discourses or kinds of language in each section. For example, the executive summary uses the discourse of the generalist, giving a concise overview of the highlights of the report. This means that readers need no specialized or technical knowledge of the subject matter to understand the report abstract. When readers move to a different part of the report, however, they may have to know more about the subject matter. For example, the discussion of research methods (how the writer gathered the data presented in the report) requires writers to speak as researchers by employing the technical terms necessary to show their methods of collecting data are sound. Therefore, when reading the research methods, readers must also read as a researcher so they can evaluate the writers' methods.

The language of a report shifts again in the results and findings section when writers speak as scientists. They discuss the important data and results and use graphs and charts to highlight the relationships that are relevant to the report subject matter.

In the implications section of a report, writers switch their language again to use the discourse of finance. They talk about what the statistics and graphs in the results section mean to demonstrate that the solution they propose is both feasible (it can be done) and superior (it is better than other possible solutions). Financial language allows writers to highlight the cost effectiveness of their solution (why it makes financial sense to choose the recommended solution). In situations where money is not the primary factor—for example, in government or nonprofit organizations—report writers use the language of ethics to highlight the moral soundness of the proposed solution(s).

Assess how well you've made these changes in discourse as you evaluate your draft in the process of revisions. You want to become skilled at shifting among different types of language, because the more smoothly you do so, the more convincing your readers will find your argument.

Another characteristic of the report genre is that it uses repetition. Reports summarize the same information at specific points throughout. For example, the abstract summarizes report highlights. Readers skim the abstract to discover the main recommendations that also appear in greater detail in the recommendations section. You can use the prose that you've drafted for one section in another section without worrying about repetition; only minor revisions might be needed. Once you have drafted the recommendations, for example, you can reuse your text to write the abstract.

Exercise 5: Analyze the Discourse in Different Sections of an Annual Report

An annual report is a good choice for illustrating how dramatically the discourse shifts from one section of a report to another.[1]

1. Read the three sample texts reproduced from the October 2014 Report of the Auditor for the Government of Alberta. Excerpt 1 (Figure 20) reproduces the first three paragraphs of the Auditor General's Message. Excerpt 2 (Figure 21) reproduces the Auditor General's discussion of "What we examined" and "What we found." Excerpt 3 (Figure 22) reproduces a more detailed discussion from page 204 of the report, where the Auditor General explains specific findings about the SIVPP (Statement of Investment Valuation Principles and Practices). In small groups or individually, examine the different features of discourse that you observe in each excerpt.

[1]Vijay Bhatia, unpublished presentation, "Discourses of and in International Arbitration Practices Across Cultures and Socio-Political Boundaries," Conference of the Canadian Association of Teachers of Technical Writing, Vancouver, B.C., June 3, 2008.

Auditor General's Message

We want to reiterate the message from our July 2014 public report regarding the need for improved results analysis reporting. This October 2014 report provides further evidence of that need—seniors care and the joint Canada—Alberta plan for oil sands monitoring.

The purpose of results analysis is to learn from what you do, so that you can do better in the future. Reporting those results helps Albertans understand what the government is achieving and how it might improve. Our July 2014 report provided a framework for three inseparable elements: governance, oversight and accountability for results. We urge users of our public reports to revisit the July 2014 report.

Good leadership encourages a clear analysis of results for significant matters, including priority initiatives. We cannot ask those we audit to tell Albertans whether they are achieving results as planned, if we do not do the same ourselves. We include our Results Analysis Report 2014 in this report (page 217).

Figure 20 Excerpt 1.

Source: October 2014, Report of the Auditor General of Alberta, http://www.oag.ab.ca/webfiles/reports/October%202014%20Report.pdf

What we examined[9]

Our audit objective was to assess the nature and quality of the first annual report (2012–2013) on the joint plan for monitoring oil sands development. We also assessed whether the results the two governments shared in the report were complete and verifiable, based on evidence that was sufficient and appropriate. To assess the quality of that evidence, we looked at the processes the department used in 2012–2013 to manage the projects for which it was responsible.

What we found

The governments of Alberta and Canada jointly released their first annual report long after the information it contained was current.

The report for 2012–2013 was released in June 2014, 15 months after the March 31, 2013 end of the first year. The 2013–2014 report on the second year of implementation has not yet been released.

The report lacked clarity and key information and contained inaccuracies. The report was not clear on:

- whether overall implementation of the plan was on track
- which of the projects committed to for 2012–2013 were completed, partly completed or not completed
- what remained to be done to implement the governments' key commitments

Figure 21 Excerpt 2.

Source: October 2014, Report of the Auditor General of Alberta, http://www.oag.ab.ca/webfiles/reports/October%202014%20Report.pdf

Similar to the accounting standards, the SIVPP also requires that day-one gains only be recognized where management can support the valuation increase through comparison to similar transactions in an observable market. We concluded that management's practice of revaluing the life settlements immediately after purchase did not comply with AIMCo's SIVPP.

All of the $325 millions of unrealized gains on these investments, up to December 31, 2013, originated from revaluing the investments through a change to the discount rate, which was different than the internal rate of return implicit in the purchase prices. Management and their agents were unable to provide adequate support for the change to the discount rate that is required by the accounting standards.

Aside from the discount rate, life expectancy is another key variable in estimating the value of the life settlements. Management has not yet reviewed whether the life expectancy assumptions underlying the valuations should also be updated.

Figure 22 Excerpt 3.

Source: October 2014, Report of the Auditor General of Alberta, http://www.oag.ab.ca/webfiles/reports/
October%202014%20Report.pdf

2. Answer the following questions:

   ■ Who is the audience for this passage?
   ■ What is the purpose of each passage?
   ■ What does each passage tell you about the genre of annual report? In other words, what can you learn about the reports as a genre or type of document based on this example?
   ■ What kind of language is used in each excerpt? In other words, what voice does the writer use in each excerpt? Does he/she speak as an expert? A generalist? A researcher? A scientist? Does this voice change from one excerpt to the next?
   ■ Do you need any kind of specialized knowledge to understand the discussion? Identify specific technical terms that the writer uses. What does this vocabulary tell you about the writer, the subject matter, and the writer's relationship to the reader?
   ■ How does the language change from one excerpt to the next?
   ■ Why do you think this change in language is important to the annual report as a genre?

3. As your instructor directs, either record enough details from your group's discussion to summarize the main points that came up in your group and present it to the whole class, or write a one-page analysis of your comparison of the discourse used in each excerpt. Make sure you answer the questions listed in item 2 above and hand in your analysis as your instructor requests.

Professional Communication Assignments

3. Write the Informal Analytical Report for Ritchie Community Centre Board of Directors

Distribute the survey that you created in Exercise 4 to the young adults at your school or at a local shopping area to gather responses. Aim for a total of 25 to 30 completed surveys. Use the discussion in this module to help you tabulate and analyze your survey responses. Write the informal report requested by Mahavira Joshi, using the responses generated by your survey. As your instructor directs, create an analytical or recommendation report. Direct the report to the members of the Ritchie Community Centre Board of Directors. As Mahavari requested, describe, summarize, and analyze the responses of your respondents. You should evaluate the options suggested in the survey results and recommend several courses of action, but do not recommend one best activity to the board (unless your instructor directs you to do so). Provide enough information about the options that the board can make an informed and wise choice in spending the grant money (or feel secure that your recommendation is the best choice).

Audience: Mahavira Joshi and the members of the Ritchie Community Centre Board of Directors

Purpose: To present the results from the survey in a report format that will allow members of the board to make good choices on how to spend the $3000 grant money

Genre: Formal report (analytical or recommendation, depending on your instructor's choice)

4. Write an Informal Informational Report on Gift-Giving Practices

Distribute the survey that you created in Exercise 3 to a selection of students on your campus. Aim for a total of 25 to 30 completed surveys. Use the discussion in the earlier section of this module on analyzing survey data to help you tabulate and interpret your survey responses. Using the information in the earlier sections on writing a report, write an informal information report describing and analyzing the gift-giving practices of the students at your institution. Direct this report to your instructor and classmates.

Audience: Your instructor and classmates

Purpose: To provide readers with information and insight about the gift-giving practices of a selection of students at your post-secondary institution

Genre: Informal information report

RESEARCH REPORTS AND OFFICE POLITICS

LO 6 Understand and manage the political elements of writing a business report

Report writing never takes place in a vacuum. Even if the report is written by one person, it should be a collaborative effort to be a successful. Collaboration comes into play through two avenues: first, most report writers need information from other employees for their research (e.g., An must work with Ben to develop the survey at Ritchie Community Centre); and second, the writer wants fellow employees to support their ideas. In most workplaces, business proceeds smoothly if the right people are consulted on a project. If you are writing a report, do not write it in isolation. Study your organization to identify whom you should consult at each stage of the development process. Should your boss see a draft of the report, or should you discuss your findings with him or her as you develop them? If you need input from fellow employees, what is the most persuasive way to ask for their help? Discuss your ideas with colleagues so they can contribute if they want to.

If you are solving a problem in the report, your coworkers will implement the solution. If they don't support your ideas, they will not act. If you bring them into the process, even at an advisory level, you help ensure that they stay involved and have chances to provide feedback. They are likely to welcome your solution because they helped develop it. Inexperienced writers who single-handedly solve a problem often find their report collecting dust on a shelf because, although their work is excellent, it ignored the office hierarchies that promote or suppress good ideas. As you write your report, consult others. If you develop a plan that they may have to act on later, discuss the plan with them early to gain their approval and support. Another bonus is that your solution is likely to improve when your coworkers offer feedback and suggestions that force you to think harder about your ideas.

MODULE SUMMARY

- Research reports pose a problem or question that needs a solution or answer. Solve the problem and answer the question through print and online sources, interviews with subject matter experts, and surveys of the population to gather opinions and preferences.

- Record complete citation information as you locate sources.

- Evaluate the reliability of your online sources.

- Surveys allow you to gather opinions and ideas from a variety of people so that you can count the results and compare them to other survey results.

- Analyze the research results, identify appropriate evidence, and draft and format the research report.

- Shift discourses as you write the different sections of a research report.

- Repeat information as necessary throughout the report.

Module 13

Design and Visuals in Business and Professional Communication

Echo/Cultura/Getty Images

LEARNING OUTCOMES

LO 1 Design and present information effectively

LO 2 Select appropriate stories for presentation through visuals

LO 3 Present visual information accurately, ethically, and effectively

GETTING STARTED

A useful component of business and professional communication is page design, which structures information visually so that readers can easily skim the document and locate key information. This module will introduce you to four useful techniques for presenting information effectively: the effective use of white space, descriptive headings, lists for multiple ideas, and visuals to highlight data and concepts. All four of these techniques are essential components of research reports (as well as other business and professional communication documents).

The first case introduces you to George Morawska, who realizes that a fact sheet would help him serve customers and boost sales at his YourPhone Kiosk location. Good fact sheet design requires attention to several important aspects of document and information design, including choosing the correct format for information and knowing the basic aspects of designing documents. In the second case you will meet Sen Wang, a Forestry student and summer intern at Natural Resources Canada, who needs to create a brochure to educate members of the general public about the pine beetle infestation in western Canada and what they can do to help prevent the beetle's eastward spread. This section shows you how to translate scientific information into visual images to ensure it reaches the broadest possible audience. Visuals include graphs, charts, tables, photographs, drawings, and so on. To communicate visually with readers, writers should choose a story to communicate through each visual. This section helps you understand how to select appropriate stories and graphs and to present information accurately and ethically.

DOCUMENT FORMAT AND DESIGN IN PROFESSIONAL COMMUNICATION

An information or fact sheet displays and compares the relevant features of several different types of items. But what does an information sheet look like? What would be the best design to display the information? If you check out the document templates that came with your word processing program, you may or may not find something that will work. If you do a quick search on the internet, you will find dozens of examples of different types of sheets, depending on whether you search for "feature sheet," "fact sheet," or "information sheet." Figure 1 is one example of a fact sheet on cloning from the Human Genome Project website. A quick glance highlights several characteristics of the fact sheet layout:

LO 1 Design and present information effectively

- A title
- Headings
- An image

The information about cloning is organized under the headings, and the photograph of Dolly the cloned sheep adds visual interest. The title informs readers about the subject of the fact sheet.

Figure 2 shows a second model for a fact sheet. It highlights other characteristics of information sheets, including:

- Topic title and logo
- Organization logo and name
- Headings
- Brief introduction to topic
- Labeled tables of information

Researching and Selecting Document Formats

Decide which format is best for your document. Should you use a fact sheet? A letter? A report? A proposal? Your choice will depend on your purpose for writing, your audience, and the situation or context. Different situations call for different types or **genres** of document. Once you have determined which genre best suits your situation, you can decide how to format and structure the document by choosing a **template** from the options supplied with your word processing program. The template supplies basic formatting to use as you compose. However, some genres are not covered in the template collection. In this case, an internet search can help you find examples of the type of format you should use. Examine five or six different examples to see the range that is possible. Look for variations that can help you present your information most clearly and effectively. Use these samples as models for structuring and presenting your writing.

Genre: The type of document used in a workplace to accomplish the goals or purposes of work

Template: An example version of a file that shows the format or structure of a document

What is cloning?

Introduction

The possibility of human cloning, raised when Scottish scientists at Roslin Institute created the much-celebrated sheep "Dolly" (*Nature* **385,** 810-13, 1997), aroused worldwide interest and concern because of its scientific and ethical implications. The feat, cited by *Science* magazine as the breakthrough of 1997, also generated uncertainty over the meaning of "cloning" –an umbrella term traditionally used by scientists to describe different processes for duplicating biological material.

Jason Benz Bennee/
Shutterstock

What is cloning? Are there different types of cloning?

When the media report on cloning in the news, they are usually talking about only one type called reproductive cloning. There are different types of cloning, however, and cloning technologies can be used for other purposes besides producing the genetic twin of another organism. A basic understanding of the different types of cloning is key to taking an informed stance on current public policy issues and making the best possible personal decisions. The following three types of cloning technologies will be discussed:

- Recombinant DNA technology or DNA cloning,
- Reproductive cloning, and
- Therapeutic cloning.

Recombinant DNA Technology or DNA Cloning

The terms "recombinant DNA technology," "DNA cloning," "molecular cloning," or "gene cloning" all refer to the same process: the transfer of a DNA fragment of interest from one organism to a self-replicating genetic element such as a bacterial plasmid. The DNA of interest can then be propagated in a foreign host cell. This technology has been around since the 1970s, and it has become a common practice in molecular biology labs today.

Scientists studying a particular gene often use bacterial plasmids to generate multiple copies of the same gene. Plasmids are self-replicating extra-chromosomal circular DNA molecules, distinct from the normal bacterial genome. Plasmids and other types of cloning vectors are used by Human Genome Project researchers to copy genes and other pieces of chromosomes to generate enough identical material for further study.

To "clone a gene," a DNA fragment containing the gene of interest is isolated from chromosomal DNA using restriction enzymes and then united with a plasmid that has been cut with the same restriction enzymes. When the fragment of chromosomal DNA is joined with its cloning vector in the lab, it is called a "recombinant DNA molecule." Following introduction into suitable host cells, the recombinant DNA can then be reproduced along with the host cell DNA.

Dolly's success is truly remarkable because it proved that the genetic material from a specialized adult cell, such as an udder cell programmed to express only those genes needed by udder cells, could be reprogrammed to generate an entire new organism. Before this demonstration, scientists believed that once a cell became specialized as a liver, heart, udder, bone, or any other type of cell, the change was permanent and other unneeded genes in the cell would become inactive. Some scientists believe that errors or incompleteness in the reprogramming process cause the high rates of death, deformity, and disability observed among animal clones.

Figure 1 Fact Sheet on cloning from the Human Genome Project website.

Source: www.ornl.gov/sci/techresources/Human_Genome/elsi/cloning.html.

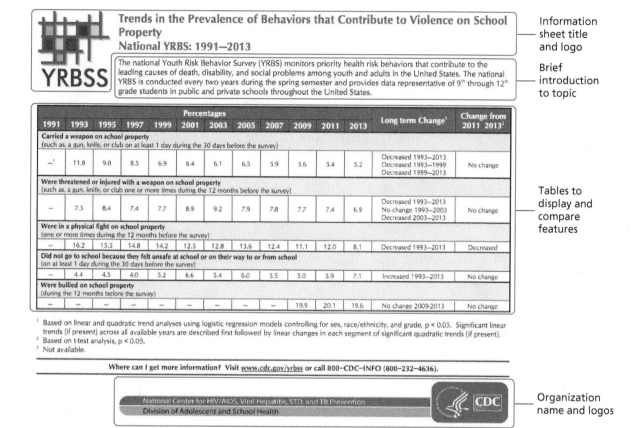

	Information sheet title and logo
	Brief introduction to topic
	Tables to display and compare features
	Organization name and logos

Figure 2 Sample feature sheet from the CDC.

Source: Trends in the Prevalence of Behaviors that Contribute to Violence on School Property, National YRBS: 1991–2013, Centers for Disease Control, http://www.cdc.gov/healthyyouth/yrbs/pdf/trends/us_violenceschool_trend_yrbs.pdf

Exercise 1: Find Examples of Three Fact Sheet Layouts

Using the internet or library, find three different examples of layouts for fact or information sheets and make printouts or photocopies. Write a half- to one-page memo to your instructor that covers the following:

- ■ Identify the features of each example that you think would be effective in your own fact sheet

- ■ Explain what these features would contribute to displaying the pertinent information effectively

Basic Components of Document Design

In business and professional communication, it is important to note how you place information on the page. Each document you write has a purpose, and readers pick it up with a goal in mind. How you present your information directly affects whether you and your readers achieve your goals.

Here are four techniques for presenting information that will help your readers quickly grasp your meaning:

1. Use white space to emphasize important points
2. Use headings that stand out
3. Use lists to emphasize multiple ideas
4. Include visuals that make data and concepts easily accessible

White space: The parts of the page that do not contain text or visuals

Use White Space

White space refers to the parts of the page that do not contain text or visuals. Arrange headings, visuals, and text on the page so that the white space around them makes them stand out. For example, the fact sheet in Figure 1 uses space between the paragraphs, around the three-point list, and around the photograph to emphasize the information in each grouping. Although there is not a lot of white space around the information on the cloning fact sheet, there is enough to make the layout visually inviting and interesting. Figure 2 uses white space around the text, images, and table so that it is easy to see the different parts of the information sheet. Visually, it makes you want to review the figures and learn more about "Youth Risk Behavior."

Use Headings That Stand Out

Subdivide your information into chunks and put a descriptive heading at the beginning of each chunk. The headings should tell readers what the section covers.

Choose a typeface for your headings that contrasts with the main text typeface and that is easy to read. Type is organized into families:

- Serif
- Sans-serif
- Slab serif
- Script
- Decorative

Serif typefaces include **Times New Roman, Palatino Linotype,** and Garamond. Their distinguishing feature is that each letter sits on little feet, or serifs, that clearly define the ends of the letters. Serif typefaces are the easiest to read in a print document.

Sans-serif typefaces are those such as **Arial,** Franklin Gothic, **Helvetica,** and Tahoma. These typefaces lack the feet, or serifs, of the serif typefaces. These typefaces give a cleaner, crisper look than serif ones, but they are harder to read in print. Online, sans-serif typefaces are easier to read and are therefore preferable in that environment.

Slab serif typefaces have broad, heavy serifs. For example, **Clarendon, Cooper Black,** and **Rockwell** are slab serif typefaces.

Script typefaces are the ones that look like handwriting or printing—for example, **Comic Sans,** *Edwardian Script,* and *Schoolhouse Cursive B.* Script typefaces can add character and tone to your document, but some script typefaces are hard to read, so choose carefully.

Decorative typefaces are the ones that are eye-catching but difficult to read, for example, **Blackmoor LET, ROSEWOOD STD,** and *Giddyup STD.* Never use a decorative typeface for more than a word or two in a document. Because of their illegibility, they are not a good choice for your title and headings, but they can add style and pizzazz if you use them properly.

How do you choose? To create an attractive contrast between the text of your document and the titles and headings, select a typeface from one "family" for the text and one from a different family for the title and headings. Research has shown that serif typefaces, such as **Times New Roman** and Palatino, are good choices for the body text of a document because most people are easily able to read them. Typefaces from the other families are more difficult to read. So choose an attractive serif typeface, such as Garamond or Palatino, for the body text, and then choose a more dramatic typeface such as **Helvetica** or **Comic Sans** for your headings. When making your choice, always consider the purpose of your document, the context for your communication, and your readers. For example, a typeface like **Comic Sans** adds an informal touch to your document—is an informal touch appropriate to the situation for which you are writing? Make a choice that suits your message.

Exercise 2: Identifying Typeface Families

Which typeface family does each of the following belong to? Serif? Sans Serif? Script? Decorative?

1. Courier
2. ERAS BOLD ITC
3. Harrington
4. Bradley Hand
5. **Playbill**
6. Baskerville Old Face
7. Blackadder ITC
8. **BlackoakStandard**
9. Eurostile

Exercise 3: Evaluating Contrasting or Conflicting Typefaces

Do these typeface combinations contrast or conflict? Identify which typeface family each word belongs to, and then decide whether the choices contrast or conflict (contrast is good; conflict is bad).

1. Free STUFF
2. Blissful **Ignorance**
3. Delicious **Garbage**
4. Recommended Solutions
5. *Woefully* Inadequate
6. Surprisingly **Interesting**

Use Lists to Emphasize Multiple Ideas   One habit to form in business and professional communication is to format the text as a list whenever you place three or more items in sequence. For example, Figure 1 uses a bulleted list for the three different methods of cloning. The formatting emphasizes the methods through the indentation and the surrounding white space.

Note the conventions for formatting lists:

- If the order of the items in the list is important, number them.
- If the order doesn't matter, use bullet points.

Include Visuals   Visuals are an essential part of business and professional communication. Look for places in your document where you can place a visual (an image, graph, diagram, or drawing) to improve your reader's understanding of your subject matter. You can use these to improve the overall look of your document by adding visual interest. But visuals are so much more useful than just acting as decoration in business and professional communication. Use them as part of your argument—facts and statistics are often much clearer when presented in a graph or table.

Exercise 4: Evaluating Page Layout in Business and Professional Documents

Collect four or five examples of business and professional writing documents. Examine each one and analyze the use of the following:

- White space
- Contrasting headings
- Lists
- Visuals

Write two or three paragraphs evaluating how effectively the various elements are used in laying out the document. Include specific examples of layout that you think are well done, as well as specific examples that could be improved.

Case 1★   YourPhone Kiosk: Using Visuals for Effective Product Presentation

Working at the YourPhone Kiosk in the Lakeside mall provided some income, especially in the summer months when it was hard to find full-time employment in an air-conditioned environment. Even though it was a dry heat, 45° C in the Okanagan Valley was still hot. George Morawska liked the phone business well enough. A constant stream of shoppers provided an interesting backdrop.

The mall traffic lightened considerably as the post-lunch crowd thinned out. George glanced down at the latest BlackBerry. The last customer at the end of the lunch rush had asked some good questions about what phone would be best for her. She had an old Nokia phone—nothing special—and a contract that had expired two years ago. George knew he had a shot at selling her something better and earning a decent commission, but the difficulty of comparing phone communication devices had made it impossible to make the sale today. What was her name, again? He glanced at the business card she'd left: Fatima Noor.

Fatima had been interested in the new BlackBerries because several people at work had them, but she also knew many people who had iPhones and various Samsung Android phones. It wasn't at all clear to a nontechnical person which one was a good fit for her.

George had started by asking her if she would use it mostly as a phone. He knew that many customers hadn't really thought out how they would use the device, and until he got them to talk about this, he was just wasting his time.

Fatima replied that she needed a phone, of course, but she also needed to keep up with her email. She noted, "I sell real estate and more and more of my clients are using email to communicate with me." She liked the idea of having a keyboard on the phone itself, which is why many of the other realtors had chosen BlackBerries. She had seen them using the predictive typing feature and thought that it might work for her.

George confirmed that this was a big advantage for those phones. He pointed out, though, that all of these devices had pluses and minuses. What Fatima would choose depended on what she would use it for most of the time. Fatima replied that she would also rely on it for her calendar and to take photos of some properties to help remember them.

George noted that most of the high-end smartphones could do all of these things, and the reviews for the best ones were more or less even. Even battery life was now pretty consistent, with the best units having enough power to get through a workday under normal circumstances. And because Fatima was a real estate agent who spent a lot of time in her car, she could always use a power adaptor to charge the phone while driving from one appointment to another.

Just then Fatima's old phone had started ringing. "Oh—that's my office," she said, glancing at her phone screen. "I've got to go, but thanks for your help. I really appreciate it. You seem to know everything about them, and it's hard for me to keep them all separate. Do you have anything that I can take with me?"

"No, but I'm here quite a bit if you want to come back. Here's my card."

"And here's mine," she said, handing it to him. "Thanks again."

As he watched her walk down the mall toward the Bay, he thought to himself, What I need is a sheet—nothing fancy—that I could hand out to customers like that. If they could see the advantages and disadvantages of each phone quickly and clearly, they would be much more likely to make a decision on the spot. And that would mean I would get credit for the sale.

> Professional Communication Assignments

1. Create a Fact Sheet for Three or Four Smartphones

Create a one-page, 8.5 × 11 inch sheet that George could use to hand out to customers such as Fatima Noor. Use different fonts for headings and for the text in the sheet. Leave plenty of white space so that readers can quickly skim and compare one device with another.

Visit a commercial website such as the following to see how they organize comparisons of different devices:

- www.shoprogers.com
- www.pcworld.com
- www.bell.ca
- www.telusmobility.com
- www.pcmag.com

Audience: Customers such as Fatima Noor, who would like to buy a new phone but lack time to research and compare their options

Purpose: To highlight the key features of three types of smartphones

Genre: Information fact sheet

2. Recommend One Particular Device That Best Meets Fatima's Needs

Analyze the information that Fatima Noor gave George to determine her needs in a cell phone and write an email that George could send her recommending which particular device would best fit her needs. Use the internet or visit a cell phone retail outlet to research the various options, then decide which one would best fit her requirements from the perspective of initial cost, ongoing expenses, service, learning curve, and features. In your message, include at least two visuals.

Audience: Fatima Noor, who would like a new cell phone but lacks the time to research and compare the main brands' features

Purpose: To recommend one brand over the others as the best fit for Fatima's needs

Genre: Email report

USING VISUALS IN BUSINESS AND PROFESSIONAL COMMUNICATION

LO 2 Select appropriate stories for presentation through visuals

Many people may think of visuals as decoration, but they are far more useful. Charts, diagrams, and tables can translate complex information into stories that readers can more quickly process and understand than textual descriptions and numbers. For example, in Case 2, Dal Blackfoot emphasizes to Sen Wang that she should use images rather than text to tell the story of the pine beetle in her brochure. He means translating the scientific data that she finds into tables, graphs, or charts so that her readers can quickly understand the importance of the information. Paragraphs of text discourage readers, especially in a brochure. Tables of data can also turn off readers when they are expected to draw their own

Province	1994	1995	1996	1997
Newfoundland and Labrador	1,047.2	2,173.8	3,315.6	4,150.0
Nova Scotia	2,679.6	4,001.6	4,848.0	5,132.9
New Brunswick	6,330.2	10,751.2	14,143.2	15,672.3
Quebec	33,056.4	48,585.7	62,596.2	76,168.5
Ontario	19,932.2	27,294.9	37,016.9	44,217.3
Manitoba	471.1	1,042.3	1,575.4	1,921.3
Saskatchewan	248.6	1,156.6	1,913.1	2,905.4
Alberta	5,482.5	10,569.1	14,031.5	16,913.1
British Columbia	63,671.4	76,477.2	89,736.8	101,178.7

Note: The values presented in this table are based on a present value calculation that assumes a zero return to capital (Present value II).

Figure 3 Statistics from Statistics Canada website comparing the value of timber stocks by province in Canada from 1994 to 1997 ($ millions). No figures were given for P.E.I., Northwest Territories, Nunavut, or Yukon.

Source: http://www40.statcan.ca/l01/cst01/envi27a.htm.

comparisons. But graphs that clearly and dramatically compare data for readers communicate with impact.

Many people enjoy learning and learn more easily when you use narratives or stories. Stories can also be persuasive because they demonstrate "why." Good visuals also tell a story clearly and concisely. But don't include a graph or chart simply for visual appeal. Also avoid using charts and figures to tell stories that everyone already knows. Instead, study your data or statistics to find something interesting and unexpected. Create a graph or chart that will accomplish a goal: it may surprise readers or it may teach them something.

For example, Figure 3 lists the value of timber stocks by province in Canada for the years 1994 to 1997. This presentation of data allows readers to assess the increase in timber value in each province over this period. As general information, this table is interesting, but each reader who examines it will notice and take away something different.

Here are three interesting "stories" that we saw in this data:

1. Although Alberta is generally considered a prairie province, it has the fourth most valuable timber stocks of any province in Canada.

2. New Brunswick has timber stocks only slightly smaller than Alberta, yet it is much smaller geographically.

3. Quebec has timber stocks nearly twice the size of Ontario, yet it covers roughly the same geographical area.

If you want readers to note something specifically from the table, you need to either point it out directly to them or choose a different method of presentation.

To show the story in item 1, instead of using a table, the comparison is more quickly and effectively displayed by using a bar chart with the prairie provinces listed in ascending order of timber stock size (see Figure 4). By removing the figures of the other provinces, you emphasize the three that you want to compare.

In contrast, Figure 5 shows timber stock values for all of the provinces that have timber stock, but the figures for Alberta are overshadowed by those of New Brunswick, Ontario, Quebec, and British Columbia. The design of Figure 5 reduces the impact of the point by providing too much information. As you can see, it is important to choose the right visual for telling your story.

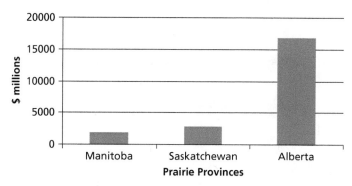

Figure 4 Bar chart comparing timber stock values in the three prairie provinces for 1997.

Source: Graph created by R. Graves, http://www40.statcan.ca/l01/cst01/envi27a.htm.

How to Choose the Right Visual for a Story

Each type of visual is best suited to presenting a different type of information or a particular relationship between data. Here are nine types of visuals:

- Bar chart
- Line graph
- Pie chart
- Dot chart
- Gantt chart
- Table
- Map
- Photograph
- Drawing

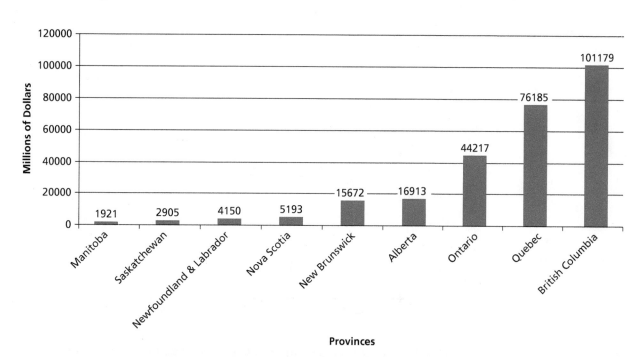

Figure 5 Bar chart comparing the value of timber stock by province in Canada in 1997.

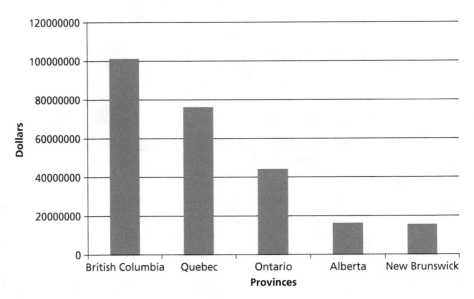

Figure 6 Five largest timber stock values in Canada for 1997.

Bar Chart   Use a bar chart to:

- Compare items
- Show change over time
- Show frequency or distribution
- Show correlation

Bar charts can show comparisons—for example, the five provinces in Canada with the largest timber stock values, as in Figure 6.

Line Graph   Use a line graph to:

- Compare items over time (as in Figure 7)
- Show frequency or distribution
- Show correlation

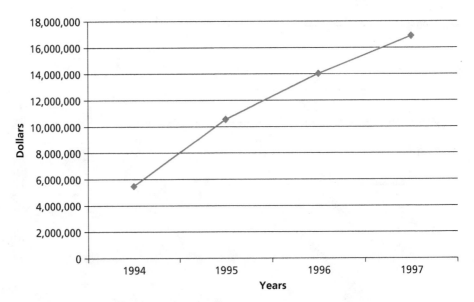

Figure 7 Line graph comparing item over time (i.e., increase in Alberta timber stock values).

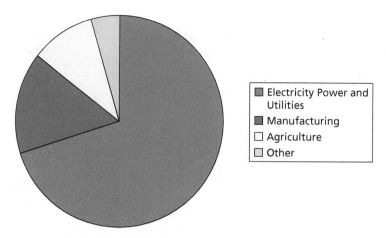

Figure 8 Pie chart showing the percentage of water used by each industrial sector.

Source: Graph by R. Graves. http://www41.statcan.ca/1762/ceb1762_000_e.htm.

A line graph is useful to emphasize the comparison between the figures that you want to illustrate. In Figure 7, the steep curve of the line graph emphasizes the fact that the value of timber stock in Alberta nearly quadrupled over a four-year period in the 1990s. Why might you want to graph these particular numbers?

This type of chart might be useful in a brochure or newsletter to show readers the phenomenal increase in the value of Alberta's timber stock in a relatively short time. This graph demonstrates the potential importance of timber stock to the Alberta economy. The information it presents could be persuasive to readers by showing residents why they should care about joining an effort to protect Alberta forests from destruction by disease or insects. This data might be used to argue, for example, the importance of halting the spread of the pine beetle from B.C.

Pie Chart   Use a pie chart to show how one part or several parts are related to the whole. To use a pie chart, your total has to add up to 100 percent. Pie charts are useful because they allow your readers to visually compare groups. They can clearly and effectively make a point about quantities. For example, in Figure 8, the pie chart format forcefully shows that electricity power and utilities are the largest users of water in the industrial sector. In comparison, manufacturing, agriculture, and other sectors use half that consumed by utilities and power generation.

Dot Chart   Use a dot or density chart to show frequency or correlation. Figure 9 is a dot chart that shows the approximate locations of coffee shops in the greater Toronto Area prepared as part of a business plan to open a Tea Emporium in the downtown lake shore area of the city. The distribution of dots illustrates both the number and distribution of potential competitors to a proposed tea shop across Toronto generally as well as in the target neighbourhood. The graphic gives an immediate sense of market penetration. In addition, the range of specific coffee shops that are named also informs readers as to the relative proportion of these shops that are chains/franchises compared to independent retailers. This graphic provides a quick overview of the data that would enable readers to understand the overall trends in this market.

Gantt Chart   Use a Gantt chart to show a timeline—for example, a schedule in a proposal or progress report. A Gantt chart is a visual display of a timetable of activities for a project or idea.

Figure 9 Dot chart showing coffee shops in and around Toronto.

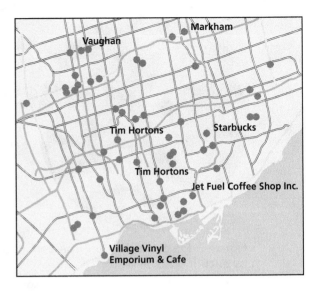

Figure 10 is a Gantt chart for a weekly status report, which requires employees to account for how they spent their time during the previous week. The employees' boss may use the status reports for recordkeeping.

The arrows visually depict the amount of time that each step took to develop the brochure. Viewers can easily see which stages of the project were most and least time consuming. They can also evaluate whether the amounts of time indicated are realistic or not.

Table   Use a table when the exact amounts are important. For example, if you are showing measurements to two decimal places, a table is the appropriate way to present the figures.

Figure 11 presents a table that shows the number of coffee shops by brand in Toronto. Because it's a visual from a business plan for a new tea shop, readers will want to know the exact number of each rather than an approximate number, so the table is the appropriate choice.

Activity	Mon. 04/06	Tues. 05/06	Wed. 07/06	Thurs. 08/06	Fri. 09/06
Find sources on pine beetles	⟷				
Read sources on pine beetles and take notes		⟷			
Decide what information to include			⟷		
Choose visuals for brochure				⟷	
Create sample page layout for brochure					⟷

Figure 10 Gantt chart documenting an employee's work on a brochure.

Brand	Number of Coffeeshops
Tim Hortons	249
Starbucks	151
Second Cup	83
Coffee Time	63
Timothy's	48
Country Style	41

Figure 11 A table showing the number of coffee shops by brand in Toronto.

Map Use a map to:

- Show location
- Compare two items

Figure 12 uses a map to show the location of the Morice Timber Supply Area in western British Columbia, the area studied by researchers Nelson, Boots, Wulder, and

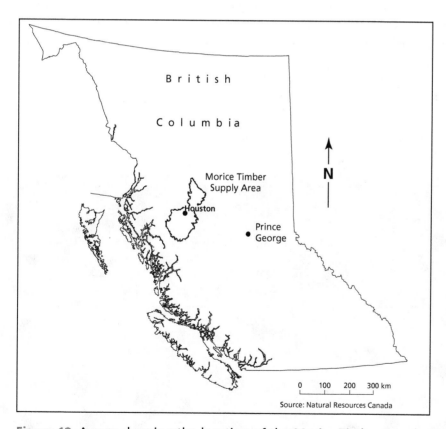

Figure 12 A map showing the location of the Morice Timber Supply Area in western British Columbia where the pine beetle infestations studies cited in this section were conducted.

Source: T. Nelson, B. Boots, and M. Wulder. Large Area Mountain Pine Beetle Infestations: Spatial Data Representation and Accuracy. Mountain Pine Beetle Initiative Working Paper 2006 – 02, Canadian Forest Service. http://www.for.gov.bc.ca/hfd/library/documents/bib97020.pdf.

Figure 13 A photograph of a longhorn beetle.

Source: Henrik Larsson/Shutterstock

Carroll. Using a map accurately pinpoints the location of the area under study. The authors also give the geographic coordinates (54° 24′ N, 126° 38′ W) for the Morice Timber Supply Area for even greater precision.

Photograph   Use a photograph to:

- Reproduce exact detail
- Show something being used

In the case of the pine beetle brochure that Sen Wang needs to create in Case 2, a photograph of the actual beetle would help readers identify the creature if they came across one. The photograph gives great detail about the beetle that would be difficult to convey through words alone.

Drawing   Use line drawings to:

- Emphasize details
- Show dimensions

In Figure 14, the schematic engineering drawing shows specific dimensions and details.

Figure 14 A sample line drawing.

Source: Molodec/Shutterstock

Conventions for Visuals

Use the conventions associated with visuals so that you are presenting the required information with them. The following are important conventions for a visual:

LO 3 Present visual information accurately, ethically, and effectively

- *Title*. Use a descriptive title with each visual so that readers know that it represents, for example, "Figure 6: Five Largest Timber Stock Values in Canada for 1997."

- *All units are labeled*. If you are using graphs or charts, make sure that the x-axis and the y-axis are clearly labeled with the units of measurement. If you include a legend, make sure that these items are also listed clearly and legibly.

- *Source of data*. If you are using data or statistics created by someone else, make sure that you include the source so that users can evaluate its validity.

- *Source of visual*. If you are using a visual that someone else created, include the source. This means at the least you should include the URL where you found the visual, if located online. If you are using the visual for purposes that are not educational (that is, associated with a school assignment), you must have permission to use it. Contact the original creator of the visual and request permission to reprint it. Sometimes you will need to pay a fee to reproduce it; other times you need only obtain written permission.

Exercise 5: Find an Interesting Story and Create a Graph to Tell It

Explore the Statistics Canada website (www.statcan.ca/menu-en.htm) until you find some data that you think is interesting and unexpected. Use a graphing program to create a chart or graph to display the interesting story that you have found. Make sure that you select the most appropriate graph to represent your data. Include all conventional labels for your graph, such as title, legend (if appropriate), data labels, source, and figure number and caption. In addition to your graph or chart, add a paragraph or two that explains the point of your visual.

Ethical Use of Visuals

Visuals should clearly and accurately represent the subject matter they are presenting. It is possible to create visuals that mislead viewers, and you should know a little bit about these techniques so that you can recognize a visual that is not giving you the straight story. Examine the bar chart in Figure 15. It reports the differences in opinion between students who support provincial tuition fee increases and those who oppose them. At first glance, the graph measures a huge disparity of opinion. However, if you look more closely, you can see that the actual range between students supporting fee increases and students opposing them is only 16 percentage points, not that far outside the survey's margin of error. It also makes it appear that many students oppose the increases, yet they are, in fact, outnumbered slightly by those who either don't know or support the increases.

The exaggeration is created by representing only 30 percentage points on the graph. At the same time, this misleading presentation diverts our attention from the fact that nearly 30 percent of students support fee increases. The misleading representation of these survey findings leave you with exactly the opposite impression from the truth: that there is a big difference of opinion on this issue among students.

Figure 15 A misleading bar chart exaggerates the differences of opinion among three groups.

Source: © Pearson Education, Inc.

Techniques for Misleading Presentation of Data

Y-Axis Does Not Start at Zero   Visuals can be misleading when the y-axis does not begin at zero. Unless they look closely, viewers may assume the graph starts at zero, so they may not recognize that the differences between the data are being exaggerated through an inaccurate presentation.

If you want to omit some of the numbers on your graph, you should start your graph at zero but create a visual break between the zero and the numbers that are relevant to your data. The break draws your readers' attention to the fact that some of the numbers in the y-axis have been omitted.

Chartjunk that misrepresents the degree of increase   Sometimes writers try to jazz up a graph by using icons or drawings—called **chartjunk**—instead of traditional bars or lines. Often this tactic can obscure or misrepresent the data being presented.

Chartjunk: Graphics added to charts to add visual interest but that distract from the data

Figure 16 uses icons instead of standard bars to illustrate the increase in pet adoptions at Red River Animal Rescue Centre. Although the graph is visually interesting, the cat images prevent readers from estimating any but the most general figures.

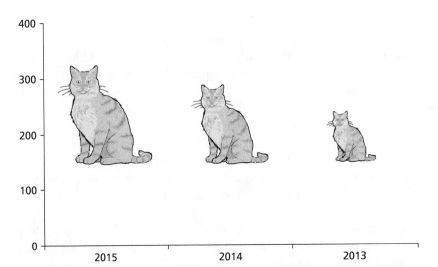

Figure 16 Pet adoptions have tripled at Red River Animal Rescue Centre over the last three years.

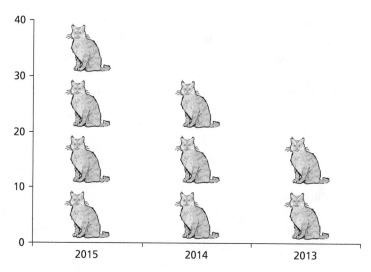

Figure 17 Red River Rescue Centre has successfully rehomed an increasing number of cats over the past three years.

It is difficult to determine the proportions between the icons to evaluate the data depicted. Similarly, the use of cat icons may distract readers from recognizing that this graph describes *all* pet adoptions, including 150 dogs, 15 rabbits, a peacock, and a pot-bellied pig in 2014.

Figure 17 uses uniformly sized icons to more accurately represent the increase in number of cat adoptions at the Red River Animal Rescue Centre. The data that it presents has been amended to show only cat adoptions so that viewers will not be misled by the choice of icons. The revision is a clearer and more accurate representation of the data being presented.

By examining other writers' visuals carefully, you can gain valuable information about how to present visual information clearly, usefully, and ethically.

Of course, sometimes the data or information that you have to present does not reflect well on your organization. In such a case, you should discuss with your supervisor the best way to approach such a situation. You will have to decide for yourself whether you are comfortable with the solutions that your supervisor may advise.

Exercise 6: Evaluating the Ethics of Some Sample Visuals

Using the Internet, find a selection of five or six visuals and evaluate the ethical presentation of the data. Alternatively, use a selection of visuals supplied by your instructor for your analysis. Examine the validity of the data supplied in each example. Assess whether the data is presented ethically. What kinds of changes would you need to make to ensure that the visual presents its data clearly and ethically? Write a memo of several paragraphs in which you include a copy of the unethical visual as well as your analysis and evaluation of its flaws and how to correct them.

Case 2★ Pine Beetle Infestation: Presenting Technical Information to a Public Audience

With 70,000 students and only 8,000 jobs, getting hired as a summer intern student at Natural Resources Canada had been a long shot—really lucky, given the lottery selection system—but it worked for Sen Wang. As a Forestry student, this was the break she needed to get a foothold in the profession. Now the fun began.

The summer internship location at the Northern Forestry Centre in Edmonton, AB, meant she had flown out of Toronto with just a weekend to find someplace to live. She had lucked out when the office turned out to be not too far from the University of Alberta campus; there was plenty of cheap student housing nearby. Maybe this would work out after all.

The first couple of weeks had been, well, boring. Lots of training videos and meeting people and trying desperately to remember names and faces—and attach the right names to the right faces. But that had changed with her first project: researching and preparing a draft of a brochure on the pine beetle.

While she knew about the problem with the pine beetle in a general way, Sen hadn't really studied it until this past week. Natural Resources had thousands of scientific publications in its database about the beetle; finding information had not been difficult. But she now realized why the administrators at the Northern Forestry Centre wanted an information brochure: almost all of the information was too technical for most people to follow.

She had found one publication that might help her get started: "Mountain Pine Beetle Mania: A Junior High Science Resource" (http://nofc.cfs.nrcan.gc.ca/bookstore_pdfs/26052.pdf). Most of it detailed how to teach kids about the pine beetle, but the section defining pine beetles might give her someplace to start. The back of the booklet listed some web resources that also promised to provide information.

Her supervisor, Dal Blackfoot, had explained, "We want to produce a brochure that brings the public up to speed on the problem and identifies the solutions currently being considered. We don't want you to bury readers in details. In fact, the real problem is to convey the basic information in as few words as possible and, if possible, through images. Use the images to tell a story about how widespread the problem is too, so include a map or graphic that shows this."

"Okay," responded Sen. She made a note on her worksheet.

"At this point you are only producing an internal document," noted Dal. He explained that her work would be the basis for a graphic designer to work from if the centre decided to distribute her brochure widely. This plan meant that Sen should include images that she found on the web, but with citations so that the graphic designer could locate the original later.

When he asked if Sen had any questions, she asked about the audience. She thought "the general public" sounded too broad: would there be a group that might be more likely to see this brochure than others? Like employees of logging companies? Or homeowners? Would people in Edmonton need this information?

"Well, that's the problem," said Dal. He explained that they wanted everyone who might come in contact with the pine beetle to have some idea of what it was. The goal of the brochure was to have readers take precautions to try to contain the pest where it was and prevent further spread.

"I see," responded Sen. "Okay, well, this should be fun. Thanks, Dal."

▷ Professional Communication Assignments

3. Create a Draft of the Pine Beetle Educational Brochure

Create a draft of Sen Wang's brochure. Use the links in Figure 18 to find information about the pine beetle. Include images that you find on the web, but remember to cite the source of the image in an attachment. You want to reach as broad an audience as possible and educate them on how best to contain the pine beetle's spread. Your brochure should include a map that shows the spread of the pine beetle so far across Canadian forests. It should also present statistical information that will help to convince readers that the pine beetle is a serious problem in western Canada's forests and that they should do what they can to help.

Government/Public Information

http://nofc.cfs.nrcan.gc.ca

www.pc.gc.ca/docs/v-g/dpp-mpb/index_e.asp
(English)

www.pc.gc.ca/docs/v-g/dpp-mpb/index_f.asp
(French)

www.for.gov.bc.ca/hfp/mountain_pine_beetle

www.forestlearn.org/watershed/e_health.htm

www.env.gov.bc.ca/bcparks
(click on MPB section)

Images

www.forestryimages.org

Parks Canada

www.pc.gc.ca/docs/v-g/dpp-mpb/index_e.asp
(English)

www.pc.gc.ca/docs/v-g/dpp-mpb/index_f.asp
(French)

Figure 18 Websites that Sen Wang found with useful information on pine beetles.

To simplify the process of creating the brochure, consider using a document template in the word processing program that you use.

Audience: Aim to reach a broad audience of readers by explaining technical terms and keeping your vocabulary simple

Purpose: To educate members of the general public to take precautions against helping the pine beetle spread into Alberta

Genre: Brochure

4. Create a newsletter to educate rural inhabitants of western Alberta

Create a newsletter (two pages, maximum) directed toward rural inhabitants of western Alberta that will persuade them to contribute to the effort to slow the spread of the pine beetle to Alberta forests and woodlots. Include information about the current range of the pine beetle, the likelihood that it will cross over into Alberta, and what readers can do to slow or stop its spread. Include images that you find on the internet, but remember to cite the source of the images in the newsletter.

Consider using a document template from your word processing program to simplify the process of designing the newsletter. Focus your attention on converting some of your information into visuals, drawings, graphs, and charts, which will help your readers understand and respond to the pine beetle infestation crisis. Include both text and visuals in the document.

Audience: Members of the general public in Alberta

Purpose: To convince them that the pine beetle is a threat to Alberta's forests

Genre: Newsletter

MODULE SUMMARY

- Choose a fact sheet when you want to offer a brief introduction to a topic.

- Choose a genre that suits your subject, purpose, and audience, and search for models of a genre on the internet.

- Use white space to emphasize important points, use headings that stand out, and include visuals.

- Translate scientific or financial data into tables, graphs, and charts to show readers the importance of the information.

- Use the proper conventions for visuals, including titles, labels, data sources, and sources.

- Use visuals ethically: don't create visuals that mislead viewers by starting the Y-axis other than at zero and avoid chartjunk that misrepresents the degree of increase.

Index

O

Objections, overcoming, 164–165, 170, 173
Office of the Privacy Commissioner of Canada, 101
Office politics, research reports and, 234
Online/electronic communications, 85–106
    analyzing, 92–93
    chat, 94
    overview of, 85–86
    printed material compared to, 94
    private information and, 101–103
    social media, 85, 86, 91
    text messaging, 85, 94
    "To" line, 87–88
    tone of, 94–95
    weblogs (blogs), 103–105
    web publications, 101–103
    See also Electronic mail (email)
Online searches
    database, 214
    key word, 209–213
    trustworthiness of, tips for evaluating, 210–211
Open-ended questions, 219–221, 224
Opinions requested in teams, 108–109
Oral communication practices, in cross-cultural communication, 134
Organizational pattern
    direct, 227–228
    in direct requests, 165–166
    indirect, 228
    in negative message, 153–154
    in negative messages, 153–154, 159
    in problem-solving persuasive messages, 171–172
    in rhetorical situations, 141

P

Page layout, 64
Paragraphs
    length of, 63
    organizing around central topic, 75–77
    topics covered in, 63
    topic sentences in, 63
    transitions in, 63–64
    writing effective, 63–64
Participation, collaboration and, 110
Persuade, 14, 17–18
Persuasion and proposal writing, 177–182
    analysis in, 181–182
    credibility in, 178
    emotional appeal in, 178–179
    logic in, 177
Persuasive messages, 163–175
    analysis in, 169–170
    direct requests in, 164, 165–169
    example of, 167
    objections, overcoming, 164–165, 170, 173
    overview of, 163–164
    problem-solving messages in, 164, 171–174
Persuasive proposals. *See* Persuasion and proposal writing
Plain language, 55, 56–67
    analyzing, 64–67
    for asking questions, 221
    principals of, 59–64

    See also Professional documents, plain language in
Politeness, in cross-cultural communication, 124, 134
Positive and informative messages
    analyzing, 149
    concluding, 144–146
    examples of, 143, 148, 149
    motivating reader through, 142–144, 146
    negative elements of, 142
    purpose of, 142
    writing, 142
    See also Informative messages
Positive emphasis, 55, 67–72
    analyzing, 70–72
    by de-emphasizing negative and stating briefly, 69
    by linking negative information to reason or reader motivator, 68–69
    by omitting trivial negatives, 71–72
    revising for, 70
    by using positive language, 68
Power distance index, 132
Power level of audience, 5
Present tense, 60
Primary audience, 2
Primary sources, 215–226
    interviews, 215–219
    surveys, 219–226
Printed material compared to online/electronic communications, 94
Privacy
    in email, 95–96
    in online/electronic communications, 101–103
Problem in research reports, 229
Problem-solution model, 182–185
Problem-solving persuasive messages, 164, 171–174
    analysis in, 173–174
    defined, 164
    example of, 171–172
    organizational pattern in, 171–172
    topics addressed in, 172
Professional documents, plain language in, 58–64
    page layout and effective communication, 64
    paragraphs, 63–64
    readers' needs, 59–60
    sentences, 61–63
    style in business communication, effective, 60–61 (*See also* Word choice)
Projects done through collaboration, 108
Proofreading email, 98, 99
Proposals, 176–195
    formatting, 186–187
    overview of, 176–177
    persuasive, 177 (*See also* Persuasion and proposal writing)
    problem statement for, drafting, 187
    questions answered by, 194–195
    in response to request for proposals, 188–194
    solicited, 177, 193–194
    unsolicited, 177, 182–186
    See also individual proposal types
Purpose
    of activity or status reports, 201
    knowing, 17
    of meeting reports, 204–205
    of message, 2, 14–18